How to Reason

A Practical Guide

+ Reasoning in the Sciences

Richard L. Epstein

Illustrations by Alex Raffi

Advanced Reasoning Forum

COPYRIGHT © 2019 by Richard L. Epstein.

ALL RIGHTS RESERVED. No part of this work covered by the copyright hereon may be reproduced or used in any form or by any means—graphic, electronic, or mechanical, including photocopying, recording, taping, Web distribution, information storage and retrieval systems, or in any other manner—without the written permission of the author.

The moral rights of the author have been asserted.

Names, characters, and incidents relating to any of the characters in this text are used fictitiously, and any resemblance to actual persons, living or dead, is entirely coincidental. *Honi soit qui mal y pense.*

Acknowledgements
I am grateful to Michael Rooney, Peter Adams, Juan Francisco Rizzo, Stipo Sentic, Marley Russell, and Sandy Nelson for their help with this project. I am grateful also to the many others who have helped over the years on *The Pocket Guide to Critical Thinking*, on which this book is based.

For more information about this book and our other publications and research, contact us:

  Advanced Reasoning Forum
  P. O. Box 635
  Socorro, NM 87801 USA
  www.AdvancedReasoningForum.org

Visit the Advanced Reasoning Forum on Facebook.

ISBN 978-1-938421-40-2   paperback
ISBN 978-1-938421-41-9   e-book (pdf)
ISBN 978-1-938421-45-7   e-book (epub)

How to Reason
and Reasoning in the Sciences

Preface

Claims
  1 Claims 2
  2 Definitions 7
  3 Subjective Claims 11
  4 Prescriptive Claims 15
  5 Concealed Claims 17

Arguments
  6 Arguments 22
  7 What's a Good Argument? 25
  8 Evaluating Premises 34
  9 Common Mistakes in Evaluating Claims . . . 41
  10 Repairing Arguments 46
  11 Too Much Emotion 56
  12 Reasoning with Prescriptive Claims 59
  13 Counterarguments 63

The Form of an Argument
  14 Compound Claims 70
  15 Valid Forms of Arguments using Conditionals . . 77
  16 General Claims 83

Numbers and Graphs
  17 Numbers 92
  18 Graphs 101

Reasoning from Experience
  19 Analogies 108
  20 Generalizing 116
  21 Cause and Effect 127

22	Cause in Populations	141
23	Inferential Explanations	149
24	Functional Explanations	160

Making Decisions

25	Evaluating Risk	166
26	Making Decisions	175

Writing Well 177

* * * * * * * * *

Reasoning in the Sciences

27	Some Examples to Start	180
28	The Scientific Method	184
29	Experiments	187
30	What Can go Wrong with an Experiment?	196
31	Models and Theories	210
32	Explanations in Science	223
33	Ways of Knowing	229

Index 231

Preface

When I first began to teach inmates at the local jail, I was told, "They aren't bad people. They just made bad decisions."
This was always said in a sympathetic tone. But it's the basis on which to blame the prisoners. They had a choice. They didn't have to end up in jail. Now they must pay. There's no empathy for their suffering; it's justice. But it's wrong. They didn't make bad decisions. They didn't make any decisions. Asked in exasperation, "But what were you thinking?" the only truthful answer they can give is "I wasn't thinking."

You, me, we're the same. We're guided by what we last heard, by our friends' approval, by impulse—our desires, our fears. Without reflection. Without even stopping to think

Here you'll learn how to reason and find your way better in life. You'll learn to see the consequences of what you and others say and do. You'll learn to see the assumptions that you and others make. You'll learn how to judge what you should believe.

Reasoning well requires judgment and the ability to imagine possibilities. The practice you need for that can come from using these ideas every day when you're studying, watching television, browsing the internet, working at your job, or talking to your friends and family. Plus, there are exercises at the end of most chapters to help you.

Because your thinking can be sharpened, you can understand more, you can avoid being duped. And, we can hope, you'll reason well with those you love and work with and need to convince, and make better decisions. But whether you will do so depends not just on method, not just on the tools of reasoning, but on your goals, your ends. And that depends on virtue.

* * * * * *

New drugs, climate change, whether cats can reason, the universe—how can we understand? Starting a science course, how can we make sense of the methods of reasoning? In the section on reasoning in the sciences here, you'll learn what an experiment is, what can go wrong with an experiment, how scientists reason with models and theories, what counts as a good explanation in science, and how to distinguish science from magic, religion, and fraud.

Cast of Characters

Claims

To reason well, to search for what is true, we need to know how to recognize what in our speech can be true or false—what we call "claims"—and what is so vague that it's just nonsense. Definitions can help us make clear what we're talking about.

Whether a sentence is too vague to be a claim depends in part on whether it's meant as a description of the world outside us or whether it's about thoughts, beliefs, or feelings. What counts as too vague depends also on whether a sentence is meant to say what is or what should be.

We'll see, too, how people can mislead us into believing a claim by a clever choice of words.

1 Claims

> **Claims** A *claim* is a declarative sentence used in such a way that it is either true or false, but not both.

To understand this or any definition we need to see examples of what fits the definition, of what doesn't fit, and what's on the border line. Only then can we begin to use the idea.

EXAMPLES
- *Dogs are mammals.*
  This is a claim.

- *2 + 2 = 5*
  This is a claim, a false one.

- *Dick is a student.*
  This is a claim, even if we don't know if it's true.

- *How can anyone be so dumb to think cats can reason?*
  This is not a claim. Questions are not claims.

- *Never use gasoline to clean a hot stove.*
  Instructions and commands are not claims.

- *I wish I could get a job.*
  Whether this is a claim depends on how it's used. If Maria who's been trying to get a job for three weeks says this to herself, it's not a claim—we don't say that a wish is true or false. But if Dick's parents are berating him for not getting a job, he might say, "It's not that I'm not trying. I wish I could get a job." Since he could be lying, in that context it's a claim.

- *There are more bacteria alive now than there were 50 years ago.*
  This is a claim, though there doesn't seem to be any way we could know whether it's true or whether it's false.

We don't have to make a judgment about whether a sentence is true or whether it's false in order to classify it as a claim. We need only judge that it is one or the other. A claim need not be an *assertion*: a sentence put forward as true by someone.

Vague sentences
Often what people say is too vague to take as a claim. There's no single obvious way to understand the words.

EXAMPLES

- *People who are disabled are just as good as people who aren't.*
  Lots of people take this to be true and important. But what does it mean? A deaf person is not as good as a hearing person at letting people know a smoke alarm is going off. This is too vague for us to agree that it's true or false.

- *Susan Shank, J.D., has joined Zia Trust Inc. as Senior Trust Officer. Shank has 20 years' experience in the financial services industry including 13 years' experience as a trust officer and seven years' experience as a wealth strategist.* —Albuquerque Journal
  April 29, 2010 and the Zia Trust website
  "Wealth strategist" looks very impressive. But when I called and asked Ms. Shank what it meant, she said, "It can have many meanings, whatever the person wants it to mean." This is vagueness used to convince you she's doing something important.

Still, everything we say is somewhat vague. After all, no two people have identical perceptions, and since the way we understand words depends on our experience, we all understand words a little differently. So it isn't whether a sentence is vague but whether it's too vague, given the context, for us to take it as a claim. In a large auditorium lit by a single candle at one end, there's no place where we can say it stops being light and starts being dark. But that doesn't mean there's no difference between light and dark.

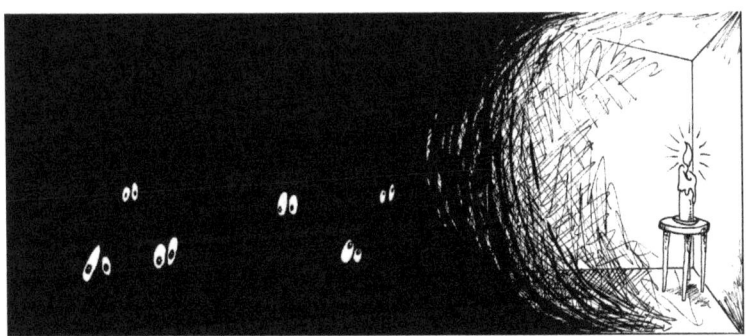

Drawing the line fallacy It's bad reasoning to argue that if you can't make the difference precise, then there's no difference.

Throughout this text we'll pick out common mistakes in reasoning and label them as a **fallacies**.

EXAMPLES

• *If a suspect who is totally uncooperative is hit once by a policeman, that's not unnecessary force. Nor twice, if he's resisting. Possibly three times. If he's still resisting, shouldn't the policeman have the right to hit him again? It would be dangerous not to allow that. So, you can't say exactly how many times a policeman has to hit a suspect before it's unnecessary force. So the policeman did not use unnecessary force.*

This argument convinced a jury to acquit the policemen who beat up Rodney King in Los Angeles in the 1990s. But it's just an example of the drawing the line fallacy.

• *Tom: My English composition professor showed up late for class today.*
  Zoe: What do you mean by late? How do you determine when she showed up? When she walked through the door? When her nose crossed the threshold?

Zoe is asking for more precision than is needed. In ordinary talk, what Tom said is clear enough to be a claim.

• *Zoe: Those psychiatrists can't agree whether Wanda is crazy or not. One says she's clinically obsessive, and the other says she just likes to eat a lot. This psychiatry business is bunk.*

Just because there are borderline cases doesn't mean there isn't a clear difference between people who are really insane and those who aren't.

A sentence is **ambiguous** if it can be understood in two or a very few obviously different ways.

EXAMPLES

• *Zoe saw the waiter with the glasses.*
Did the waiter have drinking glasses or eyeglasses, or did Zoe use eyeglasses? If we don't know which is meant, it's not a claim.

• *There is a reason I haven't talked to Robert [my ex-lover] in seventeen years (beyond the fact that I've been married to a very sexy man whom I've loved for two-thirds of that time).*
                —Laura Berman, *Ladies' Home Journal*, June 1996
The rest of the time she just put up with him?

• *Tom: Saying that having a gun in the home is an accident waiting to happen is like saying that people who buy life insurance are waiting to die. We should be allowed to protect ourselves.*

Tom, perhaps without even realizing it, is using two ways to understand "protect": physically protect vs. emotionally or financially protect.

• *Dr. E's dogs eat over 10 pounds of meat every week.*
Is this true or false? It depends on whether it means "Each of

Dr. E's dogs eats over 10 pounds of meat every week" (big dogs!) or "Dr. E's dogs together eat over 10 pounds of meat every week." It's an **individual versus group ambiguity**.

We can tolerate some vagueness, but we should never tolerate ambiguity in our reasoning, because then we really don't know what we're talking about.

Now you should know what these mean:

- Claim.
- Too vague to be a claim.
- Drawing the line fallacy.
- Ambiguous sentence.
- Individual vs. group ambiguity.

You should be ready to use these, perhaps uncertainly, but as you see them put to use in more examples and with other ideas, you'll soon be able to make them your own.

Try your hand at these!
Which of the following is a claim?
1. College is really expensive now.
2. Pass the salt, please.
3. Bill Gates founded Apple.
4. Your best friend believes that Bill Gates founded Apple.
5. A friend in need is a friend indeed.
6. The sky is blue.
7. The sky is blue?
8. Whenever Spot barks, Zoe gets mad.
9. The Dodgers aren't going to win a World Series for at least another 10 years.
10. If you don't pay your taxes on time, you'll have to pay more to the government.
11. Suzy: I feel cold today.
12. Public education is not very good in this state.
13. Men are stronger than women.
14. Americans bicycle thousands of miles every year.
15. He gave her cat food.

Answers
1. Not a claim. Too vague.
2. Not a claim. A command.
3. A claim (false).
4. A claim, but not the same as the last one.
5. What the heck does this mean?

6 *How to Reason*

6. A claim.
7. Not a claim. A question.
8. A claim.
9. A claim. We just don't know whether it's true or false and won't know for another 10 years.
10. A claim.
11. A claim. Sure it's vague, but what do you expect when talking about feelings?
12. Not a claim. Too vague.
13. Not a claim,. Too vague. Strong in what way? Can lift more? Can lift more for their body weight? Can survive trauma better?
14. Not a claim. Individual vs. group ambiguity.
15. Not a claim, ambiguous.

2 Definitions

There are two ways we can try to make clear what we say.
- Replace the entire sentence by another that is not vague or ambiguous.
- Use a definition to make a specific word or phrase precise.

> **Definitions** A *definition* is an explanation or stipulation of how to use a word or phrase.

A definition is not a claim. A definition is not true or false, but good or bad, right or wrong. Definitions tell us what we're talking about.

EXAMPLES
- *"Exogenous" means "developing from without."*
  This is a definition, not a claim. It's an explanation of how to use the word "exogenous."

- *Puce is the color of a flea, purple-brown or brownish-purple.*
  This is a definition, not a claim.

- *Lee: Maria's so rich, she can afford to buy you dinner.*
  Tom: What do you mean by "rich"?
  Lee: She's got a Mercedes.
  This is not a definition—or it's a very bad one. Some people who have a Mercedes aren't rich, and some people who are rich don't own a Mercedes. That Maria has a Mercedes might be some evidence that she's rich.

- *Fasting and very low calorie diets (diets below 500 calories) cause a loss of nitrogen and potassium in the body, a loss which is believed to trigger a mechanism in the body that causes us to hold on to our fat stores and to turn to muscle protein for energy instead.*
       —Jane Fonda's New Workout and Weight Loss Program
  Definitions aren't always labeled but are often made in passing, as with this good definition of "very low calorie diet."

- *Intuition is perception via the unconscious.* — Carl G. Jung
  This is a definition, but a bad one. The words doing the defining are no clearer than what's being defined.

- *Dogs are mammals.*
  This is not a definition. It's a claim.

- *A car is a vehicle with a motor that can carry people.*
  This is a bad definition because it's **too broad**: It covers cases that it shouldn't. For example, a golf cart would be classified as a car. So we can't use the words doing the defining in place of the word being defined.

- *Dogs are domesticated canines that obey humans.*
  This is a bad definition because it's **too narrow**.: It doesn't cover cases it should, like feral dogs in India.

Good definition For a definition to be good:

- The words doing the defining are clear and better understood than the word or phrase being defined.
- It would be correct to use the words doing the defining in place of the word or phrase being defined. That is, the definition is neither too broad nor too narrow.

- *Abortion is the murder of unborn children.*
  Here what should be debated—whether abortion is murder—is being assumed as if it were a definition.

Persuasive definitions A *persuasive definition* is a contentious claim masquerading as a definition.

- *A feminist is someone who thinks that women are better than men.*
  This is a persuasive definition.

  If you call a tail a leg, how many legs has a dog? Five?
  No, calling a tail a leg don't make it a leg.
  　　　　　　　　— attributed to Abraham Lincoln

- *Absurdity: A statement of belief manifestly inconsistent with one's own opinion.*　　— Ambrose Bierce, *The Devil's Dictionary*
  Whether you classify this as persuasive depends on how much faith you have in people.

To make a good definition, we need to look for examples where the definition does or does not apply to make sure it's not too broad or too narrow.

- *Suppose we want to define "school cafeteria." That's something a lawmaker might need in order to write a law to disburse funds for a food program. As a first go, we might try "A place in a school where students eat." But that's too broad, since that would include a room with no food service where students can take their meals. So we could try "A place in a school where students can buy a meal." But that's also too broad, since it would include a room where students could buy a sandwich from a vending machine. How about "A room in a school where students can buy a hot meal that is served on a tray"? But if there's a fast-food restaurant like Burger King at the school, that would qualify. So it looks like we need "A room in a school where students can buy a hot meal that is served on a tray, and the school is responsible for the preparation and selling of the food." This looks better, though if adopted as a definition in a law it might keep schools that want money from the legislature from contracting out the preparation of their food. Whether the definition is too narrow will depend on how the lawmakers intend the money to be spent.*

Steps in making a good definition
- Show the need for a definition.
- State the definition.
- Make sure the words make sense and are clear.
- Give examples of where the definition applies.
- Give examples of where the definition does not apply.
- If necessary, contrast it with other likely definitions.
- If necessary, revise it.

Now you can recognize and use definitions in your reasoning if you remember these ideas:
- Definition.
- Good definition.
- Persuasive definition.
- How to make a good definition.

Try your hand at these!
Classify each of the following as a definition, a persuasive definition, or neither.
If it is a definition, say what word or phrase is being defined.
1. "Dog" means "a canine creature that brings love and warmth to a human family."

10 *How to Reason*

2. Domestic violence is any violent act by a spouse or lover directed against his or her partner within the confines of the home of both.
3. Being rich means you can afford to buy a Mercedes.
4. A real fan has season tickets.
5. A conservative, in politics, is one who believes that we should conserve the political structure and laws as they are as much as possible, avoiding change.
6. A liberal is someone who wants to use your taxes to pay for what he thinks will do others the most good.
7. A killer whale has a sleek, streamlined, fusiform (tapered at both ends) body shape.

Answers
1. Persuasive definition.
2. Definition of "domestic violence."
3. Perhaps a definition of "rich," but not a good one. Better to view it as a claim.
4. Not a definition. It's a condition for someone to be a real fan.
5. Definition of "conservative," though not a good one now.
6. Persuasive definition.
7. Definition of "fusiform."

3 Subjective Claims

> **Subjective and objective claims** A claim is *subjective* if whether it's true or false depends on what someone, or something, or some group thinks, believes, or feels.
> A claim that's not subjective is *objective*.

EXAMPLES
- *All ravens are black.*
  This is an objective claim.
- *Suzy: My cat Puff is tired.*
  This is a subjective claim.
- *Suzy: It's cold outside.*
  This is too vague to be an objective claim. But if Suzy means just that it seems cold to her, it's a subjective claim. A sentence that's too vague to be an objective claim might be perfectly all right as a subjective one if that's what the speaker intended. After all, we don't have very precise ways to describe our feelings.

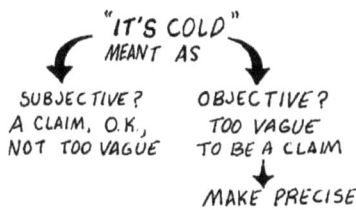

- *Wanda: I felt sick yesterday, and that's why I didn't hand in my work.*
  Wanda didn't feel sick yesterday—she left her critical thinking writing assignment to the last minute and couldn't finish it before class.
  This is a false subjective claim.
- *Lee: Calculus I is a really hard course.*
  What standard is Lee using for classifying a course as really hard? If he

means that Calculus I is difficult for him, then the claim is subjective. If Lee has in mind that about 40% of students fail Calculus I, which is twice as many as in any other course, then the claim is objective. Or Lee might have no criteria in mind, in which case it's not a claim. *If it's not clear whether subjective or objective criteria are being invoked, the sentence is too vague to be taken as a claim.*

- *Inspector: Your restaurant failed this inspection.*
Restaurant owner: That's just what you think.

  The criteria for passing a restaurant inspection include "There is an accessible sterilizing solution with test strips", "No drinks without lids are in the food preparation area", . . . each of which is objective. But despite officials trying to write regulations that are very precise and specific, for an inspector to decide whether each of those is true depends on his or her judgment. What counts as accessible? What are the boundaries of the food preparation area? Different competent inspectors might disagree. So when the restaurant owner says, "That's just what you think," he's wrong if he means that the claim is subjective, but he might be right if he means that he disagrees with the inspector's judgment about whether certain criteria are satisfied.

- *God exists.*

  Lots of people think this is subjective because there's so much disagreement about it. But whatever we mean by "God" it's supposed to be something that exists independently of people. So the example is objective: whether it's true or false doesn't depend on what anyone thinks or feels. "God exists" ≠ "I believe that God exists."

Subjectivist fallacy It's a mistake to argue that because there's a lot of disagreement about whether a claim is true it follows that the claim is subjective.

- *Wanda weighs 215 pounds.*
  This is an objective claim. Registering a number on a scale is an objective criterion.

- *Nurse: Dr. E, tell me on a scale of 1 to 10 how much your back hurts.*
  Dr. E: It's about a 7.
  This is a scale, but one that only Dr. E knows. Dr. E's claim is subjective.

- *Dick: Wanda is fat.*
  This is a subjective claim. Whether it's true depends on Dick's feeling about what is fat. But what if Wanda is so obese that everyone would consider her fat? It's still subjective, but we can note that agreement.

3 Subjective Claims 13

> ***Intersubjective claims*** A subjective claim is *intersubjective* if (almost) everyone agrees that it's true or (almost) everyone agrees that it's false.

- *There are an even number of stars in the sky.*
  This claim is objective, but no one knows how to find out whether it's true or false, and it's not likely we'll ever know.

- *There is enough oil available for extraction by current means to fulfill the world's needs for the next 63 years at the current rate of use.*
  This is objective. People disagree about it because there's not enough evidence one way or the other.

- *Zoe: Tom loves Suzy.*
  Dick: I don't think so.
  Dick and Zoe disagree about whether this subjective claim is true, but it's not for lack of evidence. There's plenty; the problem is how to interpret it.

Confusing whether a claim is objective or subjective can lead to pointless disagreements. Dick and Zoe are treating a subjective claim as if it were objective. There's no sense in arguing about taste.

Often it's right to question whether a claim is really objective. But sometimes it's just a confusion. All too often people insist that a claim is subjective ("That's just your opinion") when they are unwilling to examine their beliefs or engage in dialogue.

Now you have more tools in your reasoning kit:
- Subjective claim.
- Objective claim.
- Subjectivist fallacy.
- Intersubjective claim.

You can begin to use these if you remember:
- What's too vague to be an objective claim can still be a subjective claim.
- If it's not clear whether it's meant as subjective or objective, don't take it as a claim.
- Whether a claim is subjective or objective does not depend on:
    How many people believe it.
    Whether it's true or false.
    Whether anyone can know if it's true or false.

Try your hand at these!
Which of the following is an objective claim, a subjective claim, or no claim at all?
1. Silk insulates better than rayon.
2. Silk feels better on your skin than rayon.
3. Bald men are more handsome.
4. You intend to finish reading this book.
5. He's sick! How could someone say something like that?
6. He's sick; he's got the flu.
7. Cats enjoy killing birds.
8. (In a court of law, said by the defense attorney) The defendant is insane.
9. Zoe is more intelligent than Dick.
10. Zoe gets better grades in all her courses than Dick.
11. Suzy believes that the moon does not rise and set.
12. Spot ran to his bowl and drooled when Dick got his dog food.
13. Spot is hungry.
14. Fifty-four percent of women responding to a recent Gallup poll said they think that women do not have equal employment opportunities with men.
15. Fifty-four percent of women think that women do not have equal employment opportunities with men.
16. Dog food is more expensive at Smith's than at Albertson's

Answers
1. Objective.
2. Subjective.
3. Subjective.
4. Subjective.
5. Subjective.
6. Objective.
7. Subjective.
8. Subjective
9. Subjective.
10. Objective.
11. Subjective.
12. Objective.
13. Subjective.
14. Objective.
15. Subjective.
16. Too vague to be a claim (each kind is more expensive or overall? Individual vs. group ambiguity.)

4 Prescriptive Claims

Sometimes we want to say not only what is but what ought to be.

> **Descriptive and prescriptive claims**
> A claim is *descriptive* if it says what is.
> A claim is *prescriptive* if it says what should be.

Prescriptive claims are also called "normative," and descriptive ones are sometimes called "positive."

EXAMPLES
- *Drunken drivers kill more people than sober drivers.*
  This is a descriptive claim. It's objective.

- *There should be a law against drunk driving.*
  This is a prescriptive claim.

- *Dick: I'm hot.*
  Zoe: You should take your sweater off.
  Dick has made a descriptive claim. Zoe responds with a prescriptive one.

- *The government must not legalize marijuana.*
  This is a prescriptive claim, where "must" indicates a stronger idea than "should."

- *The government ought to lower interest rates.*
  This is a prescriptive claim.

The words "good," "better," "best," and "bad," "worse," "worst," and other **value judgments** are prescriptive when they carry with them the unstated assumption: "If it's good (preferable, . . .), then we (you) should do it; if it's bad, we (you) should not do it."

- *Texting while driving is bad.*
  This is prescriptive. It's meant that no one should text while driving.

- *Dr. E: It's just plain wrong to cheat on an exam.*
  This is prescriptive, for by "wrong" Dr. E means that his students shouldn't do it.

- *Dick: Cats are really disagreeable animals.*
  Dick is making a value judgment, but there's no "should" in it or implied. Not every value judgment is prescriptive.

Try your hand at these!
Which of these sentences is prescriptive and which descriptive or is no claim at all?
1. Dissecting monkeys without anesthetic is cruel and immoral.
2. Dissecting monkeys without anesthetic is prohibited by the National Science Foundation funding guidelines.
3. Larry shouldn't marry his sister.
4. Employees must wash their hands before returning to work.
5. Downloading a pirated copy of this textbook is wrong.
6. It's better to conserve energy than to heat a room above 68°.
7. It's about time for the government to stop bailing out the bankers.
8. Dick and Zoe have a dog named "Spot."
9. The government should raise the tax rate for the upper 1% of all taxpayers.
10. Every high school should require students to take critical thinking in 10th grade so they can improve their comprehension in all their other courses.

Answers
1. Prescriptive.
2. Descriptive.
3. Prescriptive.
4. Not a claim, a command.
5. Prescriptive.
6. Not a claim. How better?
7. Prescriptive—if a claim at all.
8. Descriptive.
9. Prescriptive.
10. Two claims. "Every high school should require students to take critical thinking in 10th grade" is prescriptive. "They (the students) can improve their comprehension in all their other courses" is a descriptive claim meant as a reason to believe the first.

5 Concealed Claims

A **slanter** is any attempt to convince using words that conceal a claim that is dubious. Persuasive definitions are slanters. A **loaded question** is a slanter, too, concealing a claim as a question.

- Lee: Why can't cats be taught to heel?
  Suzy: What makes you think cats can't be taught to heel?
  Lee poses a loaded question. Suzy answers it by pointing out and challenging the concealed claim.

- Dick: Why do all women like to shop?
  Zoe: We don't.
  Zoe has answered Dick's loaded question by denying his concealed claim.

A **euphemism** is a word or phrase that makes something sound better than a neutral description; a **dysphemism** makes it sound worse.

- Suzy: You should try to fix up Wanda with a date. Tell your friends she's Rubenesque.
  Tom: You mean she's fat.
  Suzy's used a euphemism.

- *The freedom fighters attacked the convoy.*
  "Freedom fighters" is a euphemism, concealing the claim that the guerillas are good people fighting to liberate their country and give their countrymen freedom.

- *The terrorists attacked the convoy.*
  "Terrorists" is a dysphemism, concealing the claim that the guerillas are bad people, inflicting violence on civilians for their own partisan ends without popular support.

- *The merciless slaughter of seals for their fur continues in a number of countries.*
  "Merciless slaughter" is a dysphemism; "harvesting" would be a euphemism; "killing" would be a neutral description.

- *American authorities suffered their own black eye over mistreatment of prisoners when photographs surfaced early last year showing U.S. soldiers abusing detainees at the Abu Ghraib prison on Baghdad's western outskirts.* — Associated Press, December 26, 2005
  The bias here is clear: "black eye" is a euphemism for serious damage to their reputation, and "abusing" is a euphemism for torture.

A **downplayer** is a word or phrase that minimizes the significance of a claim; an **up-player** exaggerates.

- *Zoe: Hey Mom. Great news. I managed to pass my first French exam.*
  Mom: You only just passed?
  Zoe has up-played the significance of what she did, concealing the claim "It took great effort to pass" with the word "managed." Her mother downplayed the significance of passing by using "only just," concealing the claim "Passing and not getting a good grade is not commendable."

A **weaseler** is a claim that's qualified so much that the apparent meaning is no longer there.

- *If you buy* How to Reason, *you'll get a job paying 25% more than the average wage in the U.S.**

  * Purchaser agrees to study this book four hours per day for two years.

- *[Elliot] Rappaport [a forensic psychologist] said a psychological autopsy is just like any other psychological evaluation except that the patient is missing.* —Albuquerque Journal, December 3, 2004
  That "except" qualifies the comparison away. Dogs are just like cats, except that dogs are canines and cats are felines.

- *Maria (to her boss): I am truly sorry it has taken so long for you to understand what I have been saying.*
  Maria has not apologized.

A **proof substitute** is a way to convince by suggesting you have a proof without actually offering one.

- *Dr. E to Suzy: Cats can't reason. It's obvious to any thinking person. Being around them so much must have convinced you of that. Of course some people are misguided by their emotions into thinking that felines have intelligence.*
  Dr. E didn't prove that cats can't reason, though he made it sound as if he were proving something. He was just reiterating the claim, trying to browbeat Suzy into believing it with the words "obvious," "must have convinced," "some people are misguided."

- *Suzy: Cats can so reason. It's been shown over and over that they can.*
  Unless Suzy can point to some studies, this is a proof substitute, too.

Ridicule is a particularly nasty form of proof substitute: That's so obviously wrong it's laughable.

- Dr. E: Cats can reason? Sure, and the next thing you know you'll be inviting them over to play poker.

Another way to conceal that you have no support for your claim is to **shift the burden of proof**.

- Tom: The university should lower tuition.
  Maria: Why?
  Tom: Why not?

  Tom hasn't given any reason to think his claim is true. He's only invited Maria to say why she thinks it's false, so he can attack that—which is easier than supporting his own position.

- Why wouldn't someone want laws limiting where sexual predators can live?

  Often an attempt to shift the burden of proof is given as a question that assumes a default judgment.

There are lots of other ways people try to conceal claims.

- Zoe: Where are you from?
  Harry: New York.
  Zoe: Oh, I'm sorry.

  When a concealed claim is this unpleasant, we call it an *innuendo*.

I agree. My opponent is telling the truth this time.
  Politicians specialize in innuendos.

- Scientists at McEpstein University's School of Medicine have discovered a cure for baldness.

  This supposes that baldness is a disease or at least a disability that needs to be cured.

- The homepage of the website of Los Alamos National Laboratory has the following items you can click on: Science and Technology, Working with LANL, Organization, Community, Education & Internships, Life@LANL, International.

  The homepage is a euphemism by **misdirection**. If you didn't already know that LANL is one of the main centers for nuclear weapons research in the United States, you might think from this that it is devoted solely to scientific research and applications for the betterment of humanity.

You should avoid using slanters because the other person can destroy your points not by facing your reasoning but by pointing out how you are trying to confuse people.

20   *How to Reason*

Try your hand at these!
What, if anything, is wrong in the following? If there's a concealed claim, make it explicit.
1. When are you going to start studying in this course?
2. New Mexico surveys show 60 percent of high schoolers have had sex before graduating, and only 12 percent remain abstinent until marriage.
   —*Albuquerque Journal*, January 13, 2005
3. E-mail us and we'll do our best to get back to you within 12 hours.
   —Ticketmaster's "contact us" web page
4. New Mexico had fewer than one in five—about 18 percent—of its total population living in poverty last year, while the United States remained level at about 12.5 percent. — Sean Olson, *Albuquerque Journal*, August 27, 2008
5. Knowing the law, and being perhaps a respectable, religious person, he is anxious to abstain from all appearance of evil. —*The Shepherd's Life*, W. H. Hudson, 1921
6. "In a way, we're a kind of a Peace Corps."
   —A training director of the Fort Bragg Green Beret Center, 1969
7. How many years in prison should someone get for sending a virus out on the internet that infects thousands of machines?
8. Students should be required to wear uniforms in high schools. It has been well documented that wearing uniforms reduces gang violence.
9. Maria: Wanda's so sad. She doesn't even want to get out of bed anymore. It looks like she's in another bout of blues.
10. The gaming industry in Nevada recorded another record year of profits.
11. At last our government has decided to give compensation to the Japanese who were resettled in internment camps during World War II.

Answers
1. Loaded question.
2. "only" conceals the claim that we should expect more.
3. "our best" is a weaseler
4. Nothing wrong here.
5. "appearance" conceals the claim that religious people don't really try to avoid evil.
6. "in a way" is a weaseler. In a way, cats are just like dogs.
7. Loaded question.
8. Proof substitute.
9. "sad" and "bout of the blues" are euphemisms for "depressed."
10. "gaming" is a euphemism for "gambling."
11. "at last" is a downplayer; "resettled" is a euphemism for "forcibly removed to"; and "internment camps" is a euphemism for open prisons.

Arguments

We reason to convince—others or ourselves. When we set out claims to give good reason to believe, we're making an argument.

Crucial, and most fundamental in this book, is to know what counts as a good argument. For an argument to be good, the premises—the reasons to believe—have to be plausible. But we can't expect all of those to be backed up by an argument or we'd never get started. We need standards for when to accept a claim without an argument. We also need to know some common mistakes in applying those standards.

Many arguments aren't good as stated, yet we can easily repair them. But to avoid putting words in people's mouths, we need criteria for when and how to repair an argument. Those depend in part on whether what's being argued for is a subjective claim or objective, and whether it's prescriptive or descriptive.

Finally in this section we'll see how to face challenges to our arguments by using counterarguments, and in doing so we'll see how we can show someone that his or her argument is bad—or improve ours.

6 Arguments

When we reflect on our reasons for believing a claim or when we try to convince someone by giving reasons, we're making an argument.

> **Arguments** An *argument* is an attempt to convince someone, possibly yourself, that a particular claim, called the **conclusion**, is true. The rest of the argument is one or more other claims, called the **premises**, which are given as the reasons for believing that the conclusion is true.

The nurse is trying to convince the doctor that "Your patient in Room 47 is dying" is true. She offers the premise "He's in cardiac arrest."

- *Out? Out? I was safe by a mile. Are you blind? He didn't even touch me with his glove!*

    This was said by a runner at a baseball game. He was trying to convince the umpire to believe "I was safe." He used only one premise: "He didn't even touch me with his glove." The rest is just noise.

- *Critical thinking is the most important subject you'll ever study. It will help you reason better, it will help you get a job, and it will help you make better decisions.*

    This is an argument. The conclusion is "Critical thinking is the most important subject you'll ever study." The premises are "Critical thinking will help you reason better," "Critical thinking will help you get a job," and "Critical thinking will help you make better decisions."

- *Suzy (to Tom): You can tell that economics graduates are smart. They get high-paying jobs, and they always dress well.*

    This is an attempt by Suzy to convince Tom (or maybe herself) that "Economics graduates are smart" is true. Its premises are "They get high-paying jobs" and "They always dress well."

6 Arguments 23

Dick is making an argument, trying to convince the police officer that "The accident was not my fault" is true (reworded a bit). He uses two premises: "She hit me from the rear" and "Anytime you get rear-ended it's not your fault."

• (From a label on a medication) *Follow the directions for using this medicine provided by your doctor. This medicine may be taken on an empty stomach or with food. Store this medicine at room temperature, away from heat and light.*

This is not an argument. Instructions or commands are not an attempt to convince someone that a claim is true.

Zoe's mother is attempting to convince her, but not of the truth of a claim. So there's no argument.

• *If it's OK to buy white mice to feed a pet boa constrictor, why isn't it OK to experiment on rats?*

This isn't an argument: questions aren't claims. We might construe it as an attempt to convince, taking the question as rhetorical. But before we go putting words in people's mouths, we should have a better idea of when we're justified in re-interpreting what they say.

• *Dick: You shouldn't dock your dog's tail because it will hurt her, it'll make her insecure, and she won't be able to express her feelings.*

This is an argument. The word "because" clues us to that by introducing the premises.

24 *How to Reason*

Try your hand at these!
Which of the following are arguments? If it's an argument, what are its premises and conclusion?

1. You shouldn't eat at Zee-Zee Frap's restaurant. I heard they did really badly on their health inspection last week.
2. Flo: She pulled my hair and stepped on my hand and wrecked my toy. I hate her.
3. (Advertisement) The bigger the burgers, the better the burgers, the burgers are bigger at Burger King.
4. Flo has always wanted a dog, but she's never been very responsible. She had a fish once, but it died after a week. She forgot to water her mother's plants, and they died. She stepped on a neighbor's turtle and killed it.
5. Maria: Ah-choo.
   Lee: Bless you.
   Maria: I'm just miserable. Stuffy head and trouble breathing.
   Lee: Sounds like the allergies I get.
   Maria: No, it's the flu. I'm running a fever.
6. [A review on Netflix of *Fifty Shades of Grey*—1 star out of 5] This movie plodded along like getting a root canal . . . painfully slow. Perhaps more insight into Christian Grey's psychological workings would have made the movie more interesting and engaging. I didn't read any of the books but I am wondering why all the fascination with an abusive physical relationship? It seemed to border on domestic violence and the papers are full of it with real people. Say "no" to this movie and do something better with your time . . . like bake cookies or shovel snow.
7. Look Dick! Look Zoe! See Spot. See Spot run.
8. Dick: The gas pump stopped pumping by itself.
   Zoe: I can't get it to pump any more gas.
   Dick: So the gas tank must be full.

Answers
1. Argument. Conclusion "You shouldn't eat at Zee-Zee Frap's restaurant." Premise: "I heard they did really badly on their health inspection last week." The premise is *not* "They did really badly on their health inspection last week." Big difference.
2. Not an argument.
3. Not an argument (what's the conclusion?).
4. Not an argument because not an attempt to convince.
5. Argument. Premises: Maria has a stuffy head and trouble breathing. She has a fever. Conclusion: Maria has the flu and not allergies.
6. Not an argument (what's the conclusion?).
7. Not an argument. Just great literature.
8. Argument. Conclusion: The gas tank is full. Premises: The gas pump stopped pumping by itself. Zoe can't get it to pump any more gas.

7 What's a Good Argument?

• *Dr. E is a professor. Dr. E wears a tie to class. Dr. E teaches critical thinking. So Dr. E is a vegetarian.*
> This is an awful argument. What does being a professor, wearing a tie, and teaching critical thinking have to do with Dr. E being a vegetarian?

• *All good teachers give good exams. Dr. E gives good exams. So Dr. E is a good teacher.*
> This sounds good. Should we be convinced that Dr. E gives good exams?

It isn't a matter of whether we are convinced. Bad advertisements convince, but they're not good arguments. You can give a great argument to your friend, but it won't convince her if she's weeping because her dog just died.

A good argument is one that gives good reason to believe that the conclusion is true.

This is our general guideline—but what counts as good reason?

You can say that the first argument is bad because the premises don't have anything to do with the conclusion. But that easy phrase is no guide for evaluating the second example.

The problem with the first one is that though all the premises are true, the conclusion could be false: Dr. E could be gluten intolerant; he could enjoy eating meat; he could want the woman he's dating to think he's a real man who eats steak and barbecued ribs. There's nothing in the premises that rules out those possibilities, which for all we know could be true.

The second argument sounds better. But there, too, there are likely ways the premises could be true and conclusion false: Dr. E might bore his students to tears and just copy good exams from the instructor's manual, or he might get good exams from another teacher.

> **Weak arguments** An argument is *weak* if there is some way, some possibility, for its premises to be true and conclusion false that doesn't seem unlikely.

If an argument is weak, then even if the premises are true, they don't give us good reason to believe the conclusion. A weak argument is bad.

But it isn't just that there is some possible way for the premises to be true and conclusion false. There has to be a *likely* possibility.

• [Dick heard this morning that there are parakeets for sale down at the mall. He wants to buy one, and he knows that his neighbor has a birdcage in her garage that she would give him. He wonders if it will be big enough. He reasons:]
All parakeets I've ever seen or heard or read about in bird books and the encyclopedia are under 2 feet tall. So the parakeets for sale at the mall are under 2 feet tall.

Surveying all the ways the premise could be true, we think that yes, a new supergrow bird food could have been formulated and the parakeets at the local mall are really 2 feet tall, we just haven't heard about it. Or a giant parakeet from the Amazon forest could have been discovered and brought here. Or a UFO might have abducted a parakeet, hit it with growing rays, and now it's really big. All these ways the premise could be true and the conclusion false are so unlikely that we would have very good reason to believe the conclusion if the premise is true—though the conclusion might be false.

Strong arguments An argument is *strong* if there is some way, some possibility, for the premises to be true and conclusion false, but every such possibility seems unlikely.

• *Every student at this school has paid tuition. Suzy is a student at this school. So Suzy has paid tuition.*
There isn't even one way that the premises could be true and conclusion false.

Valid arguments An argument is *valid* if there is no way, no possibility, for the premises to be true and conclusion false. An argument that is not valid is *invalid*.

Either an argument is valid or it isn't. But the strength of an invalid argument is a matter of degree according to how likely it is that the premises could be true and conclusion false.

How do we show an argument is weak? We give an example, a description of how the world could be in which the premises would be true and conclusion false. *To reason well we must use our imagination.*

7 What is a Good Argument? 27

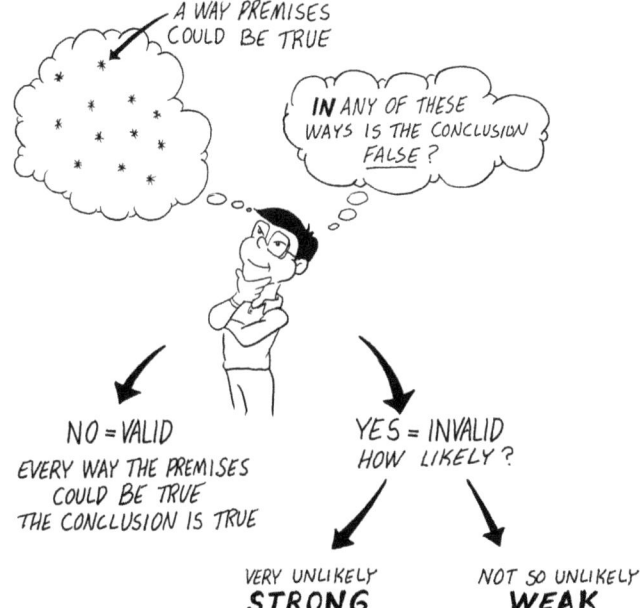

> *The conclusion follows from the premises* means that the argument is valid or strong.

For an argument to be good, it must be valid or strong. But that's not enough.

• *All textbooks are written by women.*
So the author of this textbook is a woman.
   False premise, false conclusion.

• *All textbooks are written by women. All women are human beings.*
So the author of this textbook is a human being.
   False premise, true conclusion.

From a false claim you can prove anything. So if we don't have good reason to believe the premises, then they can't give us good reason to believe the conclusion.

> **Plausible claims** A claim is *plausible* if we have good reason to believe it's true. It is less plausible the less reason we have to believe it's true. An implausible claim is also called *dubious*.

An argument is no better than its least plausible premise. But an argument could be valid or strong and have plausible premises yet still be bad.

- *Suzy:* Zeke is mean.
  Wanda: Why do you say that?
  Suzy: Because he's not nice.
  Suzy's given no reason for Wanda to believe "Zeke is mean" since "He's not nice" is not more plausible.

- *Suzy (to Dick): Every cat has a soul. So you should treat cats humanely.*
  The conclusion is plausible to Dick. But the premise is not more plausible to him. So Suzy has given Dick no more reason to believe the conclusion than he had before she spoke.

Begging the question   An argument *begs the question* if even one of its premises is no more plausible than its conclusion.

Now we can say what's needed for an argument to be good.

Tests for an argument to be good
- The premises are plausible.
- Each premise is more plausible than the conclusion.
- The argument is valid or strong.

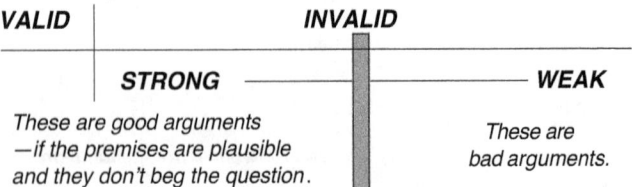

Each of these three tests can fail while the other two hold. So we can start with whichever test is easiest to judge. But why should we be interested in whether the argument is strong or valid if we don't know whether the premises are true? Compare that to applying for a home loan. A couple goes in and fills out all the forms. The loan officer looks at their answers. She might tell them right there that they don't qualify. That is, even though she doesn't know if the claims they made about their income and assets are true, she can see that even if they are true, they won't qualify for a loan. So why bother

7 What is a Good Argument? 29

to investigate whether what they said is true? On the other hand, she could tell them that they'll qualify if those claims are true. Then she goes out and makes phone calls, checks credit references and finds out if they were telling the truth.

- *Dr. E is a philosophy professor. All philosophy professors prefer dogs to cats. So Dr. E prefers dogs to cats.*
  This is a valid argument: it's impossible for the premises to be true and the conclusion false. And the conclusion is true. But it's bad because the second premise is false.

- *Dr. E is a bachelor. So Dr. E was never married.*
  There's a likely way the premise could be true and the conclusion false: Dr. E could be divorced. This is a weak argument and hence bad.

- *Whenever Spot barks, there's a cat outside. Since he's barking now, there must be a cat outside.*
  This is a bad argument: Spot might be barking at the garbageman. That doesn't show the argument is weak; it shows that the first premise is false. The argument is actually valid. But just because the argument is bad, it doesn't follow that there isn't a cat outside.

A good argument gives us good reason to believe the conclusion. But a bad argument tells us nothing about whether the conclusion is true. *A bad argument does not show that the conclusion is false or even doubtful.*

- *Maria (to her supervisor): I was told that if I put in 80 hours of overtime and have a perfect attendance record for two months, then I'll get a bonus. I've put in over 100 hours of overtime and I haven't missed a day for the last 11 weeks. So I'm entitled to a bonus.*
  The argument is valid. But we don't know if it's good because we don't know if the premises are true.

- *Student athletes should not be given special leniency in assigning their course marks because that wouldn't be treating all students equally.*
  What does "treating all students equally" mean? It means "treat everyone the same way." So the argument here is: You shouldn't treat athletes differently because you should treat everyone the same. The premise may be true, but it's just a restatement of the conclusion. The argument begs the question, so it's bad.

- *Prosecuting attorney: The defendant intended to kill Louise. He bought a gun three days before he shot her. He practiced shooting at a target that had her name written across it. He stood outside her home for two nights. He shot her twice.*

The argument is good and establishes beyond a reasonable doubt "The defendant intended to kill Louise"—if the premises are plausible. But the argument isn't valid. We don't know the defendant's thoughts, and the conclusion might be false.

- *All the dock workers at Boa Vista docks belong to the union.*
Luis has been working at Boa Vista docks for two years.
So probably Luis belongs to the union, too.

"Probably" tell us about the speaker's belief. The conclusion here is "Luis belongs to the union," and the argument is valid—regardless of what the speaker thought.

Indicator words An *indicator word* is a word or phrase added to a claim to tell us the role of the claim in an argument or what the speaker thinks about the claim or argument.

Here are some indicator words.

Conclusion indicators
  hence; therefore; so; thus; consequently; shows that

Premise indicators
  since; because; for; in as much as; due to; given that; suppose that; it follows from; on account of

Indicators of speaker's belief
  probably; certainly; most likely; I think

- *Manuel says he visited Mexico.*
He speaks Spanish and he described the towns he visited.
So Manuel really visited Mexico.

Manuel says he visited Mexico.
He speaks Spanish and he described the towns he visited.
So maybe Manuel visited Mexico.

These are the same argument. They have the same premises, and the conclusion of both is "Manuel visited Mexico." The words "so really" instead of "so maybe" lets us know that the speaker thinks the argument is valid or strong, but that doesn't make the argument valid or strong. Indicator words are not part of a claim.

Before you try your hand at some examples, review these points to make sure you can use them.

- Every good argument is valid or strong.
- Not every valid or strong argument is good.
 (It could have a dubious premise or beg the question.)

7 *What is a Good Argument?* 31

- Only invalid arguments are classified from strong to weak.
- Every weak argument is bad.
- If the conclusion of a valid argument is false, one of its premises must be false.
- A bad argument tells us nothing about the conclusion.
- Whether an argument is valid or strong does *not* depend on:
  —whether the premises are true.
  —whether we know the premises are true.
  —whether the person making the argument thinks the argument is valid or strong.

Try your hand at these!
Select the claim that makes the argument valid. You're not supposed to judge whether the claim is plausible, just whether it makes the argument valid.

1. The dogs are drinking a lot of water today. It must be hot.
    a. Dogs always drink when they are hot.
    b. Every dog will drink when the weather is hot.
    c. Hot weather means dogs will drink.
    d. Only on hot days do dogs drink a lot of water.
    e. None of the above.
2. Every Yangakuchi monitor I've had either was defective and had to be returned or else burned out in less than a year. So you'd be foolish to buy a Yangakuchi monitor.
    a. You should do what I tell you to do.
    b. Every Yangakuchi monitor will be defective or go bad.
    c. All monitors that are reliable are not Yangakuchi.
    d. None of the above.
3. Puff is a cat. So Puff meows.
    a. Anything that meows is a cat.
    b. Dogs don't meow.
    c. All cats meow.
    d. Most cats meow.
    e. None of the above.
4. Suzy is a cheerleader. So Suzy goes to all the football games.
    a. Cheerleaders get in free to the football games.
    b. Cheerleaders are expected to attend all football games.
    c. Suzy is dating Tom, who is the football captain.
    d. All cheerleaders attend all football games.
    e. None of the above.
5. If Spot gets into the garbage, Dick will hit him with a newspaper. So Dick will hit Spot.
    a. The garbage is a bad thing for Spot to get into.
    b. Whenever Spot gets into the garbage, Dick hits him.
    c. Whenever Dick hits Spot, Spot was in the garbage.

32 How to Reason

    d. Spot got into the garbage.
    e. None of the above.
6. The president is on every channel on television. So he must be making an important speech.
    a. Only presidents make important speeches on television.
    b. When the president makes an important speech on television, he's on every channel.
    c. When the president is on every channel on TV, he's making an important speech.
    d. Presidents only make important speeches.
    e. None of the above.

For the exercises below, answer the following.
   Argument? (yes or no)
   Conclusion: *Premises*:
   Classify: valid   strong ———— weak
   If not valid, show why:
   Good argument? (choose one)
   • It's good (passes the three tests).
   • It's bad because a premise is false.
   • It's bad because it's weak.
   • It's bad because it begs the question.
   • It's valid or strong, but you don't know if the premises are true, so you can't say if it's good or bad.

7. Flo's hair was long. Now it's short. So Flo must have gotten a haircut.
8. Intelligent students study hard. Zoe studies hard. So Zoe is intelligent.
9. All licensed drivers in California have taken a driver's test. Lemuel has taken a driver's test in California. So Lemuel is a licensed driver in California.
10. No dog meows. Puff meows. So Puff is not a dog.
11. Lee: My friend Judy manages a local bookstore. She drives a new Jaguar. So bookstore managers must make good money.
12. No cat barks. Buddy is not a cat. So Buddy barks.
13. What do you want to eat for dinner? Well, we had fish yesterday and pasta the day before. We haven't eaten chicken for a while. How about some chicken with potatoes?
14. Maria: Almost all the professors I've met at this school are liberals.
    Manuel: So to get a teaching job here, it must help to be a liberal.
15. Suzy: Every student who has ever taken a course from Professor Zzzyzzx has passed. So if I take his composition course, I'll pass, too.
16. Dick: Whenever the garbage gets picked up, the trash bins end up away from the curb.
    Lee: The bins haven't been moved away from the curb. So the garbage hasn't been picked up.
17. There are 30 seconds left in the football game. The 49ers have 35 points. The Dolphins have 7 points. So the 49ers will win.

Answers
1. d.
2. d.

3. c.
4. d.
5. d.
6. c.
7. Conclusion: Flo got a haircut. Premises: Flo's hair was long. Now Flo's hair is short. "So" is not part of the conclusion. Invalid: Flo might have got her hair caught in a lawn mower. But it's strong. Good if premises are plausible.
8. Weak, bad. Zoe could be dumb and that's why she studies so hard.
9. Weak, bad. Lemuel could have failed the test.
10. Valid and good.
11. Weak, bad. Judy could be married to a rich woman.
12. Weak, bad. Buddy could be a penguin or a cockroach.
13. Not an argument. So no premise or conclusion.
14. What Maria say is too vague for this to be an argument.
15. Weak, bad. Professor Zzzyzzx may have changed his grading, or the school may have required him to become harder, or he may never have had a student as bad as Suzy.
16. Valid. Good if the premises are plausible.
17. Strong. Good if the premises are plausible. But not valid.

8 Evaluating Premises

We can't ask for a justification for every premise of every argument or we'd never get started. We need criteria for when it's O.K. to accept a claim without an argument.

> **Three choices for whether to believe a claim**
> - Accept the claim as true.
> - Reject the claim as false.
> - Suspend judgment.

not believe ≠ believe is false
lack of evidence ≠ evidence it's false

Criteria for accepting an unsupported claim

Our most reliable source of information about the world is our own experience.
We need to trust our own experience because that's the best we have. Everything else is secondhand. Should you trust your buddy, your spouse, your priest, your professor, the president when what they say contradicts what you know from your own experience? That way lies demagoguery, religious intolerance, and worse. Too often leaders have manipulated the populace. All Muslims want to overthrow the U.S.? But what about my Muslim neighbor who's on the city council? You have to forget your own experience to believe the Big Lie. They repeat it over and over and over again until you begin to believe it, even when your own experience says it isn't so.

Oh, we get the idea. Don't trust the politicians. No. It's a lot closer to home than that. Every rumor, all the gossip you hear, compare it to what *you* know about the person or situation. Don't repeat it. Be thoughtful, not part of the humming crowd.

> *Who are you going to believe, me or your own eyes?* — Chico Marx

Still, there are times we shouldn't trust our own experience.

- Sgt. Carlson of the Las Vegas Police Department says, "Eyewitnesses are terrible. You get a gun stuck in your face and you can't remember anything." The police do line-ups, putting a suspect to be identified by

8 Evaluating Premises 35

a witness among other people who look a bit similar. The police have to be careful not to say anything that may influence the witness, because memory is malleable.

- *You tell the officer that the car ahead didn't put on its turn signal.*
  You think that's so, but with the rain and distractions you might have missed it. The state of the world around us can affect our observations and make our personal experience unreliable.

- *You go to the circus and see a magician cut a lady in half. You saw it, so it has to be true.*
  You don't believe it, and rightly so, because it contradicts too much else you know about the world.

- *Day after day we see the sun rise in the east and set in the west. So clearly the sun revolves around the Earth.*
  We don't accept our own experience because there's a long story, a theory of how the Earth turns and revolves around the sun. A good argument has been made for us to reject our own experience, and that argument builds on other experiences of ours.

- *Tom was asked to describe what he sees in the picture.*

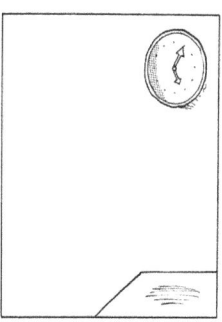

He wrote: "The guy is in the room and he spots a purse on the table. He looks around pretty shiftily and thinks that he can get away with taking the purse. So he grabs it and goes."

How does Tom know that the guy thinks he can get away with it? How does Tom know the guy grabbed the purse? Tom didn't see that. Perhaps the purse belongs to the guy's girlfriend and he was looking around for her, and then he took it to her. *Personal experience means what we perceive—not what we deduce from that.*

- *Wanda: Chinese guys are really smart. There are five of them in my calculus class and they're all getting an A.*
  It's not Wanda's personal experience that all Chinese guys are really smart but a deduction she's made from knowing five of them.

We can accept a claim made by someone we know and trust who knows about this kind of claim.
> • Maria tells Dick to stay away from the area around South Third and Westermeyer Avenue. She's seen people doing drugs there and knows two people who were mugged at that corner.
>
> Dick has good reason to believe Maria's claims.
>
> • Dick's mother tells him that he should major in business so he can get ahead in life.
>
> Should Dick believe her? She can tell him about her friends' children. But what really are the chances of getting a good job with a degree in business? It would be better to check at the local colleges where they keep records on what jobs graduates get. Dick shouldn't reject her claim; he should suspend judgment until he gets more information.

We can accept a claim made by a reputable authority we can trust as an expert on this kind of claim and who has no motive to mislead.
> • *The Surgeon General announces that smoking is bad for your health.*
>
> *The doctor hired by the tobacco company says there's no proof that smoking is addictive or causes lung cancer.*
>
> *The new Surgeon General says that heroin should be legal.*
>
> The Surgeon General is a reputable physician with expertise in public health. She's in a position to survey the research on the subject. We have no reason to suspect her motives. So it's reasonable to believe her about smoking. But is the doctor hired by the tobacco company an expert on smoking-related diseases—or an allergist or a pediatrician? He has motive to mislead. There's no reason to accept his claim.
>
> Nor is there any reason to accept what the Surgeon General says about what should be law. Though she's an authority on health, she's not an expert on law and society.

We can accept a claim put forward in a reputable journal or reference source.
> • *The* New England Journal of Medicine *is regularly quoted in newspapers, and for good reason.* Articles in it are reviewed by experts who are asked to evaluate whether the research was done to scientific standards. We have less reason to trust National Geographic because it pays for its own research in order to sell the magazine. What about Scientific American? Are the articles there reviewed by experts or are they commissioned? And anyone can incorporate as the "American Institute for Global Warming Analysis" or any other title. A name is not enough to go by.

We can accept a claim from some usually reliable media source that has no obvious motive to mislead, if the person being quoted is named. It's up to you to decide from experience whether a source is reliable. Don't trust a news report that makes that decision for you by quoting unnamed "usually reliable sources." They're not even as reliable as the person who's quoting them, and anyway they've covered themselves by saying "usually." If there's reliable information, the reporter should be able to back it up with documents or quotes. Otherwise, it's just rumor, often planted to sway opinion. *There's never good reason to believe a claim from an unnamed source.*

Look also for bias in the media because of its advertisers.

There are no absolute rules for when to accept, when to reject, and when to suspend judgment about a claim. It's a skill, weighing up these criteria in order of importance.

Criteria for judging unsupported claims

Accept The claim is known to be true from personal experience. *Exceptions*: Our memory is not good; there's a good argument against what we thought was our experience; it's not our experience but what we've concluded from it.

Reject The claim is known to be false from personal experience.

Reject The claim contradicts other claims we know to be true.

Accept The claim is made by someone we know and trust who knows about this kind of claim.

Accept The claim is made by a reputable authority we can trust as an expert about this kind of claim and who has no motive to mislead.

Accept The claim is made in a reputable journal or reference.

Accept The claim is from some media source that's usually reliable and has no obvious motive to mislead, if the person being quoted is named.

We don't have criteria for when to suspend judgment. That's the attitude we adopt whenever we don't have good reason to accept or reject a claim.

Above all, personal experience is your best guide. Don't trust others more than yourself about what you know best.

- *A Nevada couple letting their SUV's navigation system guide them through the high desert of eastern Oregon got stuck in snow for three days when their GPS unit sent them down a remote forest road.*
   —*Albuquerque Journal*, December 29, 2009

   How far down a remote snow-packed forest road do *you* have to go before you trust your own senses over your GPS unit?

Advertising

Advertisements are meant to convince you of the (often unstated) claim that you should buy the product, or frequent the establishment, or use the service. Sometimes the claims are accurate, sometimes they're not. There's nothing special about them, though. They should be judged by the criteria we've already considered. *If you think there should be more stringent criteria for evaluating ads, you're not judging other claims carefully enough.* Here are some radio ads from early 2010.

- *Gold is the only asset that's not somebody else's liability.*
   That's false. When you've paid off your car it's not someone else's liability.

- *We're Credit Card Relief . . . We've been helping people like you for more than a decade. We're an attorney-driven program.*
   This isn't true or false: "attorney-driven program" is meaningless, though it sounds impressive.

The internet

What reason do you have to believe something you read on the internet? Next time you're ready, mouth agape, to swallow what's up there on the screen, imagine your friend saying, "No, really, you believed *that*?" Don't check your brain at the door when you go online.

- *Colonial records refer to small, nearly hairless dogs at the beginning of the 19th century, one of which claims 16th-century Conquistadores found them plentiful in the region later known as Chihuahua.**

   * *Pedro Baptista Pino y Juan Lopez Cancelada, Exposición sucinta y sencilla de la Provincia del Nuevo México y otros escritos. Ed. Jesus Paniagua Perez. Valladolid: Junta de Castilla / León: Universidad de León, 2007, p. 244: "even in the desert the tiny dogs could be found, hunting rats, mice, and lizards." The footnote that follows alludes to starving Conquistadores reportedly hunting and stewing the dogs (Universidad Veracruzana, Arquivo Viejo, XXVI.2711).*

   — "Chihuahua dog," *Wikipedia*, February 2012

   You believe what you read on Wikipedia, and quote it. But this is pure fantasy written by Michael Rooney and me. There is such a book, but there's no such quote, and we made up the reference to Arquivo Viejo. What makes you think that any other entry in Wikipedia is more reliable?

Wikipedia is not an encyclopedia. Entries aren't signed, so you can't evaluate the expertise of the author. Lots of ignorant people correcting each other does not result in a reliable source. At best, Wikipedia entries are useful to stimulate our imaginations and provide references we can consult.*

Try your hand at these!
1. What three choices can we make about whether to believe a claim?
2. Our personal observations are no better than _____ .
3. What does a bad argument tell us about its conclusion?
4. When should we suspend judgment on a claim?
5. What difference is there between how we evaluate an advertisement and how we evaluate any other apparent argument?
6.

How should he respond?

Evaluate the following claims by saying whether you accept, reject, or suspend judgment.
7. Toads give you warts. (said by your mother)
8. Toads give you warts. (said by your doctor)
9. The moon rises in the west.
10. The Pacers beat the Knicks 92–84 last night. (heard on your local news)
11. They're marketing a new liposuction machine you can attach to your vacuum cleaner. (told to you by your best friend)
12. Boise-Cascade has plans to log all old-growth forests in California. (said by a Sierra Club representative)
13. The United States government was not involved in the recent coup attempt in Venezuela. (unnamed sources in the Defense Department, by the Associated Press)
14. Cats are the greatest threat to public health of any common pet. (said by the author of this book)

---

* But why trust me? See <http://chronicle.com/article/The-Undue-Weight-of-Truth-on/130704/> for an excellent critique of how ignorance can trump expertise in Wikipedia. And see <http://www.newyorker.com/archive/2006/07/31/060731fa_fact> for unmasking an editor of Wikipedia.

40 *How to Reason*

15. Cats are the greatest threat to public health of any common pet.
    (said by the Surgeon General)
16. Blood is blue without oxygen.
17. It is very unlikely that anyone could get infected with avian flu by eating thoroughly cooked chicken. *(New York Times*, Science and Health section, citing Professor William K. Hallman of Rutgers University)
18. Maxell media—offers 100 years of archival life! Delivers quality you can trust! (MacMall catalogue, 2003)
19. *Pet Healer* Pet Healer with psychic abilities to communicate with pets that have left this earthly plane. Contact 292–xxxx. Suggested donation: $25–$100.
    (*Crosswinds Weekly*, Albuquerque)

Answers
1. Accept as true. Reject as false. Suspend judgment.
2. Our memory.
3. Nothing.
4. When we don't have good reason to believe it's true or to believe it's false.
5. None.
6. The heroin user has experience finding a vein and getting high, but that doesn't make him knowledgeable about the long-term health risks.
7. Reject (common knowledge that it's false).
8. Reject. Change doctors.
9. Reject (personal experience). You did notice it rises in the east?.
10. Accept (usually reliable source).
11. Reject (personal experience and general knowledge that you can't do surgery at home, and liposuction is surgery).
12. Suspend judgment (biased source, and "all" forests seems an exaggeration).
13. Suspend judgment (unnamed source).
14. Suspend judgment (possibly biased source).
15. Accept. You can't reject this on personal experience, since no experience you have will tell you who got sick worst from which pets in the U.S.
16. Unless you're well-read on this subject, suspend judgment.
17. Accept (reliable source).
18. 100 years! How could they know that? No reason to believe.
19. If you suspended judgment, you've been conned.

9 Common Mistakes in Evaluating Claims

Sometimes we have good reason to believe a claim because it's put forward by an authority. But it's a mistake, a **bad appeal to authority**, to accept a claim when the person isn't an authority on the subject or has a motive to mislead.

> • *Zoe: What do you think of the President's new science funding plan?*
> *Tom: It's awful. It'll cut back funding on military research.*
> *They said so on that veterans' website.*
> Not everything you read on a veterans' website is true.

Though it's O.K. to suspend judgment on a claim if you don't think the person making it is a reputable authority, it's never right to say a claim is false because of who said it. That's **mistaking the person (or group) for the claim**.

> • *Tom: I don't believe the new global warming accord will help the environment. That's just another lie our president said.*
> *Dick: Come on, it's not false just 'cause he said it. Politicians don't lie all the time.*
> Tom is mistaking the person for the claim. There's no shortcut for thinking about a claim in order to evaluate whether to accept it.

> • *Zeke: There's no water shortage here in New Mexico. That's just one of those things environmentalists say.*
> Zeke is mistaking the group for the claim.

> • *Dick: This is terrible what's happening with global warming. We've got to cut back on driving.*
> *Tom: Stop driving? Are you crazy? I heard an expert on Fox News say that the evidence isn't clear that global warming is caused by humans.*
> *Dick: You believe everything you hear on Fox News?*
> *Tom: No. But since it's controversial, I figure it's best to suspend judgment.*
> You might think that suspending judgment is the best course, the most unbiased. But that's exactly what the big oil and coal companies want. If you suspend judgment on whether global warming is caused by humans using fossil fuels, you won't have reason to cut back on driving or to oppose new coal-fired electricity-generating plants. There is overwhelming evidence, given by scientists who have no obvious motive to mislead, that burning fossil fuels has caused global warming

and that global warming will get much worse and is very dangerous unless we stop using fossil fuels. That a very few scientists don't agree shouldn't count as equal to the weight of the most respected authorities and research. It's a bad appeal to authority to suspend judgment in this case. Tom is being conned, just like a lot of people were in the 1950s and 1960s when the tobacco companies trotted out their "experts" to say that it wasn't certain that smoking causes cancer.

It's also a mistake to accept a claim as true because a lot of other people believe it. That's an **appeal to common belief**.

* *Maria: All the guys at my work say that Consolidated Computers is a great investment. So I'm going to buy 500 shares—they can't all be wrong.*
Maria is making an appeal to common belief, which is just a bad appeal to authority.

The standard fare of conspiracy theorists is to think that because it's possible, it's true. **Possibility ≠ plausibility**.

* *Tom: Terrorists are attacking us by spreading disease with our money. Dollar bills are passed hand to hand more than mail, more than menus, more than a few door handles in an office building. No one gives a second thought if you handle money with gloves in the winter. Do you ever think twice when Achmed hands you your change at the convenience store? Now you know why the flu reached epidemic proportions this year.*
Suzy: Yes, yes, that could be true. And it sure explains a lot. I'm going to be real careful taking any money from Muslims now.
Tom's conspiracy theory is just feeding Suzy's prejudices and paranoia. What's possible is not necessarily plausible.

An interesting story is just that—a story, which might be worth investigating. We need evidence before we believe. Sometimes there really are conspiracies, like when the soldiers and Department of Defense tried to cover up the torture at Abu Ghraib. But with conspiracies, we can be pretty sure evidence will eventually come out.

Three may keep a secret, if two of them are dead.   — Benjamin Franklin

* *Donkeys only make that burbling noise flapping their lips when no one is around.*
A friend of mine who has donkeys and packs into the mountains with them told me this. So I was inclined to believe him—after all, he knows about

donkeys. Until I thought: How could he know if this is true? You have to be around to know whether they're burbling. Always ask:
How could they know that?

Similar mistakes in evaluating arguments
It's a mistake to say that an argument is bad because of who said it. That's **mistaking the person (or group) for the argument**.

- *Zoe: I went to Professor Zzzyzzx's talk about writing last night. He showed why the best way to start on a novel is to make an outline of the plot.*
  Suzy: Are you kidding? He could never get his published. And he doesn't even speak English good.
  Suzy is mistaking the person for the argument. Professor Zzzyzzx's argument could be good even if Suzy doubts his qualifications to make it.

To **refute** an argument is to show it's bad. When someone points out to us that the person who made an argument doesn't believe one of the premises, we reckon the argument must be bad. But that's a **phony refutation**. Judging by sincerity is mistaking the person for the argument.

- *Harry: We should stop logging old-growth forests. There are very few of them left in the U.S. They are important watersheds and preserve wildlife. And once cut, we can't re-create them.*
  Tom: You say we should stop logging old-growth forests? Who are you kidding? You just built a log cabin on the mountain.
  Tom's rejection of Harry's argument seems reasonable, since Harry's actions betray the conclusion he's arguing for. But whether they do or not (perhaps the logs came from the land that Harry's family cleared in a new-growth forest), Tom has not answered Harry's argument. Tom is not justified in ignoring an argument because of what he thinks Harry did.

  If Harry responds to Tom by saying that the logs for his home weren't cut from an old-growth forest, he's been suckered. Tom got him to change the subject, and they will be debating an entirely different claim than Harry intended. It's a phony refutation.

Whether a claim is true or false
is not determined by who said it.

Whether an argument is good or bad
is not determined by who made it.

> First, realize that it is necessary for an intelligent person to reflect on the words that are spoken, not the person who says them. If the words are true, he will accept them whether he who says them is known as a truth teller or a liar. One can extract gold from a clump of dirt, a beautiful narcissus comes from an ordinary bulb, medication from the venom of a snake.
> —Abd-el-Kader, Algerian Muslim statesman, 1858

Always ask "Why?"

Always ask "So?"

Take as authority only those whose speech indicates knowledge and awareness and whose conduct indicates trustworthiness. Rely never on the position of an authority: many fools have been promoted to high place. Human desires, wills, fears can lead to fools prospering. But wisdom will out.

Don't believe because it's comfortable. A great desire for comfort, for no challenge, can lead to the enslavement of the truth and to the enslavement of us all. If in doubt, suspend judgment. The seeker is wiser than the dogmatist.

And remember these mistakes in accepting or rejecting claims:

- Bad appeal to authority.
- Mistaking the person or group for the claim.
- Appeal to common belief.
- Mistaking the person or group for the argument.
- Phony refutation.
- Possibility ≠ plausibility.
- Forgetting to ask, "How could they know that?".

Try your hand at these!

1. When are we justified in rejecting a claim because of who said it?
2. Hypocrisy is bad. So why shouldn't we reject anything that smacks of hypocrisy?

Evaluate whether there are any mistakes in evaluating claims in these examples.

3. Suzy: I played doubles on my team for four years. It is definitely a more intense game than playing singles.
   Zoe: Yesterday on the news, Maria Sharapova said that doubles in tennis is much easier because there are two people covering almost the same playing area.
   Suzy: I guess she must be right then.
4. Mom: You shouldn't stay out so late. It's dangerous, so I want you home early.
   Son: But none of my friends have curfews, and they stay out as long as they want.
5. Manuel: Barbara said divorce'll hurt her kids' emotions.

9 Common Mistakes in Evaluating Premises   45

    Maria: But she goes out with her boyfriend every night, leaving the kids and her husband at home. She won't divorce, but she's already hurt her kids. So it doesn't matter if she gets divorced or not.

6. Zoe: You should be more sensitive to the comments you make around people.
   Dick: Of course you'd think that—you're a woman.
7. Zoe: The author of this book said that bad people always make wrong decisions. You need to have virtue to make good use of reasoning.
   Suzy: What does he know about virtue?
8. Zoe: That program to build a new homeless shelter is a great idea. We need to help get poor people off the streets so they can eventually fend for themselves.
   Suzy: How could you say that? You don't even give money to the homeless guy who was begging on the street corner there.
9. Doctor: Well, your test results show you have very high cholesterol. You need to cut back on fatty foods and get more exercise, or else you'll develop heart disease.
   Prof. Zzzyzzx: Vat are you talking? I am very good feeling. Eating meat gives me strength!
10. Zoe: That new law against panhandling is terrible. People have a right to ask for money so long as they aren't really bothering anyone.
    Tom: Sure. And I suppose you believe everything else the ACLU says.
11. Doctor: You are morbidly obese. If you don't lose some weight, you'll develop serious health problems.
    Wanda: You're just prejudiced against fat people.
12. Maria: What do you think about the new book on financial independence?
    Lee: It must be good; it's on the *New York Times* best seller list.

Answers
1. Never.
2. It's mistaking the person for the argument or claim.
3. Suzy is taking the word of an expert over her own experience.
4. The son is making a bad appeal to common practice.
5. An O.K. argument.
6. Mistaking the group (women) for the claim.
7. Suzy is right! She says she has no good reason to believe me, since I'm not an expert on virtue (I'm a logician, after all). She's not suggesting that I'm wrong but only that she has no reason to accept the claim. (Of course, if Suzy knew me better, she'd revise her opinion.)
8. Phony refutation.
9. Prof. Zzzyzzx is challenging his doctor's prescription that he needs to do those things to stay healthy. Nothing wrong with that.
10. Mistaking the group for the claim.
11. Wanda is ascribing bad motives to her doctor and using that as the basis to reject his claim. Mistaking the person for the claim.
12. Appeal to common belief (*not* authority—he isn't referring to a review). O.K., if Lee has found in the past that books on the *New York Times* best seller list are what he likes. Bad otherwise.

10   Repairing Arguments

Most arguments we encounter are not complete. But that doesn't mean they're necessarily bad.

> • Lee: *Tom wants to get a dog.*
> Maria: *What kind?*
> Lee: *A dachshund. And that's really stupid, since he wants one that will catch a Frisbee.*
>
> Lee has made an argument: Tom wants a dog that will catch a Frisbee, so he shouldn't get a dachshund. This looks bad because there's no *glue*, no claim that gets us from the premise to the conclusion. But Maria knows, just like us, that a dachshund is a lousy choice for someone who wants a dog to catch a Frisbee. They're too low to the ground, they can't run fast, they can't jump, and the Frisbee is bigger than they are so they couldn't bring it back. Any dog like that is a bad choice for a Frisbee partner. Lee just left out these obvious claims. But why should he bother to say them?

Folks usually leave out so much that if we look at only what's said when evaluating what to believe, we'll be missing too much. We can and should repair many arguments. But when are we justified in adding a premise? How do we know whether we've repaired or just added our own ideas? And how can we recognize when an argument is beyond repair? We need to make some assumptions about the person who's giving the argument.

> ***The Principle of Rational Discussion***   We assume that the other person who is discussing with us or whose argument we're considering:
> 1. Knows about the subject under discussion.
> 2. Is able and willing to reason well.
> 3. Is not lying.

Why should we invoke this principle? After all, not everyone fits these conditions all the time.

Consider condition (1). Dr. E leaves his car at the repair shop because it's running badly, and he returns later in the afternoon. The mechanic tells him that he needs a new fuel injector. Dr. E asks, "Are you sure I need a new one?" That sounds like an invitation for the mechanic to give an argument. But she shouldn't. Dr. E doesn't have the slightest idea how his engine runs, so she might as well be speaking Greek. She should try to educate Dr. E or ask Dr. E to accept her claim on trust—after all, she's an authority.

Consider condition (2). Sometimes people intend not to reason well. Like the demagogic politician or talk-show host, they want to convince you by other means and will not accept your arguments, no matter how good they are. There's no point in deliberating with them.

Or you may encounter a person who's temporarily unable or unwilling to reason well, a person who's upset or in love. Again, it makes no sense at such a time to try to reason. Calm them, address their emotions, and leave discussion for another time.

Then again, you might find yourself with someone who wants to reason well but just can't seem to follow an argument. Why try to reason? Give them a copy of this book.

What if you find that the other person is lying—not just a little white lie, but continuously lying? Then there's no point in reasoning with him except perhaps to catch him in his lies.

The Principle of Rational Discussion does not instruct us to give other people the benefit of the doubt. It summarizes the necessary conditions for us to reason with someone. Compare it to playing chess: what's the point of playing if the other person doesn't understand or won't play by the rules?

Still, most people don't follow this principle. They don't care if your argument is good. Why should you follow these rules and assume them of others? If you don't:

- You're denying the essentials of democracy.
- You'll undermine your own ability to evaluate arguments.
- You're not as likely to convince others.

If you once forfeit the confidence of your fellow citizens, you can never regain their respect and esteem. It is true that you may fool all the people some of the time; you can even fool some of the people all the time; but you cannot fool all of the people all the time.
—attributed to Abraham Lincoln

- *Dick: Cats are really dangerous pets. Look at all the evidence. See, it says so here in this medical journal, and it lists all the diseases you can catch from them, even schizophrenia. You know that lots of your friends get sick from cat allergies. And remember how Puff scratched Zoe last week? You can't deny it.*

Suzy: OK, OK. So you can reason well like Dr. E. But I still don't believe that cats are dangerous pets.

Suzy recognizes that Dick has given a good argument for cats being dangerous pets, but she still doesn't believe it. She's not judiciously suspending judgment; she's just unwilling to reason about her beloved cats.

> **The Mark of Irrationality** If someone recognizes that an argument is good, then he or she is irrational not to accept its conclusion.

It's not worthwhile to reason with people if they're irrational. Sometimes, though, we hear an argument for one side and then one for the other, and we can't find a flaw in either. Then we should suspend judgment on which conclusion is true until we can investigate more. It's not irrational to suspend judgment if you're not sure.

The Guide to Repairing Arguments

The Principle of Rational Discussion helps us formulate a guide to repairing arguments.

> **The Guide to Repairing Arguments** Given an (implicit) argument that is apparently defective, we are justified in *adding* a premise or conclusion if all the following hold:
>
> 1. The argument becomes valid or stronger.
> 2. The premise is plausible and plausible to the other person.
> 3. The premise is more plausible than the conclusion.
>
> We can also *delete* a premise that's false or dubious if doing so makes the argument no worse.

• *Lee: I was wondering what kind of pet Louis has. It must be a dog.*
Maria: How do you know?
Lee: Because I heard it barking last night.

Maria shouldn't dismiss Lee's reasoning just because the link from premises to conclusion is missing. She should ask what claim(s) are needed to make it strong, since she knows that Lee intends to and is able to reason well. The obvious premise to add is "All pets that bark are dogs." But Maria knows that's false (seals, foxes, parrots) and can assume that Lee does, too, since he's supposed to know about the subject. So she tries "Almost all pets that bark are dogs." That's plausible and with it the argument is strong and good.

We first try to make the argument valid or strong because we don't need to know what the speaker was thinking in order to do so. Then we can ask whether that claim is plausible and whether it would be plausible to the other person. By first trying to make the argument valid or strong, we can show the other person what he or she needs to assume to make the argument good.

- *No dog meows. So Spot does not meow.*
"Spot is a dog" is the only premise that will make this a valid or strong argument. So we add that. And since it's plausible, the argument is good. We don't add "Spot barks." That's true and may be obvious to the person who stated the argument, but it doesn't make the argument any better, so adding it violates condition (1) of the Guide. We repair only as needed.

- *Almost every dog barks. So Spot is a dog.*
The obvious premise to add is "Spot barks." That may be true, but it still leaves the argument weak: Spot could be a fox, or a seal, or a coyote. If the obvious premise to add leaves the argument weak, the argument is unrepairable.

- *Dr. E is a good teacher because he gives fair exams.*
To make the argument strong we need "Almost any teacher who gives fair exams is a good teacher." But that's dubious, since a bad teacher could copy fair exams from the instructor's manual. The argument can't be repaired because the obvious premise to add to make the argument strong or valid is false or dubious. But can't we make it strong by adding, say, "Dr. E gives great explanations," "Dr. E is amusing," "Dr. E never misses class"? Yes, all those are true and perhaps obvious to the person. But adding them doesn't repair this argument. It makes a whole new argument. Don't put words in someone's mouth.

- *Sure you'll get a passing grade in English. After all, you paid tuition to take the course.*
The argument is weak—and it is an argument, for the last sentence is meant as reason to believe the first. But there's no obvious repair: it's false that anyone who pays tuition for a course will pass it. The person apparently can't reason. Don't bother to repair.

- *You shouldn't eat bacon. Haven't you heard that fat is bad for you?*
The conclusion is the first sentence. But what are the premises? The speaker's question is meant as an assertion: "Fat is bad for you." That alone, though, won't give the conclusion. We need something like "Bacon has a lot of fat" and "You shouldn't eat anything that's bad for you." Premises like these are so obvious we don't bother to say them. This argument is O.K. with these obvious additions.

- *Dick: Dogs are loyal. Dogs are friendly. Dogs can protect you from burglars.*
  Maria: So?
  Dick: So dogs make great pets.
  Maria: Why does that follow?

  Maria's right. Dick's argument is missing the *glue: the link between premises and conclusion that rules out other possibilities*. What's needed here is something like "Anything that's loyal, friendly, and can protect you from burglars is a great pet." But that's exactly what Maria thinks is false: Dogs need room to run around, they need to be walked every day, they cost more to take care of than goldfish. Just stating a lot of obvious truths doesn't get you a conclusion.

- *You're going to vote for the Green Party candidate for president? Don't you realize that means your vote will be wasted?*

  The questions are meant as assertions: "You shouldn't vote for the Green Party candidate" (the conclusion) and "Your vote will be wasted" (the premise). This sounds reasonable, though something is missing. A visitor from Denmark may not know that "The Green Party candidate doesn't have a chance of winning" is true. But she may also question why that matters. We'd have to fill in the argument further: "If you vote for someone who doesn't have a chance of winning, then your vote will be wasted." And when we add that premise, we see that the argument which uses such "obvious" premises is really not good. Why should we believe that if you vote for someone who doesn't stand a chance of winning then your vote is wasted? If that were true, then who wins is the only important result of an election, rather than, say, making a position understood by people for the next election. At best, we can say that when the unstated premises are added, we get an argument one of whose premises is in need of a substantial argument. Trying to repair an argument can lead us to unstated assumptions that need to be debated.

- *Cats are more likely than dogs to carry diseases harmful to humans. Cats kill songbirds and can kill people's pets. Cats disturb people at night with their screeching and clattering in garbage cans. Cats leave paw prints on cars and will sleep in unattended cars. Cats are not as pleasant as dogs and are owned only by people who have satanic affinities. So there should be a leash law for cats just like for dogs.*

  This letter to the editor is going pretty well until the next to last sentence. That claim is a bit dubious, and the argument would be just as strong without it. So we should delete it. Then we have an argument which, with some unstated premises you can supply, is pretty good.

- *Alcoholism is a disease, not a character flaw. People are genetically predisposed to be addicted to alcohol. An alcoholic should not be fired or imprisoned but should be given treatment. Treatment centers should be established because it is too difficult to overcome the addiction to alcohol by oneself. The encouragement and direction of others is what's needed to help people, for alcoholics can find the power within themselves to fight and triumph over their addiction.*

On the face of it, "Alcoholism is a disease, not a character flaw" and "Alcoholics can find the power within themselves to fight and triumph over their addiction" contradict each other. Since both are used to get the conclusion, "Treatment centers should be established," neither can be deleted. They both can't be true, so the argument is unrepairable.

- *In a famous speech, Martin Luther King Jr. said:*

    I have a dream that one day this nation will rise up and live out the true meaning of its creed: 'We hold these truths to be self-evident— that all men are created equal'. . . . I have a dream that one day even the state of Mississippi, a desert state sweltering with the heat of injustice and oppression, will be transformed into an oasis of freedom and justice. I have a dream that my four little children will one day live in a nation where they will not be judged by the color of their skin but by the content of their character.

    . . . King is also presenting a logical argument . . . the argument might be stated as follows: "America was founded on the principle that all men are created equal. This implies that people should not be judged by skin color, which is an accident of birth, but rather by what they make of themselves ('the content of their character'). To be consistent with this principle, America should treat black people and white people alike."

    — David Kelley, *The Art of Reasoning*

    The rewriting of this passage is putting words in someone's mouth. Where did David Kelley get the premise "This implies . . . " ? Stating my dreams and hoping others will share them is not an argument. Martin Luther King Jr. knew how to argue well and could do so when he wanted. We're not going to make his words more respectable by pretending they're an argument. Not every good attempt to persuade is an argument.

- *Dick: It's a really bad idea to cut down those old growth trees.*
    Tom: What are you talking about? Are you going to let those tree-huggers tell us what to do? It's about time we took charge of our own land here instead of the federal government pushing us around

    Tom has confused whether we have the right to cut down forests with whether we should cut them down. The argument is weak; indeed, we could delete either premise and it wouldn't be any weaker. His premises are irrelevant.

> **Relevance** A premise is *irrelevant* if you can delete it and the argument isn't weaker.

• Maria (to Dick): *Parking is still difficult on campus. From 8:30 in the morning till 4 every afternoon it's impossible to find a parking place—I've spoken with all my friends, and it takes us 15 minutes, often more. And that's with a parking sticker we paid $25 to get. Without that you could look forever, or park on the street and hope not to get a ticket. Our school should build more parking lots.*

Dick agrees with all of Maria's assumptions. But still he asks, "So?" There are lots of ways her claims could be true and conclusion false: the school doesn't want to encourage more people to drive to campus; the school has no money to build parking lots; the school has an agreement with the city not to build more parking. Some general claim is needed, but there's no obvious plausible one, so we can't repair the argument.

This might seem obvious, but some assumption linking the observed behavior to the saleslady's thoughts or feelings is needed. The only one that would make the argument valid or strong is: "If a saleslady ignores a black man, then she's racist." That's implausible: She might be ignoring everyone, or she's absorbed in her book, or she's just naturally rude. The argument is unrepairable.

> **You can't get subjective from only objective** There's no good argument with subjective conclusion and only objective premises. Some premise linking observed behavior to thoughts, feelings, or beliefs is needed.

• Tom: *All CEOs of computer software companies are rich. Bill Gates is a CEO of a computer software company. So Bill Gates is rich.*
Suzy: *Gee, that's valid, just like Dr. E said. And Bill Gates is sure rich. So I guess all CEOs of computer software companies are rich.*
Suzy is **arguing backwards**. An argument is supposed to give reason to

believe that its conclusion is true, not that its premises are true. There are lots of CEOs of small software companies who are working hard just to make a living. There's no repair here.

We've seen examples where it's clear that the argument is bad and there's no point in repairing it. Let's summarize those conditions.

Unrepairable Arguments We can't repair an argument if any of the following hold:
- There's no argument there.
- There's nothing obvious to add.
- A premise is false or dubious and can't be deleted.
- The obvious premise to add would leave the argument weak.
- The obvious premise to add to make the argument valid or strong is not plausible.
- The conclusion is clearly false.

But remember: *When you show an argument is bad, you haven't shown that the conclusion is false.*

Implying and inferring

When it's clear what claim is needed to make a person's argument good, or even to make an argument, we say that the person has **implied** it; we have **inferred** it. We also say someone is implying a claim if in context it's clear from what they say that they believe it. In that case we infer that the person believes the claim.

> • *Harry: I'm not going to vote, because no matter who becomes mayor, nothing is going to get done to repair roads in this part of town.*
> A claim is needed to repair Harry's argument: "If no matter who becomes mayor nothing is going to get done to repair roads in this part of town, then you shouldn't vote for mayor." We infer this from what he said; Harry has implied it.

> • *Wendy's. Our beef is fresh. Never frozen.* — Billboard in Albuquerque.
> This ad implies "Fresh beef is better than frozen." Should you believe that?

> • *Maria: Why did you write up this exercise? It wasn't assigned.*
> *Lee: Dr. E said that all his best students hand in the optional exercises for extra credit.*
> *Maria: I better do one, too.*

Dr. E hasn't said that his students should hand in extra work to get a good grade. Lee and Maria have inferred that; they think he's implied it. If Lee complains to the department head that Dr. E is demanding more than he asked on the syllabus, Dr. E could reply that Lee was jumping to conclusions. He might say, "I've observed that my best students hand in extra-credit work—that's all I was saying. I had no intention of asking for extra assignments." Lee, however, could say that in the context in which Dr. E made the remark it was fairly obvious he was implying that if Lee wanted him to believe he's a good student, he should hand in extra work. Implying and inferring can be risky.

There are lots of tools in this chapter to help you evaluate arguments. To be able to use them, be sure you know:

- The Principle of Rational Discussion.
- The Mark of Irrationality.
- The Guide to Repairing Arguments.
- The glue in an argument.
- An irrelevant premise.
- You can't get subjective from objective.
- Arguing backwards.
- Unrepairable Arguments.
- Implying and inferring.

Try your hand at these!
1. When you show an argument is bad, what does that tell you about the conclusion?
2. If a strong argument has one false premise and 13 true premises, what choice should we make about whether to believe its conclusion?
3. How should we understand the charge that a premise is irrelevant?

Evaluate the following, saying whether it's an argument, what repair might be needed, and whether it's good or bad.

4. Dr. E is a teacher. All teachers are men. So Dr. E is a man.
5. George walks like a duck. George looks like a duck. George quacks like a duck. So George is a duck.
6. If you're so smart, why aren't you rich?
7. No cat barks. So Ralph is not a cat.
8. You're blue-eyed. So your parents must be blue-eyed.
9. Dick: When you're out, can you stop at the grocery and buy a big bag of dog food?
   Zoe: You know I'm riding my bike today.
10. Dick: Harry got into college because of affirmative action.
    Suzy: Gee, I didn't know that. So Harry isn't very bright.

11. What!? Me sexually harass her? You've got to be kidding! I never would have asked her out for a date. Look at her—she's too fat, and, besides, she smokes. I'm the boss here, and I could go out with anyone I want.
12. (From the Associated Press, July 8, 1999, about a suit against tobacco companies for making "a defective product that causes emphysema, lung cancer, and other illnesses.") The industry claimed there is no scientific proof that smoking causes any illness and that the public is well aware that smoking is risky.
13. This happened in broad daylight and that means that somebody saw something that can help catch the person responsible for this killing before there is any more violence.   —Pasadena Interim Deputy Police Chief Mike Korpal, March 11, 2010

Answers
1. Nothing.
2. If the argument is still strong without the false premise, the conclusion is likely true. Otherwise, we have no more reason to believe the conclusion than we did before we heard the argument.
3. Deleting it does not make the argument weaker, and there's no obvious way to link it to the conclusion.
4. Valid, bad, unrepairable: second premise is false.
5. Good, with the added premise: If it walks like a duck, looks like a duck, and quacks like a duck, it's a duck.
6. Not an argument. But if the speaker might mean the question as an assertion, "If you're so smart, then you'd be rich," with unstated conclusion, "You're not so smart." But the premise is false, so it's bad. Point to yourself as an example.
7. "Ralph barks" will make this valid. But we don't know if it's plausible. All we can do here is point out what's needed.
8. "(Almost) the only way you can inherit blue eyes is if both your parents are blue-eyed" is the obvious premise to add to make the argument valid. But that's false. So it's unrepairable.
9. Unstated conclusion: I can't stop at the grocery and buy dog food today. Premise needed: Zoe can't carry dog food on her bicycle. Good.
10. Can't be repaired. "(Almost) all people who are admitted to university due to affirmative action aren't bright" is false.
11. Unstated conclusion: "I didn't sexually harass her." Weak and implausible premises.
12. Unstated conclusion: Cigarettes are not a defective product that causes emphysema, lung cancer, and other illnesses. The premises in the quote contradict each other, so the argument is bad.
13. Premise needed: (Almost always) when a killing happens in broad daylight someone sees something that would help the police catch the killer. Implausible. So the argument is unrepairable.

11 Too Much Emotion

Emotions do and should play a role in our reasoning, for we can't make good decisions if we don't consider their significance in our emotional life. But that doesn't mean we should be swayed entirely by emotion. An **appeal to emotion** is an argument that depends on a premise that says you should believe or do just because you feel a certain way.

- *Suzy: Did you see that ad? It's so sad, I cried. That group says it will help those poor kids. We should send them some money.*

    To construe this as a good argument, we need to add "If you feel sorry for poor kids, you should give money to any organization that says it will help them." That's an **appeal to pity**. It's implausible: Some drug cartels help kids, too.

- *Dick (to Zoe): We should give to the American Friends Service Committee. They help people all over the world help themselves, and they don't ask whether those folks agree with their principles. They've been doing it really well for a century now, and they have very low overhead: almost all the money they get goes to those in need. All those people who don't have running water or health care need our help. Think of those poor kids growing up malnourished and sick. We've got enough money to send them $50.*

    This requires an unstated premise appealing to pity. But it isn't "Do it just because you feel sorry for someone." Rather "If you feel sorry for people, *and* you have a way to help them that is efficient and morally upright, *and* you have enough money to help, then you should send the organization money" will make the argument strong. That seems plausible, though whether it is the best use of Zoe and Dick's money needs to be considered.

- *We've got to put up a wall at the border to keep out all those Mexican rapists and thieves.*

    You've heard politicians say this. But it's just an **appeal to fear**: immigrants are less likely to commit crimes than American citizens.
    If a politician can scare you enough, maybe you'll vote for him—or her.

- *You shouldn't drive so quickly in the rain. The roads are very slippery after the first rain of the season and we could get into an accident.*

    Normally an appeal to emotion by itself is not sufficient to make a good argument. But sometimes an appeal to fear can be a good reason for a decision. An appeal to emotion that concludes you should *do* something can be good or it can be bad.

- *Wanda: This diet will work because I have to lose 20 pounds by the end of the month for my cousin's wedding.*

  This is an example of **wishful thinking**, and it's a bad argument.

Any appeal to emotion whose conclusion is a description of the world is going to be bad. Why should we believe some description is true just because we're moved by our emotions? Wishing it so don't make it so.

- *Dick: Hi, Tom. What's wrong with your car?*
  Tom: The battery's dead. Can you help me push it? Harry will steer.
  Dick: Sure.
  Zoe: (whispering) What're you doing, Dick? Don't you remember that Tom wouldn't help you fix the fence last week?

  What Zoe said isn't an argument, but we can construe it as one: "You shouldn't help Tom start his car because he wouldn't help you last week." The premise needed to make this a strong argument is "You shouldn't help anyone who has refused to help you (recently)." That's an **appeal to spite**. You decide which is better: to help or to harbor resentment.

- *On November 22, 2012, a representative of the Syrian coalition fighting the government in Syria was asked on the BBC if he condemned the execution of Syrian soldiers held prisoner by his coalition fighters. He responded by citing all the horrible things the Syrian government had done.*

  An appeal to spite often invokes the "principle" that **two wrongs make a right**. This is used to justify or excuse atrocities in war. That's a sure way for everyone's behavior to sink to the lowest level.

- *I really deserve a passing grade in your course. I know that you're a fair grader, and you've always been terrific to everyone in the class. I admire how you handle the class, and I've enjoyed your teaching so much that it would be a pity if I didn't have something to show for it.*

  "Gee," Dr. E thinks, "I guess I should pass her . . . . No, wait, she hasn't given me any reason to change her grade." The premise that's missing is "You should give a passing mark to anyone who thinks you're a great person," which is an **appeal to vanity**. It usually works with professors.

Try your hand at these!
Does the example have an appeal to emotions? Is it bad?
1. Vote for Senator Wong. He knows how important your concerns are.
2. Before you buy that Japanese car, ask whether you want to see some

Japanese tycoon get rich at your expense or whether you'd prefer to see an American kid get a meal on his plate next week.
3. Sunbathing does not cause skin cancer. If it did, how could I enjoy the beach?
4. Democracy is the best form of government. Otherwise this wouldn't be the greatest country in the world.
5. You mean that after we flew you here to Florida, paid for your lodging, showed you a wonderful time—all for free—you aren't going to buy a building site from us?
6.

> HOW DO I KNOW THAT Ms. FLETCHER WILL GO OUT WITH ME? SHE LOVES TALL MEN WHO ARE HANDSOME AND BALDING, AND BESIDES, I'M SURE I MADE A GREAT IMPRESSION ON HER. I ALWAYS IMPRESS THE LADIES WITH MY WORLDLY DEMEANOR.

Answers
1. Bad. It's just a weak argument. A politician might care about the same things you do yet be totally incompetent or greedy.
2. An appeal to spite and pity. Bad. Is it better if an American tycoon gets rich?
3. Wishful thinking. Bad.
4. Appeal to patriotism (subspecies of feel-good argument). Generic premise: You should believe that democracy is the best form of government if you love the U.S. (and think it's the greatest country). Bad.
(Samuel Johnson: "Patriotism is the last refuge of a scoundrel.")
(Ambrose Bierce: "Patriotism is the first refuge of a scoundrel.")
5. This is an appeal to guilt. Bad.
6. Wishful thinking.

12 Reasoning with Prescriptive Claims

> **Prescriptive claims and standards** A prescriptive claim either asserts a standard—this is what should be and there's nothing more fundamental to say than that—or it assumes another prescriptive claim as standard.

- *Omar: Eating dogs is bad.*
  This is a prescriptive claim, since it carries with it the assumption that we should not eat dogs.
  Zoe agreed with Omar when he said this. But did she really know what standard Omar had in mind? Certainly Omar's claim by itself is not the standard but depends on something more fundamental. Perhaps he's a vegetarian and believes "You should treat all animals humanely, and butchering animals is not humane." Zoe is likely to disagree, since she really enjoys eating a steak.
  Or Omar might believe simply "Dogs taste bad." Then he has a standard that requires a further prescriptive one, "You shouldn't eat anything that tastes bad."
  Or perhaps Omar believes "Dogs are carnivores, and we shouldn't eat carnivores." That would be a standard he might support with what he considers a more basic standard, "We should not eat anything forbidden by the standard interpretation of the Koran, and the Koran forbids eating carnivores."
  Or perhaps Omar just agrees with what most Americans think: "Dogs should be treated as companions to people and not as food."

- *It's wrong to torture children.*
  This is a prescriptive claim. It's usually taken as a standard, rather than assuming another standard.

- *Dr. Wibblitz: The university should stop doing dissection experiments on monkeys.*
  This is a prescriptive claim. Suzy agrees because she thinks that monkeys have souls and we shouldn't hurt animals with souls. But Lee disagrees, as he believes that AIDS experiments on monkeys are important. Dr. Wibblitz thinks that such experiments are important, too, yet he thinks that they are too expensive because of the new National Science Foundation regulations. Unless they can agree on a standard by which they mean to judge the claim, they cannot resolve their disagreements.

60   *How to Reason*

Debates about prescriptive claims should be about either the standard assumed or whether the claim follows from the standard. We cannot deduce a prescriptive claim from only descriptive claims, for a standard of values is needed.

> ***Is does not imply ought***   There's no good argument that has a prescriptive conclusion and only descriptive premises.

* *Smoking destroys people's health. So we ought to raise the tax on cigarettes.*
  The premise, a descriptive claim, is true. But the conclusion doesn't follow without some prescriptive premise such as "We should tax activities that are destructive of people's health." The issue then is why we should believe that.

* *The government should raise the tax rate for the upper 1% of all taxpayers.*
  This is a prescriptive claim. Before we can judge whether to accept it, we need to know what standard lies behind that "should"—what does the speaker consider a good method of taxation, and why?

* *I totally don't support prohibiting smoking in bars—most people who go to bars do smoke and people should be aware that a bar is a place where a lot of people go to have a drink and smoke. There are no youth working or attending bars and I just don't believe you can allow people to go have a beer but not to allow people to have a cigarette—that's a person's God-given right.*   — Gordy Hicks, City Councilor, Socorro, N.M.
  reported in *El Defensor Chieftain,* July 24 , 2002
  The implicit standard here for why smoking shouldn't be prohibited in bars seems to be that society should not establish sanctions against any activity that doesn't hurt youth or create harm to others who can't avoid it. The argument is just as good without the appeal to God, so by the Guide to Repairing Arguments we can ignore that. If it turns out that Hicks really does take the standard to be theological, then the argument he gives isn't adequate.

Some people—they're called **relativists**—believe that all standards, for beauty, morality, and every other value are relative to what some person or group of people believe. Most people, though, believe that at least some prescriptive claims are universally true, such as "You shouldn't torture children."

Often when you challenge people to make their standard explicit,

12 Reasoning with Prescriptive Claims 61

they'll say, "I just mean it's wrong (right) to me." Yet when you press them, it turns out they're not so happy that you disagree. What they really mean is "I have a right to believe that." Of course they do. But do they have a good *reason* to believe the claim? It's rare that people intend their moral views to be taken as just a personal standard.

> • *The problem with all these criteria is that the choice among them seems entirely arbitrary. [The author cites various conflicting standards on which to base economic policy.] ... I suspect though that the choice of a normative criterion is ultimately a matter of taste.*
> — Stephen Landsburg, *The Armchair Economist*
>
> This author seems to be a relativist. But he might just be committing the subjectivist fallacy, mistaking lack of agreement for subjectivity.

> • *The science says you've got to reduce emissions of greenhouse gases. The science says you've got to stabilize concentrations of greenhouse gases in the atmosphere. What may be subject to debate is who is to reduce how much.* —Rajendra K. Pachauri, Chairman
> U.N. Intergovernmental Panel on Climate Change
>
> The science says no such thing. Pachauri is speaking as a politician, not as a scientist, in making these judgments about where resources should be spent in light of the consequences of global warming.

When a scientist asks us to accept a prescriptive claim, he or she is no longer talking as a scientist but as someone qualified to make value judgments, playing the role of a politician, or philosopher, or priest. *No prescriptive claim follows from any scientific laws or data, for some standard—some value judgment—is required.* It's a bad appeal to authority to accept a prescriptive claim just because a scientist said it.

In evaluating reasoning that uses prescriptive claims, remember:

- A prescriptive claim states or needs a standard.
- Is does not imply ought.

Try your hand at these!
Evaluate these arguments.
1. Flo has always wanted a dog, but she's never been very responsible. She had a fish once, but it died after a week. She forgot to water her mother's plants, and they died. She stepped on a neighbor's turtle and killed it.
2. They shouldn't execute that guy tomorrow, even if he is a murderer. It's wrong to kill anyone.
3. Zoe: I want to make a lot of money.
   Zoe's mother: So you should go to law school.

4. Capital punishment executes innocent people, and it disproportionately affects minorities. States with capital punishment do not have lower murder rates than states without capital punishment. So capital punishment should be abolished.
5. Dick: We shouldn't leave the lights on when we're away.
   Zoe: Why?
   Dick: Because we should do all we can to conserve energy.
6. Zoe: We should go to Suzy's dinner party tonight.
   Dick: Why?
   Zoe: She invited us and she'll be very unhappy if we don't come.
   Dick: But I always have a miserable time at her dinner parties.
   Zoe: Look, we should go because she's our friend, and we shouldn't make our friends unhappy.

Answers
1. Unstated conclusion: "Flo should not get a dog." Prescriptive premise needed: "If you are not very responsible about animals, you shouldn't have a dog." Valid. Good.
2. Conclusion: They shouldn't execute him. Premises: He's a murderer. It's wrong to kill anyone. The first premise is irrelevant. The second premise states the standard, so whether you think the argument is good depends on whether you find it plausible.
3. Conclusion: Zoe should go to law school. Premise: Zoe wants to make a lot of money. Premise needed: "(Almost always) people who go to law school make a lot of money." That's implausible. But worse, what's the standard? "You should do what's most likely to make you lots of money"? That's even more implausible— Zoe should rob a bank? The argument is unrepairable.
4. Prescriptive premise needed: "We shouldn't do what kills innocent people, affects minorities badly more than others, and doesn't lower the murder rate." If you find that plausible, the argument is good. But that standard is also in question. Perhaps you should do what will make a lot of people feel good about getting rid of murderers even though the other premises are true.
5. The argument is valid. But whether it's good depends on whether the premise is plausible. Most folks would say yes, but others would require a further standard, and some would simply say no since they have lots of money and don't want to bother.
6. Conclusion: "We should go to Suzy's dinner party tonight," justified with the standard "We shouldn't make our friends unhappy." The argument is valid. But Dick says, "I always have a miserable time at her dinner parties," which shows that he thinks Zoe's standard is false or at least requires a substantial qualification.

13 Counterarguments

Raising objections and answering other people's objections is an important part of making and evaluating arguments.

> • *Dick: Zoe, we ought to get another dog.*
> *Zoe: What's wrong with Spot?*
> *Dick: Oh, no, I mean to keep Spot company.*
> *Zoe: Spot has us. He doesn't need company.*
> *Dick: But we're gone a lot. And he's always escaping from the yard, 'cause he's lonely. And we don't give him enough time. He should be out running around more.*
> *Zoe: But think of all the work! We'll have to feed the new dog. And think of all the time necessary to train it.*
> *Dick: I'll train him. We can feed him at the same time as Spot, and dog food is cheap. It won't cost much.*
>
> Dick is trying to convince Zoe to believe "We should get another dog." But he has to answer her objections:
> We ought to get another dog.
>   (*objection*) We already have Spot.
> The other dog will keep Spot company. (*answer*)
>   (*objection*) Spot already has us for company.
> We are gone a lot. (*answer*)
> He is always escaping from the yard. (*answer*)
> He's lonely. (*answer*)
> We don't give him enough time. (*answer*)
> He should be out running around more. (*answer*)
>   (*objection*) It will be a lot of work to have a new dog.
>   (*objection*) We will have to feed the new dog.
>   (*objection*) It will take a lot of time to train the new dog.
> I (Dick) will train him. (*answer*)
> We can feed him at the same time as Spot. (*answer*)
> Dog food is cheap. (*answer*)

Argument. Counterargument. Counter-counterargument. Objections are raised. Someone puts forward a claim that, if true, shows that one of our claims is false or at least doubtful or that our argument is not valid or strong. We then have to answer that challenge to sustain our argument. Knocking off an objection is a mini-argument within your argument; if it's not a good (though brief) one, it won't do the job.

But reasoning well isn't about winning. You could say, "I hadn't thought of that, I guess you're right." Or, "I don't know, I'll have to think about that."

In making an argument, you'll want to make it strong. You might think you have a great argument. All the premises seem obvious and they lead to the conclusion. But if you imagine someone objecting, you can see how to give better support for doubtful premises or make it clearer that the argument is valid or strong.

Refuting an argument

| It's useless to kill flies. The ones you kill will be the slowest, because the fast flies will evade you. | So you will be killing off the slowest ones and the fastest ones will remain. Over time, then, the genes for being fast will predominate. | Then with super-fast flies, it will be impossible to kill them anyway. So it's useless to kill flies. |

Zoe can't let it pass. But how do you refute an argument?

Zoe might object to one of the premises, saying that Dick won't be killing the slowest but only the ones that happen to come into their house.

Or she could agree with the premises but note that "over time" could be thousands of years, so the conclusion doesn't follow.

Or she could attack the conclusion, saying that it's not useless to kill flies because she does it all the time and it keeps their home clean.

All the ways we can show an argument is unrepairable are useful in refuting an argument. Three are fundamental.

> **Direct ways of refuting an argument**
> - Show that at least one of the premises is false or implausible.
> - Show that the argument isn't valid or strong.
> - Show that the conclusion is false.

Sometimes we can't point to any one premise that's dubious, but we know there's something wrong with the premises. They might get the conclusion that's argued for, but they get a lot more, too—so much that we can see the premises are inconsistent or lead to an absurdity.

> ***Reducing to the absurd*** To reduce to the absurd is to show that at least one of several claims is false or that collectively they are unacceptable by drawing a false or unwanted conclusion.

> • Tom: *Everyone in the U.S. should have to speak English. Everyone's got to talk the same, so we can communicate easily. And it'll unify the country.*
> Lee: *Sure. But I have real trouble understanding people from New York. So we should make everyone speak just like me, from Iowa.*
> Starting with the same premises Lee gets a claim he knows Tom won't accept. He's reduced Tom's argument to the absurd.

> *You complain that taxes are already too high and there's too much crime. And you say we should permanently lock up everyone who has been convicted of three felonies. In the places where this has been done, it hasn't reduced the crime rate. So we will have many more people who will be in jail for their entire lives. We'll need more prisons, many more. We'll need to employ more guards. We'll need to pay for a lot of health care for these people when they get old. So if you lock up everyone who has been convicted of three felonies, we'll have to pay substantially higher taxes. Since you're adamant that taxes are too high, you should abandon your claim that we should lock up forever everyone who's been convicted of three felonies.*
> The speaker is showing that the claim that taxes shouldn't be higher contradicts the claim that we should permanently lock up everyone who has been convicted of three felonies.

When you use this indirect method of refuting, be sure that the argument you use to get the false or absurd conclusion is good. Otherwise, it could be the claims you introduce that give the contradiction.

> Zoe: *I can't believe you're eating those Baken-ets fried pork skins. I thought you wanted to lose weight.*
> Dick: *Right, and the package says on the front in big letters "0 g Net Carbs".*
> Dick believes he's refuted the unstated claim that fried pork skins are fattening. But his refutation rests on an assumption that's false: If a food has no carbohydrates, it's not fattening.

One way to reduce to the absurd is to use similar premises in an argument that sounds just like the original but leads to an absurd conclusion.

> LOOK, YOUR ARGUMENT AGAINST KILLING FLIES IS BAD. I COULD USE THE SAME ARGUMENT AGAINST KILLING BACTERIA, OR AGAINST KILLING CHICKENS FOR DINNER FROM AUNT MARGERY'S HENHOUSE. THOSE CONCLUSIONS WOULD BE ABSURD.

- *You say we should leave you alone and let you cockfight because it's a tradition of your New Mexican Hispanic culture? Well, arranged marriages for 12-year-old girls were a tradition in some parts of this country. So was wife beating. We stopped those because, like cockfighting, they're cruel.*

    This refutation by analogy goes further by giving a general claim that would sanction the opposite of the conclusion, "We should stop traditions that are cruel."

There are also bad ways to try to refute. We've already seen phony refutations. The worst is **ridicule**, which ends a discussion, belittles others, and makes enemies.

- *Dr. E: I hear your department elected a woman as chairman.
Prof. Smythe: Yes, indeed. And now we're trying to decide what we should call her—"chairman," or "chairwoman," or "chairperson."
Dr. E: "Chairperson"? Why not use a neutral term that's really appropriate for the position, like "chaircreature"?*

    No argument has been given for why "chairman" shouldn't be replaced by "chairperson," although Dr. E thinks he's shown the idea is ridiculous.

In reasoning well ridicule is a worthless device: it ends arguments, belittles the other person, and makes enemies. In theory there's a big difference between reducing to the absurd and ridicule. But in practice it's difficult to distinguish them. Often, not enough of an argument is given to see how the absurd conclusion follows, so it sounds like ridicule. *If someone want us to see his comments as an argument, it's his responsibility to make that clear.* Otherwise, let's classify it as ridicule.

REDUCE TO THE ABSURD

{A, B, ..., C} — THE OTHER PERSON'S CLAIMS
(OTHER PLAUSIBLE CLAIMS)
↓
D – CONCLUSION, FALSE OR ABSURD

RIDICULE

THE OTHER PERSON'S CLAIM
HA! HA! HA! HA!

Finally, there's the all-purpose way to evade another person's argument by giving a **strawman**: putting words in someone's mouth.

- Tom: *Unless we allow the logging of old-growth forests in this county, we'll lose the timber industry and these towns will die.*
  Dick: *So you're saying that you don't care what happens to the spotted owl and to our rivers and the water we drink?*
  Tom: *I said nothing of the sort. You've misrepresented my position.*

The only reasonable response to a strawman is to say calmly, "That isn't what I said."

When objections are raised to your reasoning, you know now how to give a counterargument—unless you agree. If you want to show someone's argument is bad, you can use:

- The direct ways of refuting an argument.
- Reducing to the absurd.

But don't use:

- Phony refutation.
- Ridicule.
- A strawman.

Try your hand at these!

1. Lee: I'm going to vote for that initiative to eliminate discrimination against transgender people in hiring and getting places to live. They should be treated like everyone else. They deserve a chance to get jobs and homes.
   Tom: Are you kidding? I'm voting against it. You should, too. They don't deserve any preference over the rest of us.
2. Dick: Everyone should ride a bicycle for transportation. Cars are expensive to buy and maintain and cause a lot of pollution. A bicycle is better for your health and also for everyone else's.
   Tom: Yeah, right. I'm sure that Manuel in his wheelchair will agree with you.
3. Look, I agree with you. We have too much violence in the streets, too many drug

pushers, too little respect for the law. But our prisons are overflowing, and that's costing us a fortune. So we've got to reduce our prison population. Yet you say we should be even tougher on crime. The answer is simple. Institute a lottery among all convicted felons in jail and execute one of them every month—no appeals. That'll instill a real fear of being arrested. And it'd be fair, too.

4. Mary Ellen: Yes, yes, Dr. E. Raw food is best for you. I eat only raw food. Cooking destroys all the goodness in the food.
Dr. E: There goes 2,000,000 years of evolution.

5. Maria: You say that life begins at conception, right?
Tom: Yes. Suzy and I believe that.
Maria: So a person conceived in the U.S. should be a citizen—that's where his or her life began. So an Iranian mullah whose mother was in the U.S. from the whole time between 11 and 7 months before he was born should be able to claim citizenship in the U.S., since he was surely conceived while she was here. But you're dead set against letting more people who were born and raised outside the U.S. into the country. So the solution is that we should make sure that all women coming to the U.S. don't have sex while they're here.

6. Suzy: Suicide and euthanasia are wrong because no person should play God. That's taking over the right to decide life and death, which belongs only to God.
Manuel: But then I shouldn't push someone out of the way if a car is coming fast at her. I'd be taking over the right to decide life and death, playing God like you say.

Answers

1. Tom's presented a strawman. Lee is for equal rights, not preferences. Tom has mistakenly identified equal rights laws with affirmative action programs. Doesn't refute.
2. Tom has refuted Dick's argument by showing that the conclusion is false.
3. Reducing to the absurd. Good.
4. It isn't clear whether Mary Ellen is making an argument or just explaining why she eats only raw food. In any case, Dr. E goes directly to refuting her claim "Raw food is best for you." But to appreciate it you need to know that humans have evolved to eat cooked food, and it's now believed that eating cooked food contributed a lot to our development as a species.
5. Reducing to the absurd. Good if Maria's premises are plausible to Tom.
6. Reducing to the absurd. Suzy probably won't accept it, but it should give her pause to clarify what she means by "decide life and death."

The Form of an Argument

Much of our reasoning involves the use of "if . . . then . . . ", "not", and "or" to make new claims from old ones. In the first chapter here you'll see how to use these words well and how to avoid getting confused by misuses. In the second chapter you'll find that we can often tell whether an argument that uses these words is valid or weak just by looking at its form.

We use "all", "some", and "none" to talk in general terms. In the third chapter you'll learn how to use these well. There you'll see that many arguments that use these words are valid due just to their form, and many are weak due to their form.

The forms of the arguments that are weak are so similar to the forms of the ones that are valid that it's really easy to be misled and make bad decisions. Recognizing the forms is mostly a matter of pattern recognition.

14 Compound Claims

> **Compound claim** A *compound claim* is one that is composed of other claims but has to be viewed as just one claim.

- *Either a Democrat will win the election or a Republican will win the election.*
  This is a single claim made up of two claims "A Democrat will win the election" and "A Republican will win the election." They're joined by the word "or." Whether it's true depends on whether one or both of its parts are true. But the entire sentence is just one claim.
- *If Suzy studies hard, then Suzy will pass the exam.*
  This is just one claim, made up of the two claims "Suzy studies hard" and "Suzy will pass the exam."
- *Lee will pass his exam because he studied so hard.*
  This is not a compound claim: "because" is an indicator word that tells us that this meant as an argument.

"Or" claims

- *Dick or Zoe will go to the grocery to get eggs.*
  We can view this as an "or" claim compounded from "Dick will go to the grocery to get eggs" and "Zoe will go to the grocery to get eggs." The claims that make up an "or" claim are called the **alternatives**.
- *Either there's a wheelchair ramp at the school dance, or Manuel stayed home. But there isn't a wheelchair ramp at the school dance. So Manuel stayed home.*
  This is valid due just to its form.

> **Excluding possibilities**
> A or B + not A
> ─────────────
>   ↓   Valid
> B

In our descriptions of forms of arguments, we can use these conventions:

The letters A, B, and C stand for any claims.

The phrase "not A" stands for "a contradictory of A".

An arrow ↓ stands for "therefore".

The symbol + means an additional premise.

14 Compound Claims 71

• *Either all criminals should be locked up forever, or we should put more money into rehabilitating criminals, or we should accept that our streets will never be safe, or we should have some system for monitoring ex-convicts.* [This is all one claim: A or B or C or D.] *We can't lock up all criminals forever, because it would be too expensive. We definitely won't accept that our streets will never be safe. So either we should put more money into rehabilitating criminals, or we should have some system for monitoring ex-convicts.*

Arguments that exclude just one or more of several alternatives are valid, too.

But remember that not every valid argument is good.

False dilemma A *false dilemma* is a bad use of excluding possibilities where the "or" claim is false or dubious. Sometimes just the dubious "or" claim is called the false dilemma.

> LOOK AT THESE BILLS. YOU'RE EITHER GOING TO HAVE TO GET RID OF THOSE NASTY EXPENSIVE CIGARS OR SPOT.
>
> WHAT ARE YOU TALKING ABOUT! WE CAN'T GET RID OF SPOT!
>
> SO YOU AGREE YOU'LL GIVE UP SMOKING CIGARS.

Zoe poses a false dilemma. They could economize by not buying fast food lunches or by driving less.

• *Society can choose high environmental quality but only at the cost of lower tourism or more tourism and commercialization at the expense of the ecosystem, but society must choose. It involves a tradeoff.*
— R. Sexton, *Exploring Economics*

This is a false dilemma. Costa Rica has created a lot of tourism by preserving almost 50% of its land in parks.

Contradictories

Contradictory of a claim A *contradictory* of a claim is one that must have the opposite truth-value.

• *Spot is barking.*
A contradictory of this is "Spot is not barking."

- *Inflation will be not less than 3% this year.*
  A contradictory of this is "Inflation will be less than 3% this year," which doesn't contain "not."

> **Contradictory of an "or" claim**
> *A or B* has contradictory *not A and not B*
> **Contradictory of an "and" claim**
> *A and B* has contradictory *not A or not B*

- *Maria got the van or Manuel won't go to school.*
  A contradictory is "Maria didn't get the van, and Manuel will go to school."
- *Tom or Suzy will pick up Manuel for class today.*
  A contradictory is "Neither Tom nor Suzy will pick up Manuel for class today."

Conditional claims

> **Conditional claims** A *conditional claim* is a claim that is or can be rewritten as one of the form *If A then B* that must have the same truth-value. The claim *A* is the **antecedent** and the claim *B* is the **consequent**.

- *If Spot ran away, then the gate was left open.*
  This is a conditional, with antecedent "Spot ran away" and consequent "The gate was left open." The consequent need not happen later.
- *I'll never talk to you again if you don't apologize.*
  This is a conditional with antecedent "You don't apologize" and consequent "I'll never talk to you again."
- *Loving someone means you never throw dishes at him.*
  This is a conditional with antecedent "You love someone" and consequent "You never throw dishes at him." It's not a definition.
- *A mammal is an ungulate if it has hoofs.*
  This is not a conditional or a compound. It's a definition that uses "if" instead of "means that." We have to use our judgment to decide whether a claim is a conditional.
- *If Dick goes to the basketball game, then either he got a free ticket or he borrowed money for one.*
  This is a conditional whose consequent is also a compound claim.

14 Compound Claims 73

> **Contradictory of a conditional**
> *If A, then B* has contradictory *A but not B*

A contradictory of a conditional is *not* another conditional.

- *Zoe: I'm so worried. Spot got out of the yard. If he got out of the yard, then the dogcatcher got him, I'm sure.*
  Suzy: Don't worry. I saw Spot. He got out of the yard, but the dogcatcher didn't get him.

If   then

Contradictory

     but

- *If Spot barks, then Suzy's cat will run away.*
  Contradictory: Spot barked, but Suzy's cat did not run away.

- *If Spot got out of the yard, he was chasing a squirrel.*
  Contradictory: Spot got out of the yard, but he wasn't chasing a squirrel.

- *Bring me an ice cream cone and I'll be happy.*
  Contradictory: Despite that you brought me an ice cream cone, I'm not happy. "Despite that" is also used to make a contradictory of a conditional.

- *If cats had no fur, they would not give people allergies.*
  Contradictory: Even if cats had no fur, they would still give people allergies. "Even if" does *not* make a conditional. "Even if" is used in much the same way as "although" or "despite that."

74 *How to Reason*

> SPOT IS A GOOD DOG *EVEN IF* HE JUST MAULED YOUR CAT.
>
> SPOT IS A GOOD DOG, *ALTHOUGH* HE JUST MAULED YOUR CAT.
>
> SPOT IS A GOOD DOG *DESPITE THAT* HE JUST MAULED YOUR CAT.

Two kinds of claims are closely related to conditionals.

Contrapositive of a conditional

The *contrapositive* of *If A, then B* is *If not B, then not A*.
The contrapositive is true exactly when the original is true.

• *If Zoe does the dishes, then Dick will walk Spot.*
  Contrapositive: "If Dick doesn't walk Spot, then Zoe didn't do the dishes."

"Only if" claims

A only if B means the same as *If not B, then not A*.
Or we can say *A requires that B*.
  "Only if" does not mean the same as "if."

• *Dick will go into the army only if there is a draft.*
  This example means the same as "If there is no draft, then Dick will not go into the army" or "For Dick to go into the army requires that there will be a draft."

• *You'll get a speeding ticket only if you're going over the speed limit.*
  If you're not going over the speed limit, then you won't get a speeding ticket.
  If you get a speeding ticket, then you went over the speed limit.
    These three claims are equivalent.

Necessary and sufficient conditions

Necessary and sufficient conditions

A is necessary for B means that *If not A, then not B* must be true.
A is sufficient for B means that *If A, then B* must be true.

- *Passing an eye test is necessary but not sufficient for getting a driver's license.*
  This means "If you don't pass an eye test, you can't get a driver's license" is always true; but "If you pass an eye test, you get a driver's license" need not be true.
- *You can pass calculus only if you study hard.*
  This isn't the same as "If you study hard, you can pass calculus." Rather, studying hard is necessary, required to pass calculus; it's not sufficient. The example is equivalent to "If you pass calculus, then you studied hard." Confusing "only if" with "if" is confusing a necessary with a sufficient condition.

Here are the ideas you need to know from this chapter:

- Compound claim.
- "Or" claims and alternatives.
- Excluding possibilities.
- False dilemma.
- Contradictory of a claim.
- Conditional claims, antecedent, and consequent.
- The contrapositive of a conditional.
- "Only if" claims.
- Necessary and sufficient conditions.

Try your hand at these!
For each 1–10: • Say if it's a compound claim. • If the claim is a conditional, state the antecedent and consequent. • Write a contradictory of the claim.
1. Maria or Lee will pick up Manuel after classes.
2. Neither Maria nor Lee has a bicycle.
3. AIDS cannot be contracted by touching or by breathing air in the same room as a person infected with AIDS.
4. Zoe (to Dick): Will you take the trash out, or do I have to?
5. If Spot barks, then Puff will run away.
6. Lee will take care of Spot next weekend if Dick will help him with his English exam.
7. Loving someone means you never throw dishes at them.
8. Since 2 times 2 is 4, and 2 times 4 is 8, I should be ahead $8, not $7.
9. If Manuel went to the basketball game, then he either got a ride with Maria or he left early to wheel himself over there.
10. Drop the gun and no one will get hurt.

For the next two, state the contrapositive.
11. If Flo plays in the mud with Spot, then she has to take a bath.

76 *How to Reason*

12. If Manuel doesn't get his wheelchair fixed by Wednesday, he can't attend class Thursday. For each of the following state which of these are correct:
    (i) is necessary for (ii)   (i) is both necessary and sufficient for (ii)
    (i) is sufficient for (ii) (i) is neither necessary nor sufficient for (ii)
13. (i) Dr. E had his annual physical examination.
    (ii) Dr. E paid for an appointment with his physician.
14. (i) Manuel opened a checking account.
    (ii) Manuel wrote his first check.
15. (i) Zoe won $47 at blackjack.
    (ii) Zoe was gambling.
16. (i) Maria is divorced.
    (ii) Maria has an ex-husband.
17. (i) Suzy is over 21.
    (ii) Suzy can legally drink in this state.

Answers
1. Compound. Contradictory: Neither Maria nor Lee will pick up Manuel after classes.
2. Compound. Contradictory: Maria or Lee has a bicycle.
3. Not a compound. Contradictory: AIDS can be contracted by touching or breathing air in the same room as a person infected with AIDS.
4. Not a claim.
5. Compound. Conditional. Antecedent: Spot barks. Consequent: Puff will run away. Contradictory: Spot barked, but Puff didn't run away.
6. Compound. Conditional. Antecedent: Dick will help Lee with his English exam. Consequent: Lee will take care of Spot next weekend. Contradictory: Dick will help Lee with his English exam, but Lee will not take care of Spot next weekend.
7. Compound. Conditional. Antecedent: You love someone. Consequent: You never throw dishes at them. Contradictory: You love someone, but you do throw dishes at them.
8. Not a claim, an argument ("since" tells you that).
9. Compound. Conditional. Antecedent: Manuel went to the basketball game. Consequent: Manuel got a ride with Maria or he left early to wheel himself over there. Contradictory: Manuel went to the basketball game, but he didn't get a ride with Maria and he didn't wheel himself over there.
10. Compound. Conditional. Antecedent: You drop the gun. Consequent: No one will be hurt. Contradictory: You drop the gun but someone is hurt.
11. If Flo doesn't have to take a bath, then she didn't play in the mud with Spot.
12. If Manuel can attend class Thursday, then he got his wheelchair fixed by Wednesday.
13. Neither necessary nor sufficient.
14. (i) is necessary for (ii).
15. (i) sufficient for (ii).
16. Used to be necessary and sufficient, but now with same-sex marriages, (i) is necessary for (ii).
17. Necessary and sufficient.

15 Valid Forms of Arguments using Conditionals

Here you'll see some valid forms of reasoning using conditionals and some forms that look a lot like those but which are usually weak.

Here's an illustration for some of the examples that follow.

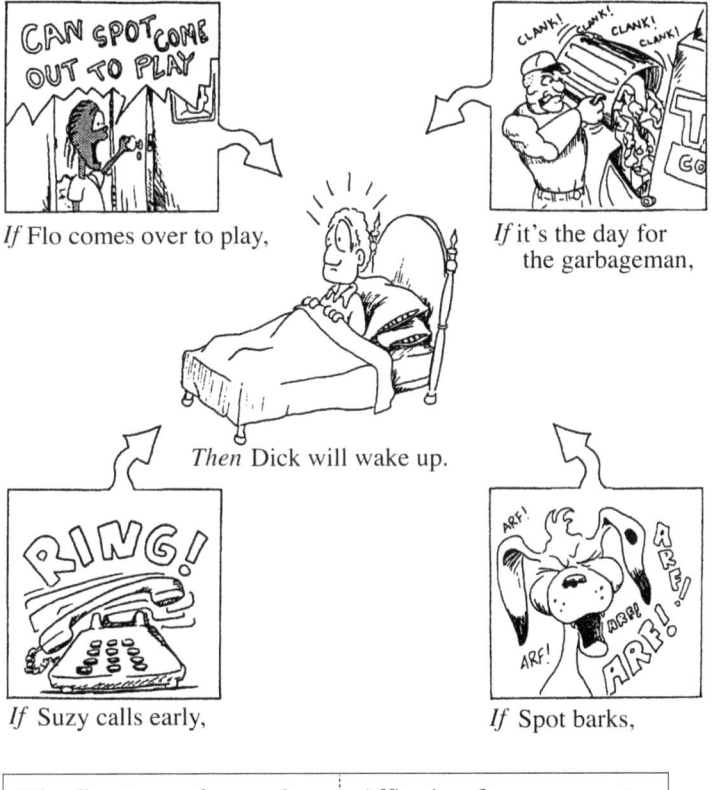

If Flo comes over to play,

If it's the day for the garbageman,

Then Dick will wake up.

If Suzy calls early,

If Spot barks,

The direct way of reasoning with conditionals	Affirming the consequent
If A, then B + A ↓ Valid B	If A, then B + B ↓ Weak A

• *If Spot barks, then Dick will wake up. Spot barked. So Dick woke up.*
This is a valid argument. It is impossible for the premises to be true and

conclusion false at the same time. It's an example of the direct way of reasoning with conditionals.

- *If Spot barks, then Dick will wake up. Dick woke up. So Spot barked.*
  This is weak. Maybe Suzy called, or Flo came over to play. It's affirming the consequent, reasoning backwards.

- Wanda: *If I go on Jane Fonda's workout and diet plan, I'll lose weight.*
  [later] Zoe: *Did you see how much weight Wanda lost?*
  Suzy: *She must have gone on that workout plan by Jane Fonda.*
  Suzy's overlooking other possibilities. Maybe Wanda has become bulimic, or had liposuction, or was really sick. Affirming the consequent is reasoning backwards.

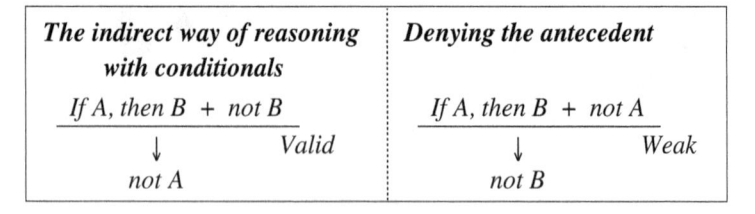

The indirect way of reasoning with conditionals	***Denying the antecedent***
If A, then B + not B	If A, then B + not A
↓ Valid	↓ Weak
not A	not B

- *If Spot barks, then Dick will wake up. Dick didn't wake up. So Spot didn't bark.*
  This is a valid argument, an example of the indirect way of reasoning with conditionals.

- *If it's the day for the garbageman, then Dick will wake up. It's not the day for the garbageman. So Dick didn't wake up.*
  This is weak. Even though the garbageman didn't come, maybe Spot barked or Suzy called early. It overlooks other possible ways the premise could be true and conclusion false.

- *If Maria doesn't call Manuel, then Manuel will miss his class. Maria did call Manuel. So Manuel didn't miss his class.*
  This is weak, denying the antecedent. The "not" in the form indicates a contradictory.

- *If Suzy doesn't call early, then Zoe won't go shopping. Zoe went shopping. So Suzy called early.*
  This is valid, an example of the indirect way. Here the contradictories don't use "not."

- *Zoe won't go shopping if Dick comes home early. Zoe went shopping. So Dick didn't come home early.*
  This is valid, an example of the indirect way.

- *When Johnny comes marching home again, the girls will all laugh and shout. Johnny died in the war. So the girls didn't laugh and shout.*
  This is a weak argument: the girls will laugh and shout anyway—they always do. It's denying the antecedent.
- *If Suzy called early, then Dick woke up. So Dick didn't wake up.*
  The obvious premise to add here is "Suzy didn't call early." But that makes the argument weak. So the argument is unrepairable.

These invalid forms of arguing are obvious confusions with valid forms, mistakes a good reasoner doesn't make. So when you see one *don't bother to repair the argument.*

Reasoning in a chain

Reasoning in a chain with conditionals If A, then B + If B, then C ↓ Valid If A, then C	*Slippery slope argument* A bad argument that uses a chain of conditionals, at least one of which is false or dubious.

- *If Dick takes Spot for a walk, then Zoe will cook dinner. And if Zoe cooks dinner, then Dick will do the dishes. So if Dick takes Spot for a walk, then he'll do the dishes. But Dick did take Spot for a walk. So he must have done the dishes.*
  This is a valid argument: reasoning in a chain with conditionals followed by the direct way of reasoning with conditionals. We conclude the last consequent because we have the first antecedent.
- *Don't get a credit card! If you do, you'll be tempted to spend money you don't have. Then you'll max out on your card. Then you'll be in real debt. And you'll have to drop out of school to pay your bills. You'll end up a failure in life.*
  This is a slippery slope argument, which you can see by rewriting it using conditionals.

Reasoning from hypotheses

One way to try to determine whether a claim is true is to see what follows from it. We make a valid or strong argument starting with the claim as premise. If we can draw a false conclusion, and we've used no other dubious premise, then we can conclude that the hypothesis is false—that's reducing to the absurd. Sometimes, though, we get only a new conditional.

> ***Hypotheses and conditionals*** If you start with an hypothesis
> *A* and make a good argument for *B*, then you've made a good
> argument for *If A, then B*.

• *Lee: I'm thinking of majoring in biology.*
*Maria: That means you'll take summer school. Here's why: You're in
your second year now. To finish in four years like you told me you
need to, you'll have to take all the upper-division biology courses
your last two years. And you can't take any of those until you've
finished the three-semester calculus course. So you'll have to take
calculus over the summer to finish in four years.*

Maria has not proved that Lee has to go to summer school. Rather, on
the assumption (hypothesis) that Lee will major in biology, Lee will have
to go to summer school. That is, Maria has proved "If Lee majors in
biology, then he'll have to go to summer school."

Here are the forms of arguments you've seen in this chapter.
- The direct way of reasoning with conditionals.
- Affirming the consequent.
- The indirect way of reasoning with conditionals.
- Denying the antecedent.
- Reasoning in a chain with conditionals.
- Slippery slope arguments.
- Hypotheses and conditionals.

If you think this is all too much to bother with, remember from the
examples how easy it is to get misled. Understand the principles, and
then it's just a matter of recognizing the patterns.

If you forget the forms, return to the basics: it's not whether the
premises and conclusion happen to be true but whether there is a way
for the premises to be true and conclusion false, and if so, how likely
that is.

Try your hand at these!
A good way to learn how to see and hear the forms is to use flashcards.
- On the back of a card, put the form (for example, If A then B; not A; so not B).
- Write whether it's valid or weak.
- On the front, put an example of that form that you've made up.
- Make three cards for each form, each card showing a different example. Some of
  the examples should have a conditional that isn't already in "if . . . then . . ." form.

15 Valid Forms using Conditionals

- Practice with your own cards.
- Practice with a friend: read to each other the examples you've made up and classify them as valid or weak.

Evaluate the following. Identify the form of the argument if it's one from this chapter.

1. Tom: Either you'll vote for the Republican or the Democratic candidate for president.
   Lee: No way I'll vote for the Democrat.
   Tom: So you'll vote for the Republican.
2. Dick: Somebody knocked over our neighbor's trash can last night. Either our neighbor hit it with her car again when she backed out, or a raccoon got into it, or Spot knocked it over.
   Zoe: Our neighbor didn't hit it with her car because she hasn't been out of her house since last Tuesday.
   Dick: It wasn't a raccoon because Spot didn't bark last night.
   Zoe: Spot! Bad dog! Stay out of the trash!
3. If Suzy breaks up with Tom, then she'll have to return his letter jacket. But there is no way she'll give up that jacket. So she won't break up with Tom.
4. Steve Pearce is a congressman who meets with his constituents regularly. If someone is a good congressman, he meets with his constituents regularly. So Rep. Pearce is a good congressman.
5. To take issue with current Israeli policy is to criticize Israel. To criticize Israel is to be anti-Israel. To be anti-Israel is to be anti-Semitic. So if you take issue with current Israeli policy, you're an anti-Semite.
6. Dr. E (on an exam day): If students don't like me, they won't show up. But all of them showed up today. So they must really like me.
7. Maria: Professor, professor, why wouldn't you answer my question in class?
   Professor Zzzyzzx: Questions in my class I do not allow. If one student I am allowing to ask a question, then others I must allow. Und then I will have lots und lots of questions to answer. Und time I won't have for mine lecture.
8. Maria: Lee will take care of Spot Tuesday if Dick will help him with his English paper.
   Manuel: (*later*) Dick didn't help Lee with his English paper, so I guess Lee didn't take care of Spot on Tuesday.
9. Only if Columbus landed in a place with no people in it could you say that he discovered it. But the Americas, especially where he landed, were populated. He even met natives. So Columbus didn't discover America. He just discovered a route to America.
10. Dick: I heard that Tom's going to get a pet. I wonder what he'll get?
    Zoe: The only pets you're allowed in this town are dogs or cats or fish.
    Dick: Well, I know he can't stand cats.
    Zoe: So he'll get a dog or fish.
    Dick: Not fish. He isn't the kind to get a pet you just contemplate.
    Zoe: So let's surprise him and get him a leash.
11. Mom: For a marriage to work, people have to have a lot in common.
    Zoe: Wrong! I know lots of miserable marriages where the people had a lot in common.

12. Zoe: You look depressed.
    Dick: I feel really low.
    Zoe: You should eat some chocolate—that always makes me feel better.
    Dick: (looking into the cupboard) Hey! There are no chocolate bars here. You must have been really depressed last week.
13. Maria: Listen to this argument I read in Steen's *Practical Philosophy for the Life Sciences,* "If the population density of a species is high in some area, then the species will not reproduce in that area. If a species doesn't reproduce in some area, it will go extinct in that area. Therefore, if the population density of a species is very high in some area, it will go extinct in that area."
    Lee: Gosh, that explains why there aren't any alligators in New York. There used to be too many of them.

Answers
1. Valid. Bad: a false dilemma. Lee could vote for the candidate for the Libertarian Party or the Green Party candidate.
2. Valid. Excluding possibilities. Good if premises are plausible.
3. Valid. Indirect way. Good.
4. Weak. Affirming the consequent. Bad.
5. Valid. Reasoning in a chain with conditionals. Bad argument and unrepairable. slippery slope and the last premise is false.
6. Valid. The indirect way. But a bad argument because the conditional is false.
7. Valid but bad: slippery slope.
8. Weak. Denying the antecedent. Bad.
9. Additional premise needed: If Columbus met natives, then where he landed was populated. Valid. Indirect way of reasoning with conditionals (rewrite the "only if " claim as an "if . . . then . . ." claim). Good.
10. Additional premises needed: If Dick heard that Tom is going to get a pet, then Tom is going to get a pet. So (1st conclusion) Tom is going to get a pet. If Tom gets a pet, then it will have to be a dog or cat or fish. So (2nd conclusion) Tom will get a dog or cat or fish. If Tom can't stand cats, then he won't get a cat. So (3rd conclusion) Tom won't get a cat. If Tom doesn't like a pet that you just contemplate, then Tom won't get a fish. So (4th conclusion) Tom won't get a fish. So (5th conclusion) Tom will get a dog. Valid, direct way (four times) and excluding possibilities. Good argument? Possibly, the premises are plausible except for one unstated premise: "If Dick heard that Tom's going to get a pet, then Tom is going to get a pet." Don't spend your money on a leash yet!
11. Not an argument. Zoe is just trying to show her Mom is wrong by stating the contradictory. But she gets the contradictory wrong.
12. Additional premises needed: There were chocolate bars in the cupboard last week. If someone ate them, it was Dick or Zoe. Someone ate them. So Dick or Zoe ate them (direct way). Dick didn't eat them. So Zoe ate the chocolate bars (excluding possibilities). If Zoe ate the chocolate bars, then she was depressed.
13. Additional premise needed: There are no alligators in New York. Steen's argument is valid (reasoning in a chain) and good, if the premises are plausible. Lee's argument is bad; it's denying the antecedent.

16 General Claims

> *All* means "Every single one, no exceptions."
> Sometimes *all* is meant as:
> "Every single one, and there is at least one."
>
> *Some* means "At least one."
> Sometimes *some* is meant as:
> "At least one, but not all."

Which of these readings is best depends on how the words are used in an argument.

- *All dogs are mammals.*
  This is a true claim.

- *All bank managers are women.*
  This is a false claim on either reading of "all."

- *All polar bears in Antarctica can swim.*
  This is a true claim if you understand "all" as "every single one."
  It is false if you understand "all" to include "at least one," since there are no polar bears in Antarctica.

- *Some dogs bark.*
  This is true on either reading of "some."

- *Some dogs are mammals.*
  This is true if you understand "some" to mean "at least one."
  But it is false if you understand "some" to include "and not all."

There are many different ways to say "all." For example, the following are equivalent:

All dogs bark.
Every dog barks.
Dogs bark.
Everything that's a dog barks.

There are also many ways to say the first reading of "some." For example, the following are all equivalent:

Some dogs can't bark.
At least one dog can't bark.
There exists a dog that can't bark
There is a dog that can't bark.

And there are many ways to say that **nothing** or **none** satisfies some condition. For example, the following are equivalent:

No dog likes cats.
Nothing that's a dog likes cats.
All dogs do not like cats.
Not even one dog likes cats.

Just as we have to be careful with "only if," we need to be careful with "only."

- *Only bank employees can open the vault at this bank. Pete is a bank employee here. So Pete can open the vault.*

    The argument is weak: Pete might be the janitor. "Only" does not mean "all." "Only bank employees can open the vault" means "Anyone who can open the vault is a bank employee."

Only   *Only S are P* means *All P are S*.

Contradictories of general claims

- *All people want to be rich.*
    Contradictory: Some people don't want to be rich.
- *Some Russians like chile.*
    Contradictory: No Russian likes chile.
- *Some women don't want to marry.*
    Contradictory: All women want to marry.
- *No cat can bark.*
    Contradictory: Some cat can bark.
- *Every cat hates to swim.*
    Contradictory: Some cat doesn't hate to swim.
- *Some whales eat fish.*
    Contradictory: Not even one whale eats fish.
- *Only dogs bark.*
    Contradictory: Some things that bark are not dogs.
    To say that just exactly dogs bark and nothing else, we could say "Dogs and only dogs bark." The contradictory of that is "Either some dogs don't bark, or some things that bark aren't dogs."

There are many ways to make general claims and many ways to form their contradictories. At best we have a partial guide.

16 General Claims

Claim	Contradictory
All *S* are *P*.	Some *S* is *P*. Not every *S* is *P*.
Some *S* are *P*.	No *S* is *P*. All *S* are not *P*. Not even one *S* is *P*.
Some *S* are not *P*.	All *S* are *P*.
No *S* is *P*.	Some *S* are *P*.
Only *S* are *P*.	Some *P* are not *S*. Not every *S* is *P*.

Some valid and weak forms of arguments with general claims

The direct way of reasoning with "all"	*Arguing backwards with "all"*
All *S* are *P* + *a* is *S* ↓ Valid *a* is *P*	All *S* are *P* + *a* is *P* ↓ Weak *a* is *S*

- *All mortgage brokers are honest. Ralph is a mortgage broker. So Ralph is honest.*

  This is valid, an example of the direct way of reasoning with "all." But though valid, it's not good. The first premise is false, as we learned in the financial crash of 2008.

- *All stockbrokers earn more than $70,000. Earl earns more than $70,000. So Earl is a stockbroker.*

  This is weak, arguing backwards with "all." Earl could be a basketball player or a mortgage broker.

Reasoning in a chain with "all"	*Reasoning in a chain with "some"*
All *S* are *P* + All *P* are *Q* ↓ Valid All *S* are *Q*	Some *S* are *P* + Some *P* are *Q* ↓ Weak Some *S* are *Q*

- *Every news website that the president reads is run by an American company. All news websites run by an American company are biased against Muslims. So the President reads only news websites that are biased against Muslims.*

  This is valid, reasoning in a chain with "all."

- *Some dogs like peanut butter. Some things that like peanut butter are human. So some dogs are human.*

  This is weak, reasoning in a chain with "some."

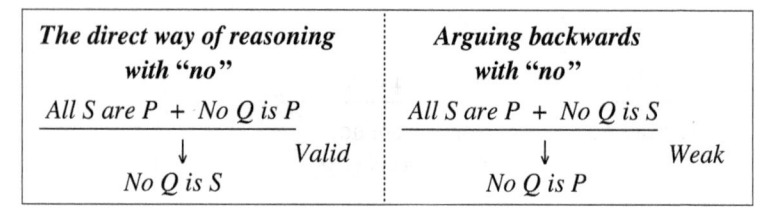

The direct way of reasoning with "no"	*Arguing backwards with "no"*
All S are P + No Q is P	All S are P + No Q is S
↓ Valid	↓ Weak
No Q is S	No Q is P

- *All corporations are legal entities. No computer is a legal entity. So no computer is a corporation.*

  This is valid, the direct way of reasoning with "no."

- *All nursing students take calculus in their freshman year. No heroin addict is a nursing student. So no heroin addict takes calculus in his or her freshman year.*

  This is weak, arguing backwards with "no."

There are lots of arguments that don't use these forms, but we can evaluate them by looking for possibilities where the antecedent could be true and consequent false.

- *Only managers can close out the cash register. George is a manager. So George can close out the cash register.*

  This is weak. "Only" does not mean "all." George could be a manager in charge of the stockroom.

- *Everyone who wants to become a manager works hard. The people in Lois' group work hard. So the people in Lois' group want to become managers.*

  This is weak. Maybe the workers in Lois' group just want a raise and not the responsibility. It illustrates a weak form: All S are Q; all P are Q; therefore, all S are P.

- *No taxpayer who cheats is honest. Some dishonest people are found out. So some taxpayers who cheat are found out.*

  This is weak. It could be that the only people who are found out are ones who steal.

• *All lions are fierce, but some lions are afraid of dogs. So some dogs aren't afraid of lions.*
  This is weak. Maybe all dogs run away before they have a chance to recognize that the lions are afraid of them.

• *Some nursing students aren't good at math. John is a nursing student. So John isn't good at math.*
  This is weak. John could be one of the many nursing students who is good at math.

• *Every dog loves its master. Dick has a dog. So Dick is loved.*
  This is valid, but none of the forms we've studied show that.

Precise generalities and vague generalities

Statistical generalities are easy to evaluate in arguments.

• *72% of all workers at the GM plant say they will vote to strike. Lulu works at the GM plant. So Lulu says he will vote to strike.*
  We can say exactly where this argument lands on the strong/weak scale: there's a 28% chance the premises could be true and the conclusion false. That's not good enough to be strong.

• *About 95% of all cat owners have cat-induced allergies. Dr. E's ex-wife has a cat. So Dr. E's ex-wife has cat-induced allergies.*
  This is a strong argument.

• *Only 4% of all workers on the assembly line at the GM plant didn't get a raise last year. Fred has worked on the assembly line at the GM plant since last year. So Fred got a raise.*
  This is a strong argument, if we know nothing more about Fred.

Most imprecise generalities, like "quite a lot" and "many," are too vague to figure in a good argument. But **almost all** and **a very few** are clear enough for us to use well in our reasoning.

• *Almost all high school principals have an advanced degree. So the principal at ARF High has an advanced degree.*
  This is a strong argument. Compare it to the direct way of reasoning with "all."

• *Almost all university professors teach every year. Mary Jane teaches every year. So Mary Jane is a university professor.*
  This is weak. Mary Jane could be a high school teacher. Compare it to arguing backwards with "all."

• *Almost all dogs like ice cream. Almost all things that like ice cream don't bark. So almost all dogs don't bark.*

This is weak. Reasoning in a chain with "almost all" is just as weak as reasoning in a chain with "some."

- *Very few army sergeants tortured prisoners in Iraq. Janet is an army sergeant. So Janet did not torture prisoners in Iraq.*
  This is a strong argument. Compare it to the direct way of reasoning with "no."

- *All truck drivers have a commercial driver's license. Only a very few beauticians have a commercial driver's license. So only a very few beauticians are truck drivers.*
  This is strong. Compare it to the direct way of reasoning with "no."

- *All professors get a paycheck at the end of the month. Only a very few people under 25 are professors. So only a very few people under 25 get a paycheck at the end of the month.*
  This is weak. Compare it to arguing backwards with "no".

- *Almost every dog loves its master. Dick has a dog. So Dick is loved.*
  This is a strong and good argument.

In this chapter you've seen how to recognize and evaluate general claims and arguments in which they appear:

- Contradictories of general claims.
- Direct way of reasoning with "all".
- Arguing backwards with "all".
- Reasoning in a chain with "all".
- Reasoning in a chain with "some".
- Direct way of reasoning with "no".
- Arguing backwards with "no".

We also saw how to evaluate arguments that use vague generalities.

Try your hand at these!
For each of 1–12 give a contradictory claim.
1. All students like to study.
2. No women are construction workers.
3. Every CEO of a Fortune 500 company is a man.
4. Not all drunk drivers get into accidents.
5. Donkeys eat carrots.
6. Only the good die young.
7. Nothing both barks and meows.
8. Tom will start every football game if he's not injured.
9. If some football player is a vegetarian, his coach will hate him.

10. All decisions about abortion should be left to the woman and her doctor.
11. The Lone Ranger was the only cowboy to have a friend called "Tonto."

For each of 12–18 select the claim that makes the argument valid. You're not supposed to judge whether the claim is plausible

12. All turtles can swim. So turtles eat fish.
    a. Anything that eats fish swims.
    b. Fish swim and are eaten by things that swim.
    c. Anything that swims eats fish.
    d. None of the above.
13. Anyone who plagiarizes is cheating. So Ralph plagiarizes.
    a. Ralph wrote three critical thinking essays in two days.
    b. Ralph cheated last week.
    c. Both (a) and (b).
    d. None of the above.
14. Pigs are mammals. So pigs eat apples.
    a. Anything that eats apples is a mammal.
    b. Pigs don't eat meat.
    c. Anything that is a mammal eats apples.
    d. None of the above.
15. All professional dancers cannot hold a day job. So no lawyer is a professional dancer.
    a. Lawyers don't usually like to dance.
    b. Dancers aren't interested in making money.
    c. Being a lawyer is a day job.
    d. Professional dancers can't write essays.
    e. None of the above.
16. Some cats chase songbirds. So some songbirds are eaten by cats.
    a. Some cats catch songbirds.
    b. Some things that chase songbirds eat them.
    c. Some songbirds attack cats.
    d. None of the above.
17. Manuel is sweating. So he must be hot.
    a. Manuel sweats when he is hot.
    b. Anyone who is hot sweats.
    c. Only Manuel sweats when he is hot.
    d. Only people who are hot sweat.
    e. None of the above.
18 Every dog chases cats. So Spot chases Puff.
    a. Spot is a dog.
    b. Puff is a cat.
    c. Puff irritates Spot.
    d. Both (a) and (b).
    e. None of the above.

Which of the following are valid arguments? For some you can refer to the forms above. But all of them can be evaluated if you return to the basics: it's not whether the premises and conclusion happen to be true but whether there is a way for the premises to be true and conclusion false, and if so, how likely that is.

19. Not every student attends lectures. Lee is a student. So Lee doesn't attend lectures.
20. Some dogs bite postal workers. Some postal workers bite dogs. So some dogs and postal workers bite each other.
21. Everyone who is anxious to learn works hard. Dr. E's students work hard. So Dr. E's students are anxious to learn.
22. No student who cheats is honest. Some dishonest people are found out. So some students who cheat are found out.
23. Only ducks quack. George is a duck. So George quacks.
24. Everyone who likes ducks likes quackers. Dick likes ducks. Dick likes cheese. So Dick likes cheese and quackers.
25. No dogcatcher is kind. Anyone who is kind loves dogs. So no dogcatcher loves dogs.
26. Dogs are mammals. Cats are mammals. Some dogs hate cats. Therefore, some dogs hate mammals.
27. Everything made with chocolate is delicious. No liquor is delicious. So no liquor is made with chocolate.

Answers

1. Some student doesn't like to study.
2. Some woman is a construction worker.
3. Some CEO of a Fortune 500 company is not a man.
4. All drunk-drivers get into accidents.
5. Some donkeys don't eat carrots.
6. Some people who die young aren't good.
7. Something both barks and meows.
8. Tom is not injured and he will not start some football game.
9. There is a football player who is a vegetarian, and his coach doesn't hate him.
10. Some decisions about abortions should not be left to the woman and her doctor.
11. Some cowboy had a friend named "Tonto," and he wasn't the Lone Ranger.
12. c.   13. d   14. c   15. c   16. d.   17. d.
18. e. (It's not "Every dog chases every cat," in which case it would be d.)
19. Invalid.
20. Invalid. It could be that dogs bite only postal workers who are cowardly and would never bite back, and the postal workers who bite dogs are so tough they never get bitten. So there could be no postal worker and dog that bite each other.
21. Invalid. Reasoning backwards with "all".
22. Invalid.
23. Invalid.
24. Invalid. And funny.
25. Valid. Reasoning backwards with "no".
26. Valid. The first premise is irrelevant.
27. Valid. The direct way of reasoning with no. If you think the conclusion is false, which premise isn't true?

Numbers and Graphs

Numbers . . . Your eyes begin to glaze over, you're in a cold sweat, . . .

With just a little study you can find your way through the numbers you meet—percentages, averages, interest rates, and all those numbers in advertisements. You'll see how numbers can be used well to inform—and how they can be used to mislead.

Graphs summarize lots of number claims. When they're done well, they allow for easy, visual comparisons. But we need to be careful reading them because they can make, and often conceal, the same kinds of mistakes we see with other comparisons using numbers.

17 Numbers

We use numbers to measure, to summarize lots of information, and then to compare.

Percentages
Percentages are used to present a summary of numbers. A percentage is a fraction of 100.

percent	fraction	ratio
26%	$26/100$	26 out of 100
92%	$92/100$	92 out of 100
18.1%	$18.1/100$	181 out of 1,000
0.2%	$.2/100$	2 out of 1,000

Sometimes percentages greater than 100 are used to indicate an increase.

400%	$400/100$	4 times as much
115%	$115/100$	1.15 times as much

- *52 out of 217 students failed Calculus I last year.*
  To calculate the percentage of students who failed, take $52/217 = 24\%$, rounded to the nearest percentage.

- *Of 81,173 women tested, 41,829 were allergic to cats.*
  In percentages, $41,829/81,173 = 51.53\%$ were allergic to cats, rounding to the nearest hundredth of a percent.

- *Last year Ralph's Pet Supply sold 412 dog collars. This year it sold 431.*
  To calculate the *increase* as a percentage of the previous year's sales, which is the *base*, take the difference and divide by the previous year's number: $(431 - 412)/412 = 4.6\%$ increase in the sale of dog collars, rounding to the nearest tenth of a percent.

- *Last month Piotr Adamowicz's Car Repair took in $59,031 in total receipts. This month it took in $51,287.*
  To calculate the *decline* in gross receipts as a percentage of last month's sales, which is the *base* of the comparison, take the difference in gross receipts and divide by the base $(59,031-51,287)/59,031 = 13.1\%$, rounding to the nearest tenth of a percent.

- *Ralph's Pet Supply buys dog collars from a wholesaler for $3.21 and sells them for $6.95.*

The store's *markup* is $3.74, which, as a percentage of the price it pays, is $3.74/3.21 = 117\%$, rounding to the nearest percent. Their *cost* as a percentage of what it sells them for is $3.21/6.95 = 46\%$.

- Last month out of the 47 rats used in Dr. Wibblitz's experiments, 17 died. This month 24 out of 52 rats died. The death rate last month was $17/47 = 36.2\%$ to the nearest tenth of a percent.

  The death rate this month is $24/52 = 46.2\%$ to the nearest tenth of a percent. The *increase* in the death rate was $(46.2-36.2)/36.2 = 27.6\%$ to the nearest tenth of a percent.

- Tom sees a stock for $60 and thinks it's a good deal. He buys it; a week later it's at $90, so he sells. He made $30—a 50% gain! His friend Wanda hears about it and buys the stock at $90; a week later it goes down to $60, so she panics and sells the stock. Wanda lost $30—that's a $33\,1/3\%$ loss.

  The same $30 is a different percentage depending on where you start, that is, depending on the base of the comparison.

  $\$90$
  $50\% \uparrow \qquad \downarrow 33\,1/3\%$
  $\$60$

- Maria: I don't know what I'm going to do. I don't have enough money to buy groceries and pay my car loan. I guess I'll have to go to Rooney-Díaz Dollars for Checks to get a loan.

  Lee How does that work?

  Maria: They give me $100 and I give them a check for $110 that they cash when my paycheck comes in—7 days from now.

  Lee: That sounds good—only 10% interest.

  Harry: Not! It's a 520% interest rate.

  Lee: Huh?

  Harry: 52 weeks in a year, so if they charged you $10 for each week, you'd owe them $520 by the end of the year. Interest rates are for the year.

  Maria: That's crazy—I only need the money for a week. I'll pay it back then.

  Harry: And if you don't, they'll let you roll the loan over and charge you the same $10 for the next week. And pretty soon you'll owe a fortune for that $100.

  Interest rates are or should be quoted per year. That's the only way we can compare them. Ask.

Mean, median, and mode

One way to present a summary of lots of numbers is by giving the mean, median, or mode of them.

94 *How to Reason*

> **Mean, median, and mode**
> The **mean** or **average** of a collection of numbers is obtained by adding the numbers, then dividing by how many items there are.
>
> The **median** is the midway mark: the same number of items above as below.
>
> The **mode** is the number most often attained.

• For the numbers 7, 9, 37, 22, 109, 9, 11:
The *average* or *mean* is calculated:
  Add $7 + 9 + 37 + 22 + 109 + 9 + 11 = 204$
  Divide 204 by 7 (the number of items) = 29.14
The *median* is 11.
The *mode* is 9.

• *It ought to be safe to cross here. I heard that the average depth is only 2 feet.*

An average is a useful figure to know only if there isn't much variation.

• *The average weight of the children in Ms. Ragini's fifth grade class is 103.7 pounds.*

Are most of the children at about that weight, or are there a lot of skinny kids and a few obese ones? More informative would be the median. Better yet, with fewer than 30 children the actual numbers can be given, along with a summary with the median.

• *The median weight of the children in Mr. Humbert's fifth grade class this year is 91 pounds and last year it was 88 pounds.*

To allow for a comparison, we need to summarize the numbers, which is best done in this case with the medians.

• *The average weight of children in New York's fifth grade classes is 101.72 pounds.*

Again, the median would be more informative. But with this large a number of children, the mode could tell us a lot, too.

• *The average wage of concert pianists in the U.S. is less than the average wage of university biology professors.*

There's not much variation in the salaries of university biology professors, but there's a huge variation in concert pianists' income ($15,000 to $2,000,000). The modes and medians would allow for a better comparison.

• *Here are the scores from Dr. E's final exam in critical thinking.*

score	52	55	57	62	75	90	92	94	95
number of students	2	4	5	4	1	4	1	7	3

The grading scale was:

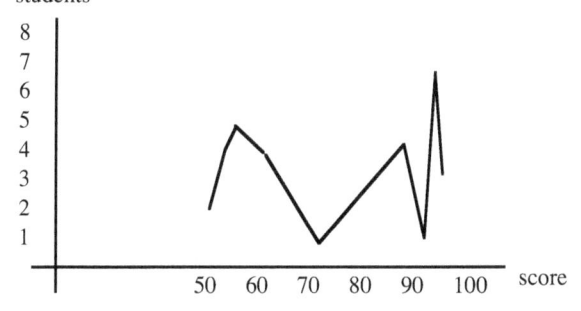

59 and below = F   60–69 = D   70–79 = C   80–89 = B   90–100 = A

When Dr. E's department head asked him how the teaching went, he told her, "Great, just like you wanted, the average mark was 75%, a C."

But she knows Dr. E too well to be satisfied. She asks him, "What was the median score?" Again Dr. E replies, "75"—as many got above 75 as below 75. But knowing how clever Dr. E is with numbers, she asks him what the mode score was. Dr. E flushes, "Well, 94." Now she knows something is fishy. When she wanted the average score to be about 75, she was thinking of a graph that looked like:

The distribution of the marks should be in a bell-shape: clustered around the median.

Unless you have good reason to believe that the average is pretty close to the median and that the distribution is more or less bell shaped, the average isn't informative.

Misleading numbers and comparisons

- *There were twice as many rapes as car thefts in our town last year.*
  So? This is a meaningless **apples and oranges** comparison: comparing different kinds of things where there's no common basis for comparing.

- *Prisons are getting worse as breeding grounds for disease in this state. There were 8% more cases of TB among prison inmates this year than last.*
  This is a misleading comparison. If the prison population increased by 16%, then it would be no surprise that the number of cases of TB is going up, though the rate (how many per 1,000 inmates) might be going down.

- *Paid attendance at Learn Your Way Out of Debt seminars is up more than 50% this year!*
  This sounded impressive to Lee until he found that last year 11 people paid for the seminars, and this year 17 did.

- *Identity Theft. Prevention & Repair Kit.*
  The fastest growing white-collar crime in the US!
  —The Attorney General's Office of New Mexico, 2007
  So it went from 5 cases to 10? Or from 5,000 to 6,000? When the base of a comparison is not given, it's just **two times zero is still zero**.

- *Once again, University of New Mexico student-athletes have made the grade. And then some.*
  The overall grade-point average for the school's 21 sports was 3.05 in the fall semester, according to the UNM registrar's office. That surpasses the previous best of 3.04, set in the spring of 2003.
  It's the eighth time in 12 semesters that the Lobos set a new standard, the figures being released Tuesday.
  — Mark Smith, *Albuquerque Journal*, February 23, 2005
  This is a two-times-zero-is-still-zero comparison. The base of the comparison should be the grade-point average for all students, which isn't given. With grade inflation it might be 3.0, so student athletes aren't better than average. Or maybe student athletes were taking easy courses —what's the grade-point average for just the courses they were taking?

- *A report on the radio says unemployment is up 10%.*
  This does not mean unemployment is *at* 10%. It means that if unemployment was 10% it is now 11%, a big increase; or if unemployment was 2%, it's now 2.2%, a small increase. Unless we know what unemployment was before, the comparison is meaningless.

• *Roadway Congestion*
Cities with highest and lowest roadway congestion index.
A value greater than 1.0 indicates significant congestion.

Highest	Index	Lowest	Index
Los Angeles	1.57	Bakersfield, Calif.	0.68
Washington	1.43	Laredo, Texas	0.73
Miami-Hialeah	1.34	Colorado Springs	0.74
Chicago	1.34	Beaumont, Texas	0.76
San Francisco	1.33	Corpus Christi, Texas	0.78

USA Today, April 13, 1999

What are they talking about? What does a "road congestion index" measure? These figures are meaningless to us.

Percentages are meant to summarize lots of numbers. *Percentages without the actual numbers are always misleading.*

• *Last term 22.857% of all Dr. Aloxomani's students failed his organic chemistry class.*

This is a case of **phony precision**. It's accurate but misleading, suggesting that there was a huge sample when it was just 8 out of 25.

• *An article in the journal* Science, *vol. 292, says that mammography screening can reduce the risk of breast cancer fatalities in women ages 50 to 74 by 25%.*

This seems like a real incentive for women that age to get tested. But the article points out that only 2 out of 1,000 women *without symptoms* are likely to die of breast cancer within the next 10 years. So reducing the risk by 25% means that at most 1 more woman in 2,000 who undergoes screening in the next 10 years might be saved.

Sometimes when we're asked to believe a claim our reaction should be *how could they know those numbers?*

• *Breast-feeding is up 16% from 1989.* — heard on National Public Radio

How could they know that number? Who was looking in all those homes? A survey? Who did they ask? Women chosen randomly? But lots of them don't have infants. Women who visited doctors? But lots of women, lots of poor ones, don't see a doctor. What does "breast-feeding" mean? Does a woman who breast-feeds one day and then stops qualify as someone who breast-feeds? Or one who breast-feeds two weeks? Six months? And up 16% from what base? Maybe NPR is reporting on a reliable survey, but without more information, it's just noise.

- *New Mexico Department of Health statistics estimate that of the 115,000 New Mexicans with diabetes, 37,000 don't know they have it.*
  —El Defensor Chieftain, Socorro, N.M., November 9, 2005
  If they don't know they have diabetes, how does the Department of Health know? There may be a good way they got this number, but we should suspend judgment unless we're willing to believe everything the Department of Health says.

Even when all the numbers are accurate, and it's all clear, the interpretation of the numbers can be skewed.

- *Harry: Did you hear that new applications for unemployment have fallen since last month and also from this month last year?*
  Dick: At last the economy is picking up.
  Or there are so many people already out of work that there aren't many left to be fired. Imagine the possibilities.

- *Another "statistic" widely quoted in feminist literature comes from the Society for the Advancement of Women's Health. It says that "only 14% (of the National Institutes of Health clinical trials funding) goes to research 52% of the population." In other words, "women-predominant" diseases, such as breast cancer, get the short end of the stick. Sounds terrible, discriminatory, unfair! But wait a minute. At least 76% of NIH clinical trial grants go to diseases that affect both sexes, such as heart disease and lung cancer. Since 76 + 14 equals 90, whether Washington lobbying groups like it or not, that means that "men-predominant" diseases are getting no more than 10% of the research money while women-predominant diseases get 14%.*
  It is just such techniques that caused Benjamin Disraeli, 130 years ago, to say that mendacity comes in only three forms, "lies, damn lies, and statistics." John Steele Gordon, USA Today, May 21, 1999

Sure, numbers make you panic. But if you understand percentages and what the mean, median, and mode are, you'll be able to find your way. Just a little caution can let you see when numbers are being badly used or used to mislead with:

- Comparisons where the base is not given.
  ("Two times zero is still zero.")
- Apples and oranges comparisons.
- Phony precision.

Try your hand at these!
1. "The birth control pill is 97% effective." What does this mean?

17 Numbers

2. Find the average, mean, median, and mode of the scores of Dr. E's students who took his critical thinking final exam: 92, 54, 60, 86, 62, 76, 88, 88, 62, 68, 81.
3. Wanda's grandfather listened to all those experts who say that over the long term the stock market is the best place to invest. So he put most of his retirement money in stocks. He just turned 70 and needs cash to retire. But the market went down 6% last week and 15% since the beginning of the year. How should he evaluate those experts' advice now?
4. [Advertisement] Our employees have a combined 52 years of experience!
5. [Advertisement for *3 Musketeers* candy bars]
   The sweetest part is finding out how little fat it has.
   (45% less fat than the average of the 25 leading chocolate brands, to be exact.)*
   *Not a low-fat food. 8 fat grams per serving for single bar vs. 15 gram average for leading chocolate brands.
6. Dick: Gee, cars are really expensive now. My uncle said he bought a new Ford Mustang in 1968 for only $2,000.
7. [On the box of a fan made by Lasco™]
   NEW   WIND RING™   30% MORE Air Velocity
8. [Concerning the way the U.S. Census Bureau operates] In 1990, 65% of the questionnaires that were mailed were filled out and returned. Census counters went back to every household that didn't mail back a form. Even then, the bureau was able to count only 98.4% of the U.S. population. — *USA Today,* April 15, 1998
9. Less than 10% of women who get breast cancer have the gene for breast cancer. Therefore, if you have the gene, there's only a 10% chance you'll get breast cancer.
10. Dick: Which section of English Lit should I take, Zoe, Professor Zzzyzzx's or Professor Øllebød's?
    Zoe: It doesn't really matter. You can't understand either, and the department info on the sections said the average mark in both their classes was a C.
11. According to Camille Scielzi, who coordinates the program, out of approximately 17,000 people who live in this county, 33 percent must exist solely on Social Security benefits that average $600 a month and 19 percent of the county residents live at or below the poverty level.   — Scott Turner, *El Defensor Chieftain,* November 12, 2015

Answers

1. It means that for every 100 women who use the contraceptive *for one year*, 3 will become pregnant.
2. average: 74.27   mean: 74.27   median: 76   mode: 88 and 62
3. The experts are right. All you have to do is wait until the stock market goes back up again—unless you die first. It's like doubling your bet on black with roulette every time you lose. You're sure to win in the long run. Unless you go broke or die first. The long run can be a very long time.
4. So? Maybe there's one employee with 50 years of experience and 48 employees with 1 month of experience.
5. It's 45% lower than the *average* of the other brands, but 24 of those other brands could actually have less fat than this candy bar if there's just one of them that has a huge amount of fat. And what are those "leading" brands? Leading where? In Brazil?

6. This is apples and oranges because it doesn't correct for inflation: $2,000 in 1968 is equivalent to what in current dollars?
7. More than . . . ?
8. If they didn't count everyone, how do they know what percentage they did count?
9. Wrong. It's just backwards. It should be: If you have breast cancer, there's less than a 10% chance you have the gene.
10. It could matter a lot! Perhaps everyone in Prof. Zzzyzzx's class got a C, while in Prof. Øllebod's class half got an A and half got an F. The median and mode are what Dick needs to know.
11. If 33% are on Social Security at $600 per month, all of those would be at the poverty level, which is more than 19%. But perhaps most of those on Social Security are getting $3,000 per month so are above the poverty level, and it's just the average that's so low. Without more information, this is all suspect.

18 Graphs

Graphs summarize lots of number claims. When they're done well, they allow for easy, visual comparisons. But we need to be careful in reading them because they can make—and often conceal—the same kinds of mistakes we've seen with other comparisons using numbers.

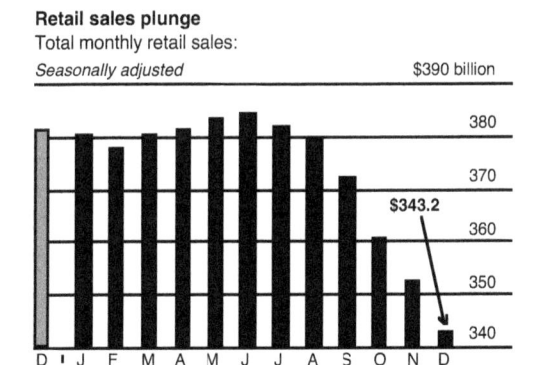

Retail sales plunge
Total monthly retail sales:
Seasonally adjusted $390 billion

[Bar chart showing monthly retail sales from D '07 through D '08, with values ranging from about 340 to 385 billion. December '08 shows $343.2 billion. Y-axis marks: 340, 350, 360, 370, 380.]

'07 | '08   Source: Department of Commerce (Associated Press, January 15, 2009)

The graph lies. The decrease from the highest sales in July to the lowest sales in December is about 11%, but the height of the bars makes it look like a decrease of 90%.

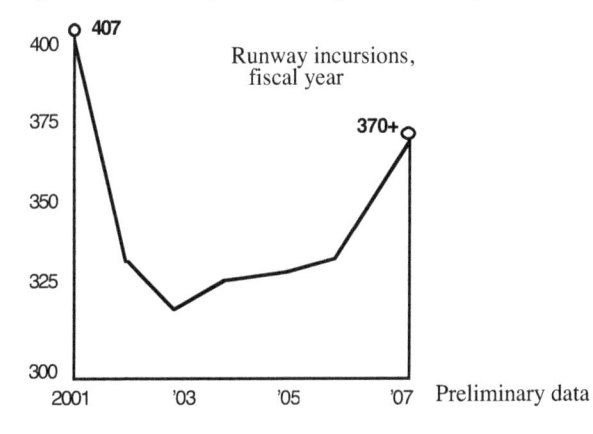

Whenever a graph doesn't show the baseline—the base of the comparison—it will exaggerate increases and decreases.

> • *Runway incursions on the increase*
>   *Incursions at U.S. airports increased 12 percent*
>   *from 2006 to 2007, almost as high as the 2001 peak.*

[Line graph titled "Runway incursions, fiscal year" showing values from 2001 (407) declining to a low around 2003, then rising to 370+ in '07 (Preliminary data). Y-axis: 300, 325, 350, 375, 400. X-axis: 2001, '03, '05, '07.]

102 How to Reason

Note: An incursion is any aircraft, vehicle or person that enters space reserved for takeoff and landing. Source: Federal Aviation Administration
— Associated Press, December 6, 2007

The figures are all there, the source is reliable, the graph is easy to read, but a 12% increase in runway incursions is depicted as a 150% increase in the heights of the points.

The spacing of the numbers on the axes can affect how we perceive changes that we're comparing. These two graphs present the same data as the previous example.

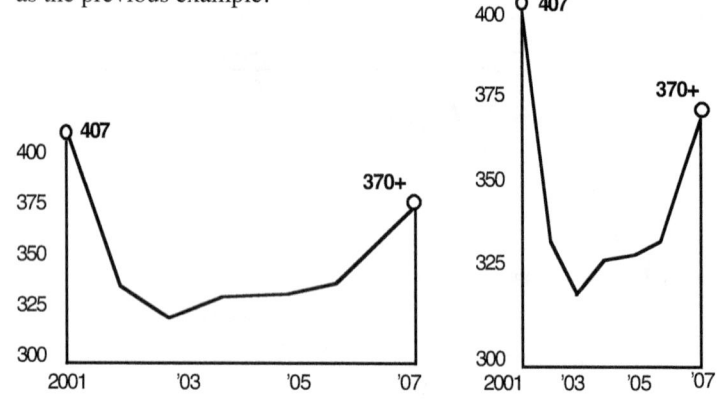

- *An economics text gives this graph.*

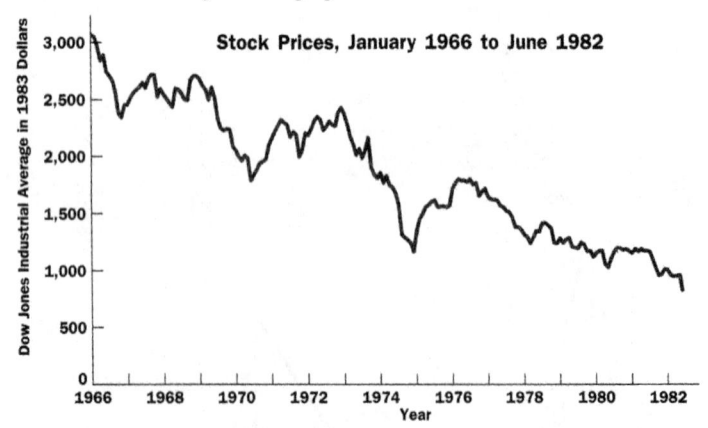

Stock Prices, January 1966 to June 1982

The text remarks that from 1966 to 1982 the prices of stocks were generally going down. Noting that from 1993 to 1998 stock prices were generally going up, the text then presents the following graph.

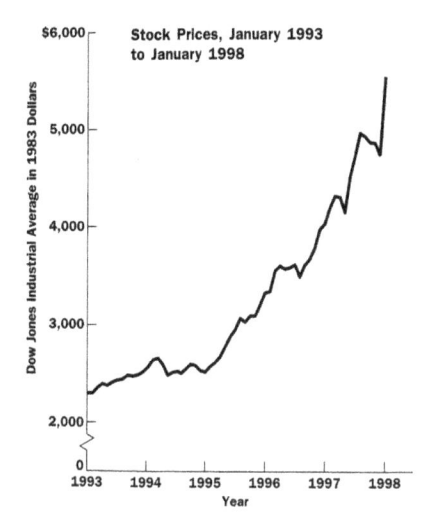

Finally, the text gives a fuller graph.

"A much longer and less-biased choice of period (1925–1998) gives a less distorted picture. It indicates that investments in stocks are sometimes profitable and sometimes unprofitable."

—W.J. Baumol and A.S. Blinder, *Economics*

104 *How to Reason*

Why is the longer period apt for comparison to the present day? If we looked at 1890 onward, we'd have a different picture still (the label "Full History" is wrong). Maybe a better comparison for investing in stocks is with the later periods because of new regulations on buying and selling stocks. The graphs do, however, compensate for inflation by stating the values in 1983 dollars—if they didn't, it would be apples and oranges.

Also note how the steepness of the increases and decreases are exaggerated in the last graph compared to the others.

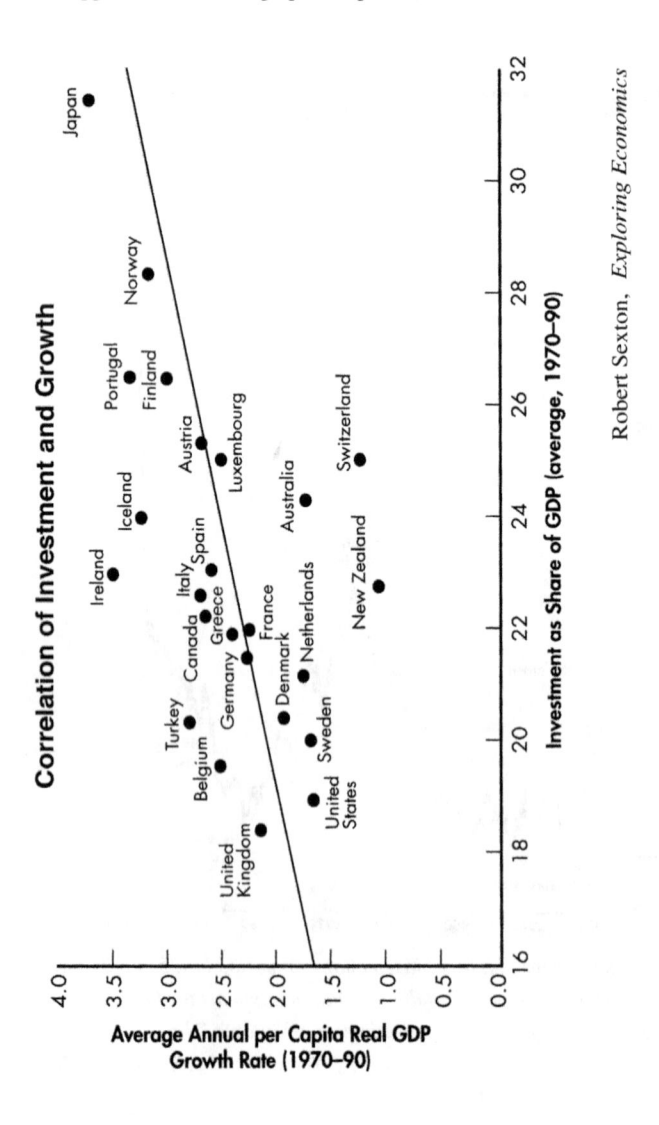

Correlation of Investment and Growth

x-axis: Investment as Share of GDP (average, 1970–90)
y-axis: Average Annual per Capita Real GDP Growth Rate (1970–90)

Countries plotted: Japan, Norway, Portugal, Finland, Ireland, Iceland, Austria, Luxembourg, Turkey, Italy, Spain, Canada, Greece, Australia, Belgium, Germany, France, Denmark, Netherlands, Switzerland, United Kingdom, Sweden, United States, New Zealand

Robert Sexton, *Exploring Economics*

By drawing the line in this graph, the author is asserting that investment and growth are correlated: Both rise together. His premises are the numbers plotted as points. But the picture doesn't obviously support that. Unless you know why and how the author is justified in drawing this line, the conclusion of this implicit argument here is just an appeal to the author's authority.

A graph is a summary of one or more claims or sometimes a whole argument. We should evaluate it by the standards we already have.

Reasoning from Experience

Arguing by analogy—"this is like that, so . . ."—is the most common way we draw on our experience. But though basic, such reasoning usually serves only as a suggestion for how to develop a good argument.

To fill out a comparison, we often need to make a claim about some group based on knowing about only a part of it. Such generalizations are not hard to evaluate once we see the criteria for what counts as a good one.

What we worry about most in our lives, though, is how to find a cause. Deciding whether to eat garlic, whether to take a job, whether to follow a doctor's advice, we need to understand whether there is cause and effect. That's not so hard to judge once we understand the criteria for what counts as cause and effect.

Often we ask "Why is this true?" An answer is typically an explanation we can judge according to clear enough criteria. But explanations about what is the function or goal of something are much harder to judge.

19   Analogies

Analogies and comparisons

> **Analogies**   A comparison becomes *reasoning by analogy* when it's part of an argument: on one side of the comparison we draw a conclusion, so on the other side we say we should conclude the same.

- *We should legalize marijuana. After all, if we don't, what's the rationale for making alcohol and tobacco legal?*
  Alcohol is legal. Tobacco is legal. Therefore, marijuana should be legal. They are sufficiently similar. This is reasoning by analogy.

- *DDT has been shown to cause cancer in rats. So there's a good chance DDT will cause cancer in humans.*
  This is reasoning by analogy with an unstated comparison: Rats are like humans. Hence, if rats get cancer from DDT, so will humans.

- *My love is like a red, red rose.*   — Robert Burns
  This is not reasoning by analogy: there's no argument.

Most reasoning by analogy is incomplete, relying on an unstated general principle. Often the value of an analogy is to uncover that principle.

- (Background: Country Joe McDonald was a rock star who wrote songs protesting the war in Vietnam. In 1995 he was interviewed on National Public Radio about his motives for working to establish a memorial for Vietnam War soldiers in Berkeley, California, his home and a center of antiwar protests in the '60s and '70s. This was his response.)
  Blaming soldiers for war is like blaming firemen for fires.

Country Joe's remark is a comparison. But it's meant as an argument:
  We don't blame firemen for fires.
  Firemen and fires are like soldiers and wars.
  Therefore, we should not blame soldiers for war.

In what way are firemen and fires like soldiers and wars? They have to be similar enough in some respect for Country Joe's remark to be more than suggestive. We need to pick out important similarities that we can use as premises.

Firemen and fires are like soldiers and war
    wear uniforms
    answer to chain of command
    cannot disobey superior without serious consequences
    fight (fires/wars)
    work done when fire/war is over
    until recently only men
    lives at risk in work
    fire/war kills others
    firemen don't start fires—soldiers don't start wars
    usually like beer

That's stupid: Firemen and soldiers usually like beer. So?

When you ask "So?" you're on the way to deciding if the analogy is good. It's not just any similarity that's important. There must be some crucial, important way that firemen fighting fires is like soldiers fighting wars, some similarity that can account for why we don't blame firemen for fires that also applies to soldiers and war. Some of the similarities listed don't seem to matter. Others we can't use because they trade on an ambiguity, like saying firemen "fight" fires.

We don't have any good guide for how to proceed—that's a weakness of the original argument. But if we are to take Country Joe McDonald's remark seriously, we have to come up with some principle that applies to both sides.

The similarities that seem most important are that both firemen and soldiers are involved in dangerous work, trying to end a problem/disaster they didn't start. We don't want to blame someone for helping to end a disaster that could harm us all.

(‡)   Firemen are involved in dangerous work.
    Soldiers are involved in dangerous work.
    The job of a fireman is to end a fire.
    The job of a soldier is to end a war.
    Firemen don't start fires.
    Soldiers don't start wars.

But even with these added to the original argument, we don't get a good argument for the conclusion that we shouldn't blame soldiers for wars. We need a general principle:

    You shouldn't blame someone for helping to end a disaster
    that could harm others if he didn't start the disaster.

This general principle seems plausible, and it yields a valid argument.

But is the argument good? Are all the premises true? This is the point where the differences between firemen and soldiers might be important.

The first two premises of (‡) are clearly true, and so is the third. But is the job of soldiers to end a war? And do soldiers really not start wars? Look at this difference:

> Without firemen there would still be fires.
> Without soldiers there wouldn't be any wars.

Without soldiers there would still be violence. But without soldiers—any soldiers anywhere—there could be no organized violence of one country against another ("What if they gave a war and nobody came?" was an antiwar slogan of the Vietnam War era).

So? The analogy shouldn't convince. The argument has a dubious premise.

We did not prove that soldiers should be blamed for wars. As always, when you show an argument is bad you haven't proved that the conclusion is false. You've only shown that you have no more reason than before for believing the conclusion.

Perhaps the premises at (‡) could be modified, using that soldiers are drafted for wars. But that's beyond Country Joe's argument. If he meant something more, then it's his responsibility to flesh it out. Or we could use his comparison as a starting place to decide whether there is a general principle, based on the similarities, for why we shouldn't blame soldiers for war.

Steps in evaluating an analogy
- Is this an argument? What is the conclusion?
- What is the comparison?
- What are the similarities?
- Can we state the similarities as premises and find a general principle that covers the two sides?
- Does the general principle really apply to both sides? Do the differences matter?
- Are the premises really true?
- Is the argument valid or strong?

• *It's wrong for the government to run a huge deficit, just as it's wrong for any family to overspend its budget.*
> The unstated assumption behind this analogy is that what is good for a person or family is also what is good for a country. Without more premises, though, this is unconvincing. There are very big differences between a family and a country: a family doesn't have to repair roads, it can't put up tariffs, nor can it print money. The **fallacy of composition**

is to argue that what is true of the individual therefore is true of the group, or what is true of the group is therefore true of the individual. The differences between a group and an individual are typically too great for such an analogy to be good.

- *For at least three years in California, about every third teacher hired was brought aboard under an emergency permit, a provisional license that enables people who possess college degrees, but no teaching credentials, to work.*

  "We wouldn't allow a brain surgeon to learn on the job," says Day Higuchi, president of the United Teachers Los Angeles, a 41,000-member teachers union. "Why is it OK to let someone who doesn't know what they're doing teach our kids?" — USA Today, August 30, 1999

  This is an argument, with conclusion (stated as a rhetorical question) that it isn't O.K. to let someone teach who isn't trained as a teacher. Higuchi, however, needs another premise: "If someone doesn't have a teacher's credential, then they don't know what they're doing teaching," which is not so clearly true. The comparison of a brain surgeon with a teacher has too many dissimilarities to be convincing: a teacher saying "Oops" is nothing like a brain surgeon saying "Oops."

- *Suzy: This candy bar is really healthy. Look, on the label it says "All natural ingredients."*
  Dick: Lard is all natural, too.

  Dick is refuting Suzy's argument that the candy bar is healthy by using an analogy: the same unstated principle would give a good argument for lard being healthy, which we know is false.

- *According to a Food and Drug Administration statement, "the question of a relationship between brain tumors and aspartame was initially raised when the agency began considering approval of this food additive in the mid-1970s." However, aspartame was approved for use in 1981.*

  Since it is an effective insecticide and rodenticide, I can't see any justification for human consumption.

  Richard Fagerlund, *Albuquerque Journal*, May 9, 2009

  This is an analogy from the ill effects of a chemical on rodents and insects to the ill effects on humans. But what are the similarities between those and humans that matter, and why don't the differences matter? We can refute this argument by noting that chocolate will kill dogs but it's fine (actually great!) for humans.

- [About the suggestion that the government should do nothing to rescue the big automakers from going bankrupt in 2008.] *It's easy to demonize the American auto industry. It has behaved with the foresight of a crack addict for years. But even when people set their own house on fire, we still dial 9-1-1, hoping to save lives, salvage what we can and protect the rest of the neighborhood.*

Bob Herbert, *The New York Times*, November 15, 2008

The comparison here is between someone setting his house on fire and automakers running their business badly. But the differences are immense. In particular, fires are immediately physically dangerous. We shouldn't be convinced by Herbert's suggestion that the government should rescue the automakers.

• *Downloading computer software from someone you don't know is like accepting candy from a stranger.*

This becomes an analogy when you consider the conclusion on one side that your mother probably told you: you shouldn't accept candy from a stranger. That suggests we should conclude: you shouldn't download (accept) computer software from someone you don't know. This looks pretty good, though we need to come up with a general principle that covers both sides.

• *a. Suppose that good, highly reliable research is announced showing that a liquid derived from eyes removed without anesthetic from healthy cats when applied to human skin reduces wrinkles significantly. Would it be justifiable to do further research and manufacture this oil?*

b. Same as (a) except that the liquid is drunk with orange juice and significantly reduces the chance of lung cancer for smokers.

c. Same as (a) except the liquid is mixed with potatoes and eaten and significantly reduces the chance of heart disease and lengthens the lives of women.

d. Same as (a) except that when drunk the liquid kills off all viruses harmful to humans.

If you said "yes" for some and "no" for others, what differences are there? If you said the same for all, did you reason by analogy? What general principle did you use? Would it apply if we replaced "cats" with "dogs"? Evaluating the analogies and disanalogies can lead to insight about our ethical assumptions.

Analogies and the law

Most analogies are not made explicit enough to serve as good arguments. But in the law, analogies are presented as detailed, carefully analyzed arguments, with the important similarities pointed out and a general principle stated.

Laws are often vague, or situations come up which no one ever imagined might be covered by the law. Do the tax laws for mail-order purchases apply to the internet? Similarities or differences have to be pointed out, general principles enunciated. Then those principles have to be respected by other judges. That's the idea of precedent or common law.

> The basic pattern of legal reasoning is reasoning by example. It is reasoning from case to case. It is a three-step process described by the doctrine of precedent in which a proposition descriptive of the first case is made into a rule of law and then applied to a next similar situation. The steps are these: Similarity is seen between cases; next the rule of law inherent in the first case is announced; then the rule of law is made applicable to the second case.
>
> Edward H. Levi, *An Introduction to Legal Reasoning*

But why should a judge respect how earlier judges ruled? Those decisions aren't actually laws.

Imagine getting thrown in jail for doing something that's always been legal, yet the law hasn't changed. Imagine running a business and suddenly finding that something you did, which before had been ruled safe and legal in the courts, now leaves you open to huge civil suits because a judge decided differently this week. If we are to live in a society governed by laws, the law must be applied consistently. It's rare that a judge can say that past decisions were wrong.

Only a few times has the Supreme Court said that all rulings on one issue, including rulings the Supreme Court made, are completely wrong. Brown vs. the Board of Education said that segregation in schools, which had been ruled legal for nearly a hundred years, is now illegal. Roe vs. Wade said that having an abortion, which had been ruled illegal for more than a century, is now legal. Such decisions are rare. They have to be. They create immense turmoil in the ways we live. We have to rethink a lot. And we can't do that regularly.

So what does a judge do when she's confronted by fifteen cases that were decided one way, the case before her falls under the general principle that was stated to cover those cases, yet her sense of justice demands that she decide this case the other way? She looks for differences between this case and those fifteen others. She tweaks the general principle just enough to get another principle that covers all those fifteen cases but doesn't include the one she's deciding. She makes a new decision that now must be respected or overthrown.

114 *How to Reason*

Try your hand at these!
Here are comparisons to evaluate. Note that there may be more than one argument in some of them.

1. You wouldn't buy a kitten at a pet store to give to your dog. Why, then, do you consider it acceptable to buy white rats for your boa constrictor?
2. Zoe: (*while driving*) Don't throw that banana peel out the window.
   Dick: Don't worry, it's biodegradable.
   Zoe: So is a newspaper.
3. Dick: Zoe, let's get married.
   Zoe: I've told you before, Dick, I won't get married until we sleep together.
   Dick: But that would be wrong. I won't sleep with you before we get married.
   Zoe: Would you buy a car without a test drive?
   Dick: Why buy the cow when the milk's free?
4. Dick: Congratulations on getting away with the shoplifting.
   Zoe: What are you talking about?
   Dick: Didn't you just install Adobe Acrobat on your computer from Tom's copy?
5. If killing is wrong, why do you punish murderers by killing them?
6. Tom: Colleges should be run like a business. Then they'd be more efficient, would cost less, and the education would be better because competition would be rewarded and bad teaching would be penalized.
7. When a trout rising to a fly gets hooked on a line and finds himself unable to swim about freely, he begins with a fight which results in struggles and splashes and sometimes an escape. Often, of course, the situation is too tough for him.
   In the same way the human being struggles with his environment and with the hooks that catch him. Sometimes he masters his difficulties; sometimes they are too much for him. His struggles are all that the world sees and it naturally misunderstands them. It is hard for a free fish to understand what is happening to a hooked one.

   —Karl A. Menninger, *The Human Mind*
8. Zeke: Boy, did you screw up.
   Dick: That is so unnecessary.
   Zeke: So is ice cream. But if it gives you pleasure, why not do it?
9. When Spot gets a bad cut, he licks the wound and it gets better quickly.
   So when Dick gets a bad cut, should he:
   Let Spot lick it? Lick it himself?

Answers
1. It seems that the conclusion is "It's not (morally?) acceptable to buy white rats to feed to your boa constrictor." A search for a general principle will lead to a dead-end because the differences are too great: Someone buys white rats to *feed* to their boa constrictor, since otherwise the snake will die. It must have live food.
2. Zoe is refuting Dick's argument that it's O.K. to throw a banana peel out the window by showing the same argument would justify throwing a newspaper out the window.
3. There are three arguments here:
   a. Dick says that you shouldn't sleep with someone before marriage because it's wrong. That's weak because "wrong" is too vague and/or subjective. A prescriptive standard is needed.

b. Zoe argues that she and Dick should sleep together in analogy with test driving a car before buying it. The analogy is weak: you can't hurt a car by test driving it (or if you do, insurance will make it O.K.), but you can hurt someone by sleeping with him or her and then not committing to the person. It also assumes "The (almost) sole reason for getting married is sex."

c. Dick then argues that Zoe and he should not sleep together in analogy with getting free milk from a cow and then not buying it. The analogy is not so weak. It depends on the claim "The only reason Zoe would marry me is for sex," and after Zoe's last argument that's not implausible.

4. The conclusion here is that sharing a program that you haven't purchased is theft. The comparison is to shoplifting. Even though you may think that the conclusion is true, this argument shouldn't convince, as there are too many differences.

5. This is not an analogy. It's questioning whether the person believes the general principle he or she espouses.

6. Tom is confusing the ideal perpetrated by business people with reality. Big businesses have lots of incompetent employees, take risks with money that a person who is being trusted shouldn't, and are plenty inefficient. Moreover, Tom isn't taking into account the big difference between businesses and colleges: businesses are out to make money, while a college's goal is (purportedly) to educate students. Consider the differences between consumers and students.

7. This beautiful piece doesn't get better by treating it as an argument. There's no obvious conclusion. It's an attempt to get you to imagine the lives of others, to instill empathy.

8. Zeke is trying to justify that it's O.K. to make snide remarks. The unstated premise he seems to assume is: If it feels good, do it. That's implausible, not least because of this comparison. Eating ice cream gives you pleasure but doesn't harm anyone else.

20 Generalizing

> **Generalizations** A *generalization* is an argument in which we conclude a claim about a group, called the **population**, from a claim about some part of it, the **sample**. Sometimes the general claim that is the conclusion is called the generalization. Plausible premises about the sample are called the **inductive evidence** for the generalization.

- *In a study of 5,000 people who owned pets in Anchorage, Alaska, dog owners expressed higher satisfaction with their pets and with their own lives. So dog owners are more satisfied with their pets and their own lives than other pet owners.*
  Sample: The 5,000 people who were surveyed in Anchorage.
  Population: Pet owners everywhere.

- *Of potential customers surveyed, 72% said that they liked "very much" the new green color that Yoda plans to use for its cars. So about 72% of all potential customers will like it.*
  Sample: The group of potential customers who were interviewed.
  Population: All potential customers. This is a *statistical* generalization.

- *Every time the minimum wage is raised, there's squawking that it will cause inflation and increase unemployment. And every time it doesn't. So watch for the same bad arguments again this time.*
  The unstated conclusion is that raising the minimum wage will not cause inflation or increase unemployment. This is a generalization from the past to the future.
  Sample: All times in the past that the minimum wage was raised.
  Population: All times it was raised or will be raised.

- *The doctor tells you to fast from 10 p.m. At 10 a.m. she gives you glucose to drink. Forty-five minutes later she takes some of your blood and has it analyzed. She concludes you don't have diabetes.*
  Sample: The blood the doctor took.
  Population: All the blood in your body.

- *Maria goes to the city council meeting with a petition signed by all the people who live on her block requesting that a street light be put in. Addressing the city council, she says, "Everyone on this block wants a street light here."*
  This is not a generalization. There's no argument from some to more.

20 Generalizing 117

Representative samples

What constitutes a good generalization? If we have a sample that's just like the entire collection, we can trust a generalization we make from it.

> *Representative sample* A sample is *representative* if no one subgroup of the whole population is represented more than its proportion in the population. A sample is **biased** if it is not representative.

How can we get a representative sample? You might think we can get one by making sure we have no intentional bias when we choose it. That's called **haphazard sampling**. It's not reliable.

• *For his sociology class, Tom decided he'd try to determine the attitudes of students about sex before marriage by giving a questionnaire to the first 20 students he met coming out of the student union.*

Tom had no intentional bias in choosing his sample. But there's no reason to believe it's representative. Those students might all be coming from a meeting of the Green Party, or the student Bible Society, or . . . .

• *Zoe reckons she can do better. She enlists three of her friends to hand out the questionnaire to the first 20 students they meet coming out of the student union, the administration offices, and the largest classroom building at 9 a.m., 1 p.m., and 6 p.m.*

Trying harder to get rid of intentional bias won't guarantee that a sample is representative. Perhaps all the players on the intercollegiate sports teams were gone for the day. They need a better way to choose a sample.

> *Random sampling* A sample is *chosen randomly* if at every choice there is an equal chance for any of the remaining members of the population to be picked.

• *Tom assigns a number to each student listed in the student directory, writes the numbers on slips of paper, puts them in a fishbowl, and has Suzy draw out one number at a time. Then he gives his questionnaire to the students whose numbers are drawn.*

Probably this would be a random selection. A simpler way to get a random selection is to use prepared tables of random numbers you can find online. For Tom's survey he can take the list of students from the directory, and if the first number on the table is 413, he would pick the 413th student on the list; if the second number is 711, he'd pick the 711th student on the list; and so on, until he has a sample that's big enough.

Random sampling is very likely going to yield a sample that's close to being representative. That's because of the **law of large numbers**, which says, roughly, that if the probability of something occurring is X percent, then over the long run the percentage of times that happens will be about X percent.

> • *The probability that a fair coin when flipped will land heads is 50%. So though you may get a run of 8 tails, then 5 heads, then 4 tails, then 36 heads to start, in the long run, repeating the flipping, eventually the number of heads will tend toward 50%.*
>
> • *Of the 20,000 students at Tom's school, 500 are vegetarians. So the chance that one student picked at random would be a vegetarian is: 500/20,000 = 1/40. If Tom were to pick 300 students at random, the chance that half of them would be vegetarians is very, very small. It's very likely, however, that 7 or 8 (about 1/40 of 300) will be vegetarians.*

Dick is confused about the law of large numbers. The ball could land on red 100 times in a row, yet black could even out by coming up just one more time than red every 100 spins for the next 10,000 spins.

The **gambler's fallacy** is to reason that a run of events of a certain kind makes a run of contrary events more likely to even up the probabilities. The long run can be very long indeed.

> *In the long run we're all dead.* — John Maynard Keynes

If we choose a large sample randomly, the chance is very high that it will be representative, since the chance of any one subgroup being over-represented is small—not nonexistent, but small. It doesn't matter if we know anything about the composition of the population in advance. After all, to know how many homosexuals there are, and how many married women, and how many men, and . . . you'd need to know almost everything about the population in advance. But that's what we do samplings to find out.

With a random sample we have good reason to believe the sample is representative. A sample chosen haphazardly might give a representative sample, but we have no good reason to believe it will.

Weak Argument	*Strong Argument*
Sample is chosen *haphazardly*. Therefore, the sample is representative.	Sample is chosen *randomly*. Therefore, the sample is representative.
Lots of ways the sample could be biased.	Very unlikely the sample is biased if it's large enough.

> • *We recruited participants at six busy locations in Zurich, Switzerland. Eligible participants were randomly approached and asked whether they would agree to take part in the study. We approached 272 pedestrians, and 185 (68%) were willing to take part. . . .*
>
> *In this sample, Swiss citizens did not know more than a third of MMK [minimum medical knowledge]. We found little improvement from this low level within groups with medical experience (personal or professional), suggesting that there is a consistent and dramatic lack of knowledge in the general public about the typical signs of and risk factors for important clinical conditions.*
>
> "Do Citizens Have a Minimum Medical Knowledge? A Survey"
> L. Bachmann, F. Gutzwiller, M. Puhan, J. Steurer, C. Steurer-Stey, and G. Gigerenzer, *BMC Medicine*, vol. 5, no. 14, 2007

This is just haphazard sampling. There's no reason to believe that the people interviewed are representative of all Swiss, much less "the general public." Yet this was published in a peer-reviewed journal, although one that's only online and has an ad for "Science Singles" at the top of its homepage.

The sample is big enough

For us to have confidence that a sample is representative, the sample has to be big enough. How big? Roughly, the idea is to measure how much more likely it is that the generalization is going to be accurate as we increase the number in our sample.

> • *If Lee wants to find out how many people in his class of 300 biology students are spending 10 hours a week on the homework, he might ask*

15 or 20. *If he interviews 30, he might get a better picture. But there's a limit. After he's asked 100, he probably won't get a much different result if he were to ask 150. And if he's asked 200, it's not likely his generalization will be different if he asks 250.*

- *Of the 20,000 students at Tom's school, 500 are vegetarians. If Tom chooses randomly just 8 students to interview, one might be a vegetarian, and from that tiny sample he might mistakenly infer that 12% of the students at his school are vegetarians.*

- *The makers of Doakes toothpaste proudly announce that users reported a 25% reduction in cavities, as certified by an independent laboratory.*
  This sounds impressive until you look up the study and find that the researchers followed only 12 people. With such a small sample, by chance they might find that the six people who used the toothpaste got 3 cavities and the other six got 4.

Generalizing from a sample that's obviously too small is called a **hasty generalization** based on **anecdotal evidence**. Often we can rely on common sense to evaluate whether a sample is big enough. But when we generalize to a very large population, say 2,500, or 25,000, or 250,000,000, how big the sample should be cannot be explained without at least a mini-course on statistics. In evaluating statistical generalizations, we have to expect that the people doing the sampling have looked at enough examples, which is reasonable if it's a respected organization or a well-known polling company. Surprisingly, 1,500 is typically adequate for a sample size when surveying all adults in the United States.

How big the sample needs to be depends also on how much **variation** there is in the population regarding the aspect you're investigating. If we know in advance that there's very little variation, then a small sample chosen haphazardly will do. When there's lots of variation or you don't know how much variation there is, you need a large sample, and random sampling is the best way to get that.

- *It's incredible how much information they can put on a CD. I just bought one that contains six movies.*
  This is a good generalization. The unstated conclusion is that every CD can contain as much information as this one that has the movies on it. There is little variation in the production of CDs for computers, so a sample of one is sufficient.

The sample is studied well
A large representative sample can still lead to a bad generalization if the sample isn't studied well.

> • *The doctor taking your blood to see if you have diabetes won't get a reliable result if her test tube isn't clean or she forgets to tell you to fast the night before. You won't find out the real attitudes of students about tuition if you ask a biased question. Picking a random sample of bolts won't help you determine whether the bolts are O.K. if all you do is inspect them by eye and not with a microscope or a stress test.*

> • *Surveys on sexual habits are notorious for being inaccurate. Invariably women report that the number of times they engaged in sexual intercourse with a man in the last week, or month, or year is much lower than the reports that men give of sexual intercourse with a woman during that time. The figures are so different that it would be impossible for both groups to be answering accurately.*

Generally, questionnaires and surveys are problematic because questions need to be formulated without bias and the interviewer has to rely on the respondents answering truthfully.

> • *One of the questions on the* "Official 2015 Democratic Party Survey":
>   *"Do you support his [President Obama's] plan to close other*
>   *tax loopholes to simplify the tax code so that corporations*
>   *and the ultra-wealthy will pay their fair share?"*
> There's no reason to believe any generalization from such a biased question. This is propaganda masquerading as a survey.

> • *Maria asked all but three of the 36 people in her class whether they've ever used cocaine. Only two said "yes." So Maria concludes that almost no one in the class has used cocaine.*
> This is a bad generalization. The sample is big enough and probably representative, but it's not studied well. People are not likely to admit to a stranger that they've used cocaine. An anonymous questionnaire is needed.

> • *More than four million people younger than 21 drove under the influence of drugs or alcohol last year, according to a government report released Wednesday. That's one in five of all Americans aged 16 to 20.*
>   —Associated Press, December 30, 2004
> We don't know whether they used an anonymous questionnaire, so we have no reason to accept their generalization.

Now we can summarize what's needed for a good generalization.

> ***Premises needed for a good generalization***
> - The sample is representative.
> - The sample is big enough.
> - The sample is studied well.

The margin of error and the confidence level
It's never reasonable to believe a statistical generalization with a conclusion that is too precise.

> • *In a survey, 27% of the people in Nantucket who were interviewed said they wear glasses. So 27% of all people in Nantucket wear glasses.*
> No matter how many people in Nantucket are surveyed, short of all of them, we can't be confident that exactly 27% of all people in the town wear glasses. Rather, "27%, more or less, wear glasses" is the right conclusion.

That "more or less" can be made fairly precise according to a theory of statistics. The **margin of error** gives the range in which the actual number for the population is likely to fall. The **confidence level** measures how strong the argument is for the statistical conclusion, where the survey method and responses are taken as premises.

> • *The opinion poll says that when voters were asked their preference, the incumbent was favored by 53% and the challenger by 47%, with a margin of error of 2% and a confidence level of 95%. So the incumbent will win tomorrow.*
> From this survey they're concluding that the percentage of all voters who favor the incumbent is between 51% and 55%, while the challenger is favored by between 45% and 49%. "The confidence level is 95%" means that there's a 95% chance it's true that the actual percentage of voters who prefer the incumbent is between 51% and 55%. If the confidence level were 70%, then the survey wouldn't be reliable: there would be a 3-out-of-10 chance that the conclusion is false. Typically, if the confidence level is below 95%, results won't be announced.

The bigger the sample, the higher the confidence level and the lower the margin of error. The problem is to decide how much it's worth in extra time and expense to increase the sample size in order to get a stronger argument.

> • *With a shipment of 30 insulating tiles, inspecting 3 and finding them OK would normally allow you to conclude that all the tiles are OK. But if*

they're for the space shuttle, where a bad tile could doom the spacecraft, you'd want to inspect each and every one of them.
Risk doesn't change how strong an argument we have, only how strong an argument we want before we'll accept the conclusion.

• *Flo: Every time I've seen a stranger at Dick's gate, Spot has barked. So Spot will always bark at strangers at Dick's gate.*
This is a bad generalization. The sample is chosen haphazardly, so there's no reason to believe it's representative.

• *Dick: Why does the phone always ring when I'm in the shower?*
Selective attention is a common mistake in generalizing. We note only what's unusual and forget the other times.

• *In a test of 5,000 cattle from Manitoba, none of them were found to be infected with mad cow disease. So it's pretty likely that no cattle in Canada have mad cow disease.*
This is a bad generalization. There's no reason to think that the sample is representative. At best the evidence could lead to a conclusion about all cattle in Manitoba.

• *Suzy: My grandmother was diagnosed with cancer seven years ago. She's refused any treatment that was offered to her over the years. She's perfectly healthy now and doing great. The treatments for cancer are just a scam to get people's money.*
This is a bad generalization from anecdotal evidence.

• *Dick: A study I read said people with large hands are better at math.*
 Suzy: I guess that explains why I can't divide.
Perhaps the study was done carefully with a random sample. But you don't need a study to know that people with large hands do better at math. Babies have small hands, and they can't even add. "All people" is the wrong population to study.

• *Lee: Every rich person I've met invested heavily in the stock market. So I'll invest in the stock market, too.*
This is a confused attempt to generalize. Perhaps Lee thinks that the evidence he cites gives the conclusion that if you invest in the stock market, you'll get rich(er). But that's arguing backwards, confusing (1) "If you invest in the stock market, you'll get rich" with (2) "If you're rich, then you invested in the stock market." The population for (1) is all investors in the stock market, not just the rich ones. It's a case of selective attention.

• *Suzy: I've been studying this astrology book seriously. I think you should definitely go into science.*
 Lee: I've been thinking of that, but what's astrology got to do with it?

> Suzy: Your birthday is in late January, so you're an Aquarian?
> Lee: Yeah, January 28.
> Suzy: Well, Aquarians are generally scientific but eccentric.
> Lee: C'mon. That can't be right.
> Suzy: Sure it is. Copernicus, Galileo, and Thomas Edison were all Aquarians.

This is a bad generalization based on anecdotal evidence. It's selective attention, reasoning backwards.

- *A "Quality of Education Survey" was done by the Las Cruces, New Mexico, school district in 2012. Forms were sent out to the parents of 25,000 students, and the public was invited to fill out forms online. The numbers of respondents were:*

Parents 6,448	Guardian of student 300
Staff at school 176	Other relative of student 64
No response 2,380	Other interested party 39
Teacher at school 303	Not known 31

The responses were grouped together. One of the questions was "The school staff maintains consistent discipline that is conducive to learning." The results were:

Strongly agree	30.71%	Strongly disagree	2.88%
Agree	54.17%	No opinion	3.58%
Disagree	7.16%	No response	1.47%

There's no reason to think that the sample is representative, despite the large number of responses. There's no reason to think that those who responded know what goes on in the school.

- *Of the chimpanzees fed one-quarter pound of chocolate per day in addition to their usual diet, 72% became obese within two months. Therefore, it is likely that most humans who eat one-quarter pound of chocolate per day in addition to their usual diet will become obese within two months.*

A generalization is needed to make this analogy good: 72% of all chimpanzees, more or less, will become obese if fed one-quarter pound of chocolate per day in addition to their usual diet. Whether this will be good depends on whether the researchers can claim that their sample is representative. The analogy then needs a claim about the similarity of chimpanzee physiology to human physiology in order to be a good argument. Trying to formulate such a claim will make it clear that it isn't the same quantity of chocolate but the amount relative to the body weight of the chimpanzees and the humans that should be the same.

20 *Generalizing* 125

You've learned what generalizations are, and now you can evaluate them using what you've seen here:
- Population and sample.
- Inductive evidence.
- Representative sample and biased sample.
- Haphazard sampling and random sampling.
- Gambler's fallacy.
- Anecdotal evidence.
- Three premises needed for a good generalization.
- The margin of error and the confidence level.
- Selective attention.

Try your hand at these!
For 1–11, say whether it's a generalization, If it is, identify the sample and population, and then evaluate whether it's good.

1. German shepherds have a really good temperament. I know because lots of my friends and my sister have one.
2. Maria: Look! That dry cleaner broke a button on my blouse again. I'm going to go over there and complain.
3. Maria to Suzy: Don't bother to ask Tom to do the dishes. My brother's a football player, and no football player will do the dishes.
4. Manuel: Are those refried beans?
   Maria: Yes.
   Manuel: I can't believe you'd cook those for dinner. Don't you remember I had terrible indigestion the last time you made them?
5. Harry: Don't go to Seattle in December. It rains there all the time then.
6. You don't have to worry about getting the women's gymnastic team in your van. I saw them at the last meet, and they're small enough to fit in.
7. From our study it appears that bald men are better husbands.
8. Socialized medicine in Canada isn't working. I heard of a man who had colon cancer and needed surgery. By the time doctors operated six months later, the man was nearly dead and died two days later.
9. Manuel to Maria: Lanolin is great for your hands—you ought to try it. It's what's on sheep wool naturally. How many shepherds have you seen with dry, chapped hands?
10. Lee: When I went in to the health service, I read some women's magazine that had the results of a survey they'd done on women's attitudes towards men with beards. They said that they received over 10,000 responses from their readers to the question in their last issue, and 78% say they think that men with beards are really sexy! I'm definitely going to grow a beard now.
11. In 2015, Public Policy Polling asked 532 Republican primary voters across the U.S. if they supported or opposed bombing Agrabah: 30% supported bombing, 13% opposed bombing, and 57% said they were not sure.

12. The mayor of a town of 8,000 has to decide whether to spend town funds on renovating the park or hiring a part-time animal control officer. She gets a reputable polling organization to do a survey.
   a. The results of the survey are 52% in favor of hiring an animal control officer and 47% in favor of renovating the park, with 1% undecided, and a margin of error of 3%. The confidence level is 98%. Which choice will make the most people happy? Should she bet on that?
   b. The results are 61% in favor of hiring an animal control officer and 31% in favor of renovating the park, with 8% undecided, and a margin of error of 9%. The confidence level is 94%. Which choice will make the most people happy? Should she bet on that?

Answers
1. Generalization. Sample: The German shepherds the speaker has met. Population: All German shepherds. Anecdotal evidence. Bad.
2. Not a generalization.
3. Is the sample Maria's brother, or other football players she knows? Since we can't identify the sample, it's not O.K. to call this a generalization.
4. Generalization: Manuel will get sick this time. Sample: The last time Manuel ate refried beans cooked by Maria. Population: All times Manuel eats refried beans cooked by Maria. Anecdotal, but considering the risk, it's good enough to convince Manuel.
5. Possibly generalizing, but could be just repeating a general claim he's heard. We can't identify the sample, so don't treat it as a generalization.
6. Not a generalization.
7. The study may have been a generalization, but the sample and the population are not given here, so we can't treat it as one. Besides, it's too vague.
8. This is just a hasty generalization.
9. Maria should ask Manuel how many shepherds he knows.
10. No reason to think the sample is representative. Lee doesn't even have reason to think the sample is representative of the women who read that magazine. After all, they may have got only 10,000 out of 200,000 sent out, and mostly women who like men with beards responded.
11. Agrabah is a fictional city from Disney's *Aladdin*.
12. a. Too close to call. b. Hire the animal control officer. Even with the huge margin of error and large number of undecided, we can be confident that most people prefer that.

I TALKED TO ALL THE PEOPLE WHO LIVE ON THIS STREET AND EVERYONE WHO HAS A DOG IS REALLY HAPPY. SO IF I GET MY MOM A DOG, SHE'LL BE HAPPY, TOO.

21 Cause and Effect

Describing causes and effects
What exactly is a cause? Last night Dick said:

> Spot made me wake up.

Spot caused Dick to wake up. But it's not just that Spot existed. It's what he was doing that caused Dick to wake up:

Spot's barking caused Dick to wake up.

So Spot's barking is the cause? What kind of thing is that? The easiest way to describe the cause is to say:

> Spot barked.

The easiest way to describe the effect is to say:

> Dick woke up.

Causes and effects can be described with claims.

Causal claims A *causal claim* is a claim that is or can be rewritten as *X causes (caused) Y*. A **particular** causal claim is one in which a single claim can describe the (purported) cause, and a single claim can describe the (purported) effect. A **general** causal claim is a causal claim that generalizes many particular causal claims.

• *Spot caused Dick to wake up.*
  This a particular causal claim, where the purported cause can be described by the single claim "Spot was barking" and the purported effect by "Dick woke up." We might generalize from this particular cause and effect to the claim "Very loud barking by a dog near someone when he is sleeping

causes him to wake up, if he's not deaf." That's a general causal claim. For it to be true, lots of particular causal claims have to be true.

- *The speeding ticket Dick got made his auto insurance rate go up.*
  This is a particular causal claim. The purported cause is "Dick got a speeding ticket," and the purported effect is "Dick's auto insurance went up."

- *Speeding tickets make people's auto insurance rates go up.*
  This is a general causal claim. For it to be true all particular causal claims like the previous example have to be true.

- *Penicillin prevents serious infection.*
  What is the cause? The existence of penicillin? No, it's that penicillin is administered to people in certain amounts at certain stages of their infections. What's a "serious infection"? This is too vague to count as a causal claim.

- *Lack of rain caused the crops to fail.*
  The purported cause here is "There was no rain," and the purported effect is "The crops failed." This example is true of a few years ago in the Midwest. A cause need not be something active; almost any claim that describes the world could describe a cause.

Necessary conditions for cause and effect

What conditions are needed for a causal claim to be true?

The cause and effect both happened.
That is, the claim describing the cause and the claim describing the effect are both true. We wouldn't say that Spot's barking caused Dick to wake up if Spot didn't bark or Dick didn't wake up.

It's (nearly) impossible for the cause to happen and the effect not to happen.
It has to be (nearly) impossible for the claim describing the cause to be true and the claim describing the effect to be false. It can't be just coincidence that Dick woke up when Spot barked.

That's the same condition for an argument to be valid or strong. But here we're not trying to convince anyone that the conclusion is true: we know that Dick woke up. What we can carry over from our study of arguments is how to look for possibilities—ways the premises could be true and the conclusion false—to determine if there is cause and effect. As with arguments, we'll often need to supply unstated premises to show that the effect follows from the cause.

- *A lot has to be true for it to be impossible for "Spot barked" to be true and "Dick woke up" to be false:*
   Dick was sleeping soundly up to the time that Spot barked.
   Spot barked at 3 a.m.
   Spot was close to where Dick was sleeping.

   We could go on forever. But as with arguments, we state what we think is important and leave out the obvious. If someone challenged us, we could add "There was no earthquake at the time"—but we just assume that as part of the normal conditions.

Normal conditions   The *normal conditions* for a causal claim are the obvious and plausible claims that are needed to establish that the relation between the purported cause and the purported effect is valid or strong.

- *Very loud barking by a dog that's near someone who is sleeping causes him to wake up, if he's not deaf.*
   For a general causal claim like this one, the normal conditions won't be specific just to the one time Spot woke Dick but will be general.

The cause precedes the effect.
We wouldn't accept that Spot's barking caused Dick to wake up if Spot began barking only after Dick woke up. The cause has to precede the effect. That is, "Spot barked" became true before "Dick woke up" became true.

The cause makes a difference.
If there were no cause, there would be no effect.

- *Dr. E has a desperate fear of elephants. So he buys a special wind chime and puts it outside his door to keep the elephants away. He lives at 6,000 feet above sea level in a desert, and he confidently claims that the wind chime causes the elephants to stay away.*
   After all, ever since he put up the wind chime he hasn't seen any elephants.
   Why are we sure the wind chime being up did not cause elephants to stay away? Because even if there had been no wind chime, the elephants would have stayed away. Which elephants? All elephants. The wind chime works, but so would anything else. Having the wind chime doesn't make a difference.

There is no common cause.
We don't say that night causes day. That's because there's a common cause of both "It was night" and "It is now day," namely, "The Earth is rotating relative to the sun."

> • *Dick: Zoe is irritable because she can't sleep properly.*
> *Tom: Maybe it's because she's been drinking so much espresso that she's irritable and can't sleep properly.*
> Tom hasn't shown that Dick's causal claim is false by raising the possibility of a common cause. But he does put Dick's claim in doubt. We have to check the other conditions for cause and effect to see which causal claim seems most likely.

In summary, here are the conditions required for a causal claim to be true when cause and effect are described by claims.

Necessary conditions for cause and effect
- The cause and effect both happened (both claims are true).
- The cause precedes the effect.
- It's (nearly) impossible for the cause to happen (be true) and the effect not to happen (be false), given the normal conditions.
- The cause makes a difference: if the cause had not happened, the effect would not have happened, given the normal conditions.
- There is no common cause.

These are necessary conditions. In practice, however, we treat them as sufficient, too. Here's an example.

The cat made Spot run away.

Cause What is the cause? It's not just the cat. How can we describe it with a claim? Perhaps "A cat meowed close to Spot."

Effect Spot ran away.

Cause and effect each happened The effect is clearly true. The cause is highly plausible: almost all things that meow are cats.

Cause precedes effect Yes.

It's (nearly) impossible for the cause to be true and effect false
What needs to be assumed as "normal" here? Spot is on a walk with Dick. Dick is holding the leash loosely enough for Spot to get away. Spot chases cats. Spot heard the cat meow. We could go on, but this seems enough to guarantee that it's unlikely that the cat could meow near Spot and Spot not chase it.

The cause makes a difference Would Spot have run away even if the cat had not meowed near him? Apparently not, given those normal conditions, since Dick seems surprised that Spot ran off. Perhaps he would have, though, even if he'd only seen the cat. But that apparently wasn't the case. So let's revise the cause to be "Spot wasn't aware a cat was near him, and the cat meowed close to Spot." Now we can reasonably believe that the cause made a difference.

Is there a common cause? Perhaps the cat was hit by a meat truck and lots of meat fell out, and Spot ran to that? No, Spot wouldn't have barked. Nor would he have growled.

Perhaps the cat is a hapless bystander in a fight between dogs, one of which is Spot's friend. We do not know if this is the case. So it is possible that there is a common cause, but it seems unlikely.

Evaluation We have good reason to believe the original claim on the revised interpretation that the cause is "Spot wasn't aware a cat was near him, and the cat meowed close to Spot, and Spot heard it."

These are the steps we should go through to establish a causal claim. If we can show that one of them fails, though, there's no need to check all the others.

Common mistakes in reasoning about cause and effect

Tracing the cause too far back in time
It's sometimes said that the cause must be close in space and time to the effect. But the astronomer is right when she says that a star shining caused the image on the photograph, even though that star is very far away and the light took millions of years to arrive. The problem isn't

how distant in time and space the cause is from the effect. *When we trace a cause too far back, the problem is that the normal conditions begin to multiply.* When you can't even imagine what the normal conditions are, you know you've gone too far back.

> • My mother missed the sign-up to get me into Kernberger Preschool, and that's why I've never been able to get a good job.
> This is tracing the cause too far back.

Reversing cause and effect
If reversing cause and effect sounds just as plausible as the original claim, investigate the evidence further before making a judgment.

> • Suzy: Sitting too close to the TV ruins your eyesight.
> Zoe: How do you know?
> Suzy: Well, four of my grade-school friends used to sit really close to the TV, and all of them wear really thick glasses now.
> Zoe: Maybe they sat so close because they had bad eyesight.
> Zoe hasn't shown that Suzy's claim is false. But her suggestion that cause and effect are reversed raises sufficient doubt not to accept Suzy's claim without more evidence.

Looking too hard for a cause
We look for causes because we want to understand, so we can control our future. But sometimes the best we can say is that it's **coincidence**.

> • Before your jaw drops open in amazement when a friend tells you a piano fell on her old piano teacher the day after she dreamt she saw him in a recital, remember the law of large numbers: if it's possible, given long enough, it'll happen. After all, most of us dream, say, one dream a night for at least 100 million adults in the U.S. That's 700 million dreams per week. With the elasticity in interpreting dreams and what counts as a "dream coming true," it would be amazing if a lot of dreams didn't "accurately predict the future."

But doesn't everything have a cause? Shouldn't we look for it? For much that happens in our lives we won't be able to figure out the cause. We just don't know enough. We must, normally, ascribe lots of happenings to chance, to coincidence, or else we have paranoia and end up paying a lot of money to phone psychics.

> • *A woman in New York cuts her hand with a sharp knife. At just that moment her mother in Montana 2,500 miles away feels a pain in the same hand. Coincidence?*
> Yes. That's what coincidence is.

Post hoc ergo propter hoc ("after this, therefore because of this") It's a mistake to argue that there is cause and effect just because one claim became true after another.

> • *Lee: I scored well on that last exam and I was wearing my red-striped shirt. I'd better wear it every time I take an exam.*
> This is *post hoc* reasoning.

> • *A recent study showed that everyone who uses heroin started with marijuana. So smoking marijuana causes heroin use.*
> And they probably all drank milk first, too. Without further evidence this is just *post hoc* reasoning.

Claiming that a correlation by itself establishes cause and effect is the **correlation-causation fallacy**. It's just a pumped-up version of *post hoc* reasoning or reversing cause and effect.

The best way to avoid making common mistakes in reasoning about cause and effect is to experiment. Conjecture possible causes, then by experiment eliminate them until there's only one. Check that one. Does it make a difference? If the purported cause is eliminated, is there still the effect? Often we can't do an experiment, but we can do an imaginary one. That's what we always do in reasoning well: *Imagine the possibilities*.

> • *Disappointing job creation, Hungary woes send markets reeling*
> — Headline, Associated Press, June 5, 2010
> Every day newswriters pick out what they consider the most prominent piece of good news if the market went up, or bad news if the market went down, and ascribe the change in the stock market to that. That's just *post hoc* reasoning.

> • *Flo: Salad makes you fat. I know 'cause Wanda's really fat and she's always eating salad.*
> Flo has reversed cause and effect.

> • *Zoe: My life's a mess. I've never really been happy since all those years ago in school you told Sally that I hated her cat. She believed your stupid joke and made sure I wasn't a cheerleader. I'll never be a cheerleader. It's your fault I'm so miserable now.*
> *Dick: There, there.*

Zoe is tracing the cause too far back. Dick rightly doesn't try to reason with her because he remembers the Principle of Rational Discussion.

- *Money causes counterfeiting.*
This is a general causal claim covering every particular claim like "That there was money in this society caused this person to counterfeit the currency." We certainly have lots of evidence. But it's tracing the cause too far back. There being money in a society is part of the normal conditions for the effect that someone counterfeited currency.

- *When more and more people are thrown out of work, unemployment results.*   — President Calvin Coolidge
This isn't cause and effect. It's a definition.

- (Advertisement by the Iowa Egg Council in the Des Moines, Iowa, International Airport)
Children who eat breakfast not only do better academically, but they also behave better.   Archives of Pediatric and Adolescent Medicine
They're hoping you'll believe that the correlation means there's cause and effect. But you know to look for other possibilities. In particular, there could be a common cause: their parents are richer and/or spend more time with them, which is why they get breakfast and do better academically and behave better.

- *Maria: Fear of getting fired causes me to get to work on time.*
What is fear? The purported cause here is "Maria is afraid of getting fired," and the effect is "Maria gets to work on time."

 Is it possible for Maria to be afraid of getting fired and still not get to work on time? Certainly, but not, perhaps, under normal conditions: Maria sets her alarm; the electricity doesn't go off; the weather isn't bad; Maria doesn't oversleep; . . . .

 But doesn't the causal claim mean it's because she's afraid that Maria makes sure these claims will be true or that she'll get to work even if one or more is false? She doesn't let herself oversleep due to her fear. In that case, how can we judge whether what Maria said is true? It's easy to think of cases where the cause is true and effect false. So we have to add normal conditions. But that Maria gets to work regardless of conditions that aren't normal is what makes her consider her fear to be the cause.

 Subjective causes are often a matter of feeling, some sense that we control what we do. They are often too vague for us to classify as true or false.

- *Dick: Hold the steering wheel.*
Zoe: What are you doing? Stop! Are you crazy?
Dick: I'm just taking my sweater off.

21 Cause and Effect   135

Zoe: I can't believe you did that. It's so dangerous.
Dick: Don't be silly. I've done it a thousand times before.
  Crash . . . Later
Dick: You had to turn the steering wheel!? That made us crash.
   The purported cause is that Zoe turned the steering wheel; the effect is that the car crashed. The necessary criteria are satisfied. But Zoe's turning the steering wheel is a **foreseeable consequence** of Dick making her take the wheel, which is the real cause. The normal conditions are not just what has to be true before the cause but also what will normally follow the cause.

- *The Treaty of Versailles caused World War II.*
   The purported cause is "The Treaty of Versailles was agreed to and enforced." The purported effect is "World War II occurred." To analyze a conjecture like this, an historian will write a book. The normal conditions have to be spelled out. She has to show that it was a foreseeable consequence of the enforcement of the Treaty of Versailles that Germany would re-arm. But was it foreseeable that Chamberlain would back down over Czechoslovakia? More plausible is that the signing of the Treaty of Versailles is *a* cause, not *the* cause of World War II. When several claims together are taken *jointly* as the cause, we say that each describes **a cause** or is a **causal factor**.

- *Tom: The only time I've had a really bad backache is right after I went bicycling early in the morning when it was so cold last week. Bicycling never bothered me before. So it must be the cold weather that caused my back to hurt after cycling.*
   The purported cause is "It was cold when Tom went cycling," the effect is "Tom got a backache." The criteria seem to be satisfied. But Tom may have overlooked another cause. He also had an upset stomach, so maybe it was the flu. Or maybe it was tension, since he'd had a fight with Suzy the night before. He'll have to try cycling in the cold again to find out. Even then he may be looking too hard for *the* cause, when there may be several causes jointly. Another possibility: Tom will never know for sure.

- Dick: Wasn't it awful what happened to old Mr. Grz?
  Zoe: You mean those tree trimmers who dropped a huge branch on him and killed him?
  Dick: You only got half the story. He'd had a heart attack in his car and pulled over to the side. He was lying on the pavement when the branch hit him and he would have died anyway.
   What's the cause of death? Mr. Grz would have died anyway. So the tree branch falling on him wouldn't have made a difference. But the tree branch falling on him isn't a foreseeable consequence, part of the

normal conditions of his stumbling out of his car with a heart attack. It's an *intervening cause*.

* *Poltergeists are making the pictures fall down.*
  To accept this, we have to believe that poltergeists exist. That's dubious. Worse, it's not **testable**: how could you determine if there are poltergeists? Dubious claims that aren't testable are the worst candidates for describing a cause.

* *Lee: Look at this. Alcoholism has to be genetic. They did a study and found that 20% of children with an alcoholic parent grew up to be alcoholics, while only 5% of children without an alcoholic parent grew up to be alcoholics.*
  Lee has fallen into the **fallacy of looking at only one end**. Looked at the other way, 80% of children with an alcoholic parent didn't grow up to be an alcoholic. That seems to show that alcoholism isn't genetic. He's also committed the **single-cause fallacy**: looking for a single cause when there are many causal factors. Perhaps genetics predisposes a person to be an alcoholic, but there's a lot more involved: how the parents acted at home, the culture of drinking the child grew up in, the availability of alcohol, emotional and physical setbacks in life, and more.

* *Running over nails causes your tires to go flat.*
  This sounds right, but it's false. Lots of times we run over nails and our tires don't go flat. What's correct is: "Running over nails *can cause* your tires to go flat." That is, if the conditions are right, running over a nail will cause your tire to go flat. In the next chapter we'll look at the difference between "causes" and "can cause."

* *Zoe: Every time I wash my car, it rains within 12 hours.*
  Suzy: Well, don't wash your car today. I want my picnic to be fun.
  Behind Suzy's comment is a general causal claim: "Zoe's washing her car causes it to rain." We just laugh. Of course there's no connection.
  But suppose it was always clear and forecast to be sunny for the next two days when Zoe washed her car. And it always rained within six hours. And this happened 30 times over two years. We'd have pretty good evidence for Zoe's claim.
  Still, we'd be suspicious. Constant conjunction (correlation) isn't enough to convince us that if the cause weren't true, the effect wouldn't be true. The conjunction might be coincidence or the result of a common cause. My pulse is evidence that I'm breathing, occurring always in conjunction with it, and if I had no pulse I wouldn't be breathing. But my having a pulse is not the cause of my breathing.

21 Cause and Effect

We want a general principle that connects cause and effect, some glue for the inference. The constant conjunctions give us motive to find one, but until we do, we're apt to dismiss the causal claim as *post hoc* reasoning.

Since he was adopted by staff members as a kitten, Oscar the Cat has had an uncanny ability to predict when residents are about to die. Thus far, he has presided over the deaths of more than 25 residents on the third floor of Steere House Nursing and Rehabilitation Center in Providence, Rhode Island. His mere presence at the bedside is viewed by physicians and nursing home staff as an almost absolute indicator of impending death, allowing staff members to adequately notify families. Oscar has also provided companionship to those who would otherwise have died alone. For his work, he is highly regarded by the physicians and staff at Steere House and by the families of the residents whom he serves.
—David M. Dosa, M.D. *New England Journal of Medicine*, July 26, 2007

This is very sweet and mysterious. How does Oscar the Cat know the person is going to die? But reversing cause and effect is just as plausible given the evidence: Oscar the Cat visiting the person causes the person to die. Mysteries merit further investigation, not slack-jawed acceptance.

There's a lot here, but it all fits together when you understand:

- (Purported) cause and effects can be described with claims.
- Particular causal claim and general causal claim.
- Normal conditions.
- Common cause.
- Necessary conditions for cause and effect.
- Tracing the cause too far back.
- Reversing cause and effect.
- Coincidence.
- *post hoc ergo propter hoc*.
- Correlation-causation fallacy.
- Foreseeable consequence.
- Causal factor.
- Intervening cause.
- Fallacy of looking at only one end.
- Single-cause fallacy.

Try your hand at these!

For 1–9, if appropriate, rewrite the sentence as a causal claim—that is, one that uses the word "causes" or "caused." If it's a particular causal claim, describe the purported cause and the purported effect with claims.

1. The police car's siren got me to pull over.
2. Because you were late, we missed the beginning of the movie.
3. The onion's smell made me cry.
4. Dogs make great pets.
5. I better not get the pizza with anchovies because every time I do, I get heartburn.
6. Someone ringing the doorbell made Spot bark.
7. Coffee keeps me from getting a headache in the afternoon.
8. If it weren't for my boyfriend, I'd have no problems.
9. Our airplane took off from gate number thirteen. No wonder we're experiencing so much turbulence.

For the following, decide whether it's a causal claim. If it is, describe the (purported) cause and effect with claims. Then evaluate it, as in the example on pp. 130–131.

10. Maria: I had to slam on the brakes because some idiot pulled out in front of me.
11. Zeke abuses animals because his parents abused him.
12. Suzy: My feet hurt so bad the other day when I was cheerleading. My feet have never hurt at the other cheerleading events, but I was wearing new shoes. So it must have been my new shoes.
13. Marriage is the chief cause of divorce.
14. I've got to go to the game. The only time I wasn't in the bleachers this season, they lost.
15. Zoe: The dark sky makes me really depressed today.
16. The emphasis on Hollywood figures in the media causes people to use drugs because people want to emulate the stars.
17. Maria: It's awful what's happened to Zeke.
    Lee: Why? What happened? I haven't seen him for ages.
    Maria: He started using drugs. It's because he was hanging out with that bad bunch.
18. Suzy: Eating potato chips and sitting on the couch must be healthy. All the guys on the football team do it.
19. Dr. E: My students don't like the material at the end of this course. That's why so many have missed class the last weeks of classes.
20. Zoe belched loudly in the shower with the bathroom window open, and she and Dick haven't seen Spot since. He must have run away because she belched.

21 Cause and Effect   139

Answers
1. The police car's siren caused me to pull over Particular. Cause (stated as a claim): The police car had its siren going near me. Effect (stated as a claim): I pulled over.
2. Your being late caused us to miss the beginning of the movie. Particular. Cause (stated as a claim): You were late. Effect (stated as a claim): We missed the beginning of the movie.
3. The onion's smell caused me to cry. Particular. Cause (stated as a claim): The onion smelled. Effect (stated as a claim): I cried.
4. Not a causal claim.
5. Not a causal claim. Inductive evidence is offered for a generalization that might be used in establishing a general causal claim.
6. Someone ringing the doorbell caused Spot to bark. Particular. Cause (stated as a claim): Someone rang the doorbell. Effect (stated as a claim): Spot barked.
7. Drinking coffee causes me not to get a headache in the afternoon. General. Perhaps too vague: how much coffee?
8. An attempt to make a general causal claim, but too vague.
9. Our airplane taking off from gate number 13 caused us to experience turbulence. Cause: Our airplane took off from gate number 13. Effect: We had a lot of turbulence on the flight.
10. Someone pulling in front of Maria caused her to slam on her brakes. Cause: Someone pulled in front of Maria. Effect: Maria slammed on her brakes. Cause and effect true? Apparently so. Cause precedes effect? Yes. It's nearly impossible for the cause to be true and effect false? Yes, given some plausible normal conditions. Cause makes a difference? It seems so, but we need to know more about what was happening at the time. Was Maria paying attention? Common cause? Possibly, if the other driver was trying to avoid hitting someone. Evaluation: Plausible if nothing else unusual was happening at the time.
11. This is too vague to be a causal claim. How did Zeke's parents abuse him? What do you mean that Zeke abuses animals? Even if this could be made precise, it would be practically impossible to specify the normal conditions.
12. Wearing new shoes caused Suzy's feet to hurt when she was cheerleading. Cause: Suzy wore new shoes cheerleading. Effect: Her feet hurt. Cause and effect true? Suzy ought to know. Cause precedes effect? Yes. It's nearly impossible for the cause to be true and effect false? We need to know the normal conditions. Was everything like it usually is when Suzy is cheerleading? Apparently so, from what she says. Cause makes a difference? Suzy says it did, by comparing it to all the other times when she didn't have sore feet. Common cause? None apparent. Evaluation: Pretty plausible.
13. This is tracing too far back. Getting married is part of the normal conditions for getting a divorce.
14. It's a general causal claim. Anecdotal evidence. *Post hoc* reasoning. No reason to believe it.
15. The dark sky caused Zoe to be depressed. Cause: The sky is dark. Effect: Zoe is depressed. Cause and effect true? Apparently so. Cause precedes effect? Yes. It's nearly impossible for the cause to be true and effect false? Can't say. We'd need to

know a lot more about Zoe's psyche or else rely on a generalization that Zoe gets depressed every time it's dark in similar circumstances. Cause makes a difference? Perhaps, but we need to know what happened to Zoe before that might have made her depressed. Common cause? None. Evaluation: Suspend judgment until we know more.
16. Too vague to be a claim.
17. Zeke hanging out with a bad bunch caused him to start using drugs. Cause: Zeke started hanging out with a bad bunch. Effect: Zeke started using drugs. Evaluation: This might be *post hoc* reasoning. Or it could be overlooking a common cause: perhaps it was because Zeke wanted to start using drugs that he began to hang out with the bad bunch. We need to know more.
18. This is a general causal claim. Possibly reversing cause and effect or a common cause. They play football, so they're healthy and like to watch TV and are hungry a lot. No reason to think the causal claim is true.
19. This is an example of egotism: Dr. E thinks that it's something he does, and he's overlooking another cause, namely, at the end of the term students have a lot of work and cut classes to do that. There's no reason to believe the causal claim.
20. This is just *post hoc ergo propter hoc*. A possible cause is being overlooked. Perhaps someone left the gate open, or someone let him out, or . . .

22 Cause in Populations

Cause-in-population studies
When we say smoking causes lung cancer, what do we mean? If you smoke a cigarette, you'll get cancer? If you smoke a lot of cigarettes this week, you'll get cancer? If you smoke 20 cigarettes a day for 40 years, you'll get cancer? It can't be any of these, since there are lots of people who did all that yet didn't get lung cancer, and the effect has to (almost) invariably follow the cause.

Cause in a population is usually explained as meaning that given the cause, there's a higher probability that the effect will be true than if the cause had not occurred. In this example, people who smoke have a much higher probability of getting lung cancer. But really we're talking about cause and effect just as we did before. Smoking lots of cigarettes over a long period of time will cause (inevitably) lung cancer. The problem is that we can't state, we have no idea how to state, nor is it likely that we'll ever be able to state the normal conditions for smoking to cause cancer. Among other factors, there are diet, where one lives, exposure to pollution and other carcinogens, and one's genetic inheritance. But *if we knew exactly* we'd say: "Under the conditions ___ , smoking ___ (number of) cigarettes every day for ___ years will result in lung cancer."

Since we can't specify the normal conditions, the best we can do is point to the evidence that convinces us that smoking is a cause of lung cancer and get an argument with a statistical conclusion: "People who continue to smoke two packs of cigarettes per day for 10 years are __% more likely (with margin of error __%) to get lung cancer."

How do we establish a cause-in-population claim?

Controlled experiment: cause-to-effect
This is our best evidence. We choose 10,000 people at random and ask 5,000 of them never to smoke and 5,000 of them to smoke a pack of cigarettes every day. We have two samples, one composed of those who are administered the cause, and one of those who are not, the latter called the **control group**. We come back 20 years later to check how many in each group got lung cancer. If a lot more of the smokers got lung cancer, and the groups were representative of the population as a whole, and we can see no other common thread among those who got

lung cancer, we'd be justified in saying that smoking causes lung cancer.

Of course such an experiment would be unethical, so we use rats instead and then argue by analogy. Whether that's more ethical is another issue.

Uncontrolled experiment: cause-to-effect Here we take two randomly chosen samples of the general population for which we have factored out other known possible causes of lung cancer, such as working in coal mines. One of the groups is composed of people who say they never smoke. The other group is composed of people who say they smoke. We follow the groups and 20 years later check whether those who smoked got lung cancer more often. Since we think we've accounted for other common threads, smoking is the remaining common thread that may account for why the second group got cancer more often.

This is a cause-to-effect experiment, since we start with the suspected cause and later see if the effect followed. But it is uncontrolled. Some people may stop smoking, some may begin, people have quite varied diets—there may be a lot we'll have to factor out in trying to assess whether it's smoking that causes the extra cases of lung cancer.

Uncontrolled experiment: effect-to-cause Here we look at as many people as possible who have lung cancer to see if there is some common thread that occurs in (almost all) their lives. We factor out those who worked in coal mines, we factor out those who lived in high pollution areas, those who have cats, ... If it turns out that a much higher proportion of the remaining people smoked than in the general population, we have good evidence that smoking was the cause (the evaluation of this requires a knowledge of statistics). This is uncontrolled because how they got to the effect was unplanned, not within our control. And it is an effect-to-cause experiment because we start with the effect in the population and try to account for how it got there.

> • *Barbara smoked two packs of cigarettes a day for 30 years. Barbara now has lung cancer. Barbara's smoking caused her lung cancer.*
> Is it possible for Barbara to have smoked two packs of cigarettes each day for 30 years and not get lung cancer? We can't state the normal conditions. So we invoke the statistical relation between smoking and lung cancer to say it is unlikely for the cause to be true and effect false.
> Does the cause make a difference? Could Barbara have gotten

lung cancer even if she had not smoked? Suppose we know that she wasn't a coal miner, didn't work in a textile factory, didn't live in a city with a very polluted atmosphere, and didn't live with a heavy smoker—all conditions that are known to be associated with a higher probability of getting lung cancer. Then it is possible for Barbara to have gotten lung cancer anyway, since some people who have no other risks do get lung cancer. But it is unlikely, since few of those people do.

We have no reason to believe that there is a common cause. Maybe people with a certain biological make-up feel compelled to smoke, and that biological make-up also contributes to their getting lung cancer independently of their smoking. But we've no evidence, and before cigarette smoking and coal use became popular, lung cancer was rare.

So assuming a few normal conditions, "Barbara's smoking caused her lung cancer" is as plausible as the strength of the statistical link between smoking and lung cancer and the strength of the link between not smoking and not getting lung cancer. We must be careful, though, that we do not attribute the cause of the lung cancer to smoking just because we haven't thought of any other cause, especially if the statistical link isn't very strong.

- Zoe: *I can't understand Melinda. She's pregnant and she's drinking.*
 Dick: *That's all baloney. I asked my mom, and she said she drank when she was pregnant with me. And I turned out fine.*
 Zoe: *But think how much better you'd have been if she hadn't.*

 Zoe doesn't say but alludes to the cause-in-population claim that drinking during pregnancy causes birth defects or poor development of the child. That has been demonstrated: many cause-in-population studies have been done that show there is a higher incidence of birth defects and developmental problems in children born to women who drink during pregnancy than to women who do not drink, and those defects and problems do not appear to arise from any other common factor.

 Dick, however, makes a mistake. He confuses a cause-in-population claim with a general causal claim. He's right that his mother's experience would disprove the general causal claim, but it has no force against the cause-in-population claim.

 Zoe's confusion is that she thinks there is a perfect correlation between drinking and physical or mental problems in the child, so that if Dick's mother had not drunk he would have been better, even if Zoe can't point to the particular way in which Dick would have been better. But the correlation isn't perfect; it's only a statistical link.

- *Lack of education causes poverty. Widespread poverty causes crime. So lack of education causes crime.*

We often hear words like these, and some politicians base policy on them. But they're too vague. How much education constitutes "lack of education"? How poor do you have to be? How many poor people constitute "widespread poverty"? Researchers make these sentences more precise and analyze them as cause-in-population claims, since we know they couldn't be true general causal claims. There are people with little education who've become rich, and lots of poor people are law-abiding citizens. Indeed, during the worst years of the Depression in the 1930s, when there was more widespread poverty than at any time since in the U.S., there was less crime than any time in the last 20 years. This suggests it would be hard to find a precise version of the second sentence that is a true cause-in-population claim.

• *The number of teenagers giving birth declined 2 percent in the United States in 2008, reversing two years of increases, as older teens may have delayed starting a family because of the recession.*
   —*Albuquerque Journal*, March 7, 2010

The author conjectures a cause-in-population claim on nothing more than *post hoc* evidence.

• *Women who imbibe a little wine, beer or spirits every day are less likely than teetotalers to see their memories and other thinking powers fade as they age, according to the largest study to assess alcohol's impact on the brain. The study of more than 12,000 elderly women found that those who consumed light to moderate amounts of alcohol daily had about a 20 percent lower risk of experiencing problems with their mental abilities later in life.*

   "Low levels of alcohol appear to have cognitive benefits," said Francine Grodstein of the Brigham and Women's Hospital in Boston, senior author of the study, which is being published in today's New England Journal of Medicine. *"Women who consistently were drinking about one-half to one drink per day had both less cognitive impairment as well as less decline in their cognitive function compared to women who didn't drink at all."*

   While the study involved only women, the findings probably hold true for men, although previous research indicates that men seem to benefit from drinking slightly more—one to two drinks per day, researchers said.

   The findings provide the latest evidence that indulging in alcohol, long vilified as part of an insalubrious lifestyle, can actually help people live longer, healthier lives. While heavy drinking clearly causes serious problems for many people, recent research has found that drinking in moderation protects the heart.   —*Washington Post,* January 15, 2005

Correlation does not establish cause and effect. It could be the reverse here: elderly women who are mentally alert prefer to have something to drink to slow them down to sleep better. Or there could be a common cause. It's not even clear from this article whether this was a cause-to-effect or effect-to-cause study. More studies are needed, at least from the little we learn in this write-up.

- *The US Bureau of Labor Statistics data from 2001 show the following:*

Education and Lifetime Income

Highest Education Level Achieved	Lifetime Income (40 years)
Bachelor's Degree	$1,667,700
Associate Degree	$1,269,850
High School Graduate	$994,080
Not High School Graduate	$630,000

Higher levels of education payoff in lifetime income in a big way.

It is interesting to note that this relationship between education and earnings potential has been known since the 1970's, and has been consistently demonstrated by government surveys. In fact the difference in income level with education has grown significantly over the years. The Bureau of the Census has suggested that the gap in earnings between those with higher education and those with lower education will continue to grow in the future. The US Bureau of Labor Statistics has also shown that the unemployment rate steadily drops with higher levels of education. Unemployment for non-high school graduates was 6.5% in 2000, 3.5% for high school graduates, and 2.3% for those with an associate degree.

Education makes a difference!

Education Online, 2010, www.education-online-search/articles/special_topics/education_and_income/.com

There's a clear correlation between income and level of education. The website claims that this means getting more education is the cause of earning more ("payoff," "education makes a difference"). But people who finish more schooling are brighter, are either wealthier or can figure out how to get money for their education, are willing to work hard and to persevere. People like that are likely to earn more than other folks whether they get more education or not. Without more evidence, more studies that factor out these possible common causes, this is just *post hoc* reasoning.

Try your hand at these!
Explain what's wrong in 1–4.

1. Suzy: Vegetarians get cancer much less than meat eaters.

Manuel: Oh, yeah, so how come Linda McCartney, a well-known vegetarian, died from cancer when she was only in her 50s?

2. Dick: Hey, Zoe. Listen to this. A Roper survey said wine drinkers are more successful than those who don't drink. Frequent wine drinkers, it says, earn about $67,000 a year, while occasional drinkers earn about $40,000. People who don't drink at all earn a little more than $30,000. You want to be successful, don't you?
Zoe: You're not going to get me to start drinking wine that way.

3. Maria: Wives of servicemen suffer domestic abuse at the rate of 2 to 5 times that of other women.
Suzy: Boy, I sure hope Tom doesn't join the army.

4. [Advertisement] Studies have shown that three cups of Cheerios® a day with a low-fat diet can help lower cholesterol.

Analyze the following by answering:
What causal claim is at issue?
Which type of cause-in-population experiment, if any, was done?
Evaluate the evidence for the causal claim.
How would you further test the claim?

5. Late nights may make teens more prone to depression and suicidal thoughts by depriving them of sleep, a Columbia University study said.

Teens whose parents let them go to bed past midnight were 24 percent more likely to be depressed and 20 percent more likely to have contemplated suicide than peers whose parents set bedtimes at or before 10 p.m., the researchers said in the journal *Sleep*. Earlier set bedtimes may be protective because they increase the likelihood of getting enough sleep, they said.   — *Albuquerque Journal*, January 2, 2010

6. (From the transcript for National Public Radio's *All Things Considered*, May 15, 2001)
ROBERT SIEGEL, host: An article reached us today with the title "Survival in Academy Award-winning Actors and Actresses." It is not about casting or contracts. It's actually in the *Annal of Internal Medicine*, and it's about survival. Dr. Donald Redelmeier and his colleague Sheldon Singph found that actors and actresses who have won Oscars live, on average, 3.9 years longer than other performers who have never won Oscars. Dr. Redelmeier is in Toronto and joins us now. Dr. Redelmeier, how did you conduct this study?
DR. DONALD REDELMEIER: What we did is, we identified every actor and actress who's ever been nominated for an Academy Award in either a supporting role or a leading role over the full history of the Academy Awards since 1929.
SIEGEL: What does this tell you? What do you think is the cause of the greater longevity among those actors and actresses who won Academy Awards?
DR. REDELMEIER: One possible theory is that winning an Academy Award improves a person's self-esteem and gives them a much greater resilience to the normal stressors that confront us on a day-to-day basis. And that, in turn, causes changes in the hypothalamic, pituitary, adrenal glands of the body or the immun- ological systems, and so that much less damage occurs over the years.
SIEGEL: If this is true, do you think we should find then that, say, the Academy

Award winners among the film editors or the special effects people would also outlive their colleagues or do you think it requires the adulation that only star actors and actresses get to add the extra 3.9 years to a life span?

DR. REDELMEIER: Well, more research is always needed. Another possibility is that it isn't due to a person's internal biology, but it reflects their external behavior — i.e., that stars live lives under continuous scrutiny, and so because of that, they need to sleep properly every night, eat a balanced diet at every meal, exercise regularly every day in order to preserve their glamorous image. And so it's those external behaviors rather than the internal peace of mind that confers a much greater survival benefit than is generally appreciated.

7. In the mid-1970s a team of researchers in Great Britain conducted a rigorously designed large-scale experiment to test the effectiveness of a treatment program that represented "the sort of care which today might be provided by most specialized alcoholism clinics in the Western world." [reference supplied]

The subjects were one hundred men who had been referred for alcohol problems to a leading British outpatient program, the Alcoholism Family Clinic of Maudsley Hospital in London. The receiving psychiatrist confirmed that each of the subjects met the following criteria: he was properly referred for alcohol problems, was aged 20 to 65 and married, did not have any progressive or painful physical disease or brain damage or psychotic illness, and lived within a reasonable distance of the clinic (to allow for clinic visits and follow-up home visits by social workers). A statistical randomization procedure was used to divide the subjects into two groups comparable in the severity of their drinking and their occupational status.

For subjects in one group (the "advice group"), the only formal therapeutic activity was one session between the drinker, his wife, and the psychiatrist. The psychiatrist told the couple that the husband was suffering from alcoholism and advised him to abstain from all drink. The psychiatrist also advised the husband to stay on his job (or return to it) and encouraged the couple to attempt to keep their marriage together. There was a free-ranging discussion and advice about the personalities and particularities of the situation, but the couple was told that this one session was the only treatment the clinic would provide. They were told in sympathetic and constructive language that the "attainment of the stated goals lay in their hands and could not be taken over by others."

Subjects in the second group (the "treatment group") were offered a year-long program that began with a counseling session, an introduction to Alcoholics Anonymous, and prescriptions for drugs that would make alcohol unpalatable and drugs that would alleviate withdrawal suffering. Each drinker then met with a psychiatrist to work out a continuing outpatient treatment program, while the social worker made a similar plan with the drinker's wife. The ongoing counseling was focused on practical problems in the areas of alcohol abuse, marital relations, and other social or personal difficulties. Drinkers who did not respond well were offered in-patient admissions, with full access to the hospital's wide range of services.

Twelve months after the experiment began, both groups were assessed. No significant differences were found between the two groups. Furthermore, drinkers in the treatment group who stayed with it for the full period did not fare better than those

who dropped out. At the twelve-month point, only eleven of the one hundred drinkers had become abstainers. Another dozen or so still drank but in sufficient moderation to be considered "acceptable" by both husband and wife. Such rates of improvement are not significantly better than those shown in studies of the spontaneous or natural improvement of chronic drinkers not in treatment.
—Herbert Fingarette, *Heavy Drinking: The Myth of Alcoholism as a Disease*

Answers
1. Manuel is confusing a cause in population claim with a general causal claim.
2. This may be reversing cause and effect: if you've got more money, you can enjoy wine. There's no reason to think that this correlation establishes cause and effect, as Dick seems to think it does.
3. Suzy thinks that being in the army causes men to abuse their wives. But there's a possible common cause that hasn't been ruled out: men who are prone to abuse their wives like violence and hence are more likely to join the Army.
4. A low-fat diet all by itself can help lower cholesterol. So the purported cause doesn't obviously make a difference. Anyway, three cups of Cheerios is a lot of Cheerios. Eating three cups of grated celery will fill you up just as well. It's almost a weaseler.
5. Causal claim: Late nights for teens *can cause* them to have depression. Type of cause-in-population experiment: we're not told. We have no idea how the sample was chosen, nor how large it was, nor if it was studied well. But even were we to know, there's no reason here to believe the causal claim. There may be a common cause: parents who don't care enough for their children to supervise them and set bedtimes cause their children to be depressed.
6. (At first Redelmeier says it's a conjecture, but then as the interview goes on, he speaks as if it's established by his research.) Winning an Academy Award can cause a person to live longer. Uncontrolled: cause-to-effect. No reason to believe the claim. The mechanism that Redelmeier postulates is just as true for the losers as for the winners. Just as likely are: (1) Healthy people are better actors and actresses, and/or (2) being nominated for but not getting an Academy Award is bad for your health. Siegel actually proposes a test: expand the sample. Try to rule out the other possibilities by seeing if winning an Academy Award is the only common thread.

    You think they'd be able to find an interviewer who knows the basics about cause and effect.
7. Causal claim: Giving long-term programs of counseling, AA, drugs that make alcohol unpalatable, and drugs alleviating withdrawal cause people to stop being alcoholic. Controlled cause-to-effect. It looks like it was very well done and established that the claim is false for the population studied (London alcoholics). Further tests? Repeat the study in different areas with different samples of people.

23 Inferential Explanations

Why does the sun rise in the east? How does electricity work? How come Spot gets a bath every week? Why didn't you give me an A on the last exam? We give explanations as answers to lots of different kinds of questions. Our answers can be as varied as the questions. We can tell a story, a myth about how the world was created. We can write a scientific treatise on how the muscles of the esophagus work. We can give instructions for how to play a guitar. We can draw a map.

In this chapter we'll consider explanations that are meant to answer the question "Why is this true?"

> ***Inferential explanations*** An answer to the question "Why is claim E true?" that can be understood as "Because A, B, C, . . . are true" is an *inferential explanation*. Sometimes just the claims A, B, C, . . . are called the *explanation* of E. The claim E is called the claim being explained, and the claims A, B, C, . . . are called the **explanatory claims**.

- *Zoe: Why is Spot limping?*
   Dick: *Here, I see. It's because he's got a thorn in his paw.*
     This is an inferential explanation: "Spot has a thorn in his paw" is meant to explain "Spot is limping."

Necessary conditions for an inferential explanation to be good

The claim that's meant to be explained is very plausible.
We can't explain what's dubious.

- Dick: *Why is it that most people who call psychic hot lines are women?*
   Zoe: *Wait a minute, what makes you think more women than men call psychic hot lines?*
     Dick has posed a loaded question, and Zoe has responded appropriately, asking for an argument to show that "More women than men call psychic hot lines" is true.

The explanation is valid or strong.
The truth of the claim that's being explained is supposed to follow from the claims doing the explaining. So the relation between those claims

should be valid or strong, like the relation between the premises and conclusion of a good argument.

> • *Dogs lick their owners because dogs aren't cats.*
> This is a bad explanation. The relation of "Dogs aren't cats" to "Dogs lick their owners" is neither valid nor strong, and there's no obvious way to repair it.

The claims doing the explaining are plausible.
In an inferential explanation the claims doing the explaining are supposed to make clear why the claim we are explaining is true. They can't do that if they aren't plausible.

> • *The sky is blue because there are blue globules very high in the sky.*
> This is a bad explanation because "There are blue globules very high in the sky" is not plausible.

But *a good inferential explanation will have at least one claim among those that do the explaining that is less plausible than what's being explained.* Otherwise it wouldn't explain, it would be an argument, a way to convince.

> Zoe offers a good explanation of why Dick has a headache:
> Anyone who drinks that much is going to have a headache.
> Therefore (explains why), Dick has a headache.

Judged as an argument, however, this is bad, for it begs the question: it's a lot more obvious to Dick that he has a headache than that anyone who drinks that much is going to have a headache.

The explanation answers the right question.
Questions are often ambiguous, and a good explanation to one reading of a question can often be a bad explanation to another. If a question is ambiguous, that's a fault of the person asking the question. We can't be expected to guess correctly what's meant. An explanation is bad

because it answers the wrong question *if* it's very clear what question the person is asking.

Flo gave a good explanation—to the wrong question.

The explanation is not circular.
We can't explain why a claim is true by just restating the claim in other words.

- *Zoe: Why can't you write today, Dick?*
  Dick: Because I've got writer's block.
  This is a bad explanation: "I've got writer's block" just means you can't write.

Necessary conditions for an inferential explanation to be good
For the inferential explanation E because of $A, B, C, \ldots$
to be good, the following must hold:

- E is very plausible.

- The inference "$A, B, C, \ldots$ therefore E" is valid or strong, possibly with respect to some other plausible claims.

- Each of $A, B, C, \ldots$ is plausible, but at least one of them is not more plausible than E.

- $A, B, C, \ldots$ answer the right question.

- The explanation is not "E because of D" where D is E itself or a simple rewriting of E.

Often we say that an explanation is *right* or *correct* rather than "good" and *wrong* rather than "bad." Note that these are necessary conditions for an inferential explanation to be good. There's no agreement on sufficient conditions. That requires judgment.

Repairing explanations

Explanations, just as arguments, are often incomplete. We don't reject them out of hand without trying to see if they can be repaired. We can invoke the Principle of Rational Discussion to get a guide to repairing explanations like the Guide to Repairing Arguments.

> ***The Guide to Repairing Inferential Explanations*** Given an (implicit) inferential explanation that is apparently defective, we are justified in adding a further explanatory claim if all of the following hold:
> - The explanation becomes stronger or valid.
> - The claim is plausible and would seem plausible to the other person.
> - The claim does not make the explanation circular.
>
> We may delete an explanatory claim if that doesn't make the explanation worse.

Causal explanations

When an inferential explanation is given in terms of cause and effect, *if it's good causal reasoning and it answers the right question, the explanation is good; otherwise it's bad.*

- Suzy: *Why did Dick wake up?*
  Zoe: *Because Spot was barking.*
  This is a good causal explanation (see p. 127).

- *Dick recovered from his cold in one week because he took vitamin C.*
  This is a causal explanation, but not a good one. The purported cause does not clearly make a difference.
  > *Proper treatment will cure a cold in seven days, but left to itself a cold will hang on for a week.* —Henry G. Felsen

- Zoe: You say that this argument is bad. But why?
  Dr. E: *It's bad because it's weak, for example, Sheila could have been a rabbit or a herring.*
  Dr. E knows what he's talking about, and this is a good inferential explanation. But it's not a causal one. Explanations in terms of rules or criteria aren't causal.

- Zoe: *Why did you call your coffeehouse The Dog & Duck?*
  Owner: *Why not?*

Shifting the burden of proof is just as bad for explanations as for arguments.

- *Zoe: Why was Tom so unpleasant to us today?*
  Dick: Oh, don't mind him. He was just out of sorts.
  This looks circular, but it's worse. Being out of sorts indeed makes people rude—if we had a clear idea of what "being out of sorts" means besides acting rudely. The purported explanation is too vague or circular.

- *Suzy: Why did Dick just get up and leave the room like that in the middle of what Tom was saying?*
  Zoe: Because he wanted to.
  This is a bad explanation. Wanting to leave the room when Tom is talking is something unusual and requires further explanation. An explanation is **inadequate** if it leads to a further "Why?" Even if the claims doing the explaining are obviously true, they may not be enough.

- *Dick: Why did that turtle cross the road?*
  Lee: Because its leg muscles carried it.
  This is bad because it's the wrong kind of answer. Normally we'd understand Dick to be asking for a **behavioral explanation**: claims about the motives or beliefs or feelings of a person or creature. What's been given is a premise about the physical makeup of the turtle, a physical explanation. It answers the wrong question.

    On the other hand, "To get to the other side" would be an inadequate explanation. Since we don't know what the turtle's motives are, or indeed if it has any, it's unlikely we can give a good answer to Dick.

- *Psychiatrist: Where is Dr. E? It's time for his appointment.*
  Receptionist: Don't you remember? He said he wouldn't be coming anymore.
  Psychiatrist: He is resisting the understanding that I am bringing him.
  Receptionist: But he says it's because he can't afford your fee.
  Psychiatrist: Ah! There, there's the proof that his unconscious is resisting, because I know he could borrow money from his rich uncle.
  Psychiatrists often make their explanations immune to testing. If anything counts as resistance, if everything can be explained in terms of unconscious motives, there's no way to test. We might as well say that a patient won't come because gremlins are inhabiting his psyche, though that might be less effective in getting a patient to continue treatment and pay the bills.

    If a claim explains everything, it explains nothing. This is a bad causal explanation. *Untestable claims are the worst candidates for a good explanation.*

- Zoe: *My mom is always hot and irritable now.*
  Dick: *Why's that?*
  Zoe: *She's going through menopause.*
  This is a good causal explanation because there's good cause-in-population evidence that most women who go through menopause have those symptoms.

- Dick: *Why won't Spot eat his dog food today?*
  Zoe: *He hasn't been hungry all day.*
  Dick: *I don't think so. He just ate the doggie treat I gave him.*
  Dick has shown that Zoe's explanation is not good by showing that the claim doing the explaining is false.

- Zoe: *Why did the lights just go out?*
  Dick: *The transformer down the street must have blown again. I'll have to call the electric company.*
  Zoe: *Don't bother. I can see the lights are still on where Flo lives, and the street lights are working.*
  Zoe has used reducing to the absurd to refute Dick's explanation. If Dick's explanation were right, then from the same claim we could conclude, "The street lights and all the lights on the block are out." That claim is false. So his claim must not be true. So it's a bad explanation.

- Dr. E: *I won't accept your homework late.*
  Maria: *But I had a meeting I had to attend at work.*
  Dr. E: *So? I don't count problems with employment as an excuse for handing in late work.*
  Maria has explained why she did not hand in the homework on time. She thinks she's also given an excuse, but Dr. E disabuses her of that. An explanation is not an excuse.

Arguments and explanations

Dick, Zoe, and Spot are out for a walk in the countryside. Spot runs off and returns after five minutes. Dick notices that Spot has blood around his muzzle. And they both really notice that Spot stinks like a skunk. Dick turns to Zoe and says, "Spot must have killed a skunk. Look at the blood on his muzzle. And he smells like a skunk."

Dick has made a good argument:

> Spot has blood on his muzzle. Spot smells like a skunk.
> *Therefore*, Spot killed a skunk.

Dick has left out some premises he knows are obvious to Zoe and him:

23 *Inferential Explanations* 155

Spot isn't bleeding.
Skunks aren't able to fight back very well.
Dogs try to kill animals by biting them.
Normally when Spot draws a lot of blood from an animal that's smaller than him, he kills it.
Only skunks give off a characteristic skunk odor that drenches whoever or whatever is near if they are attacked.

Zoe replies, "Oh, that explains why he's got blood on his muzzle and smells so bad." She takes the same claims and views them as an explanation, a good explanation, relative to the same unstated premises:

Spot killed a skunk
explains why Spot has blood on his muzzle and smells like a skunk.

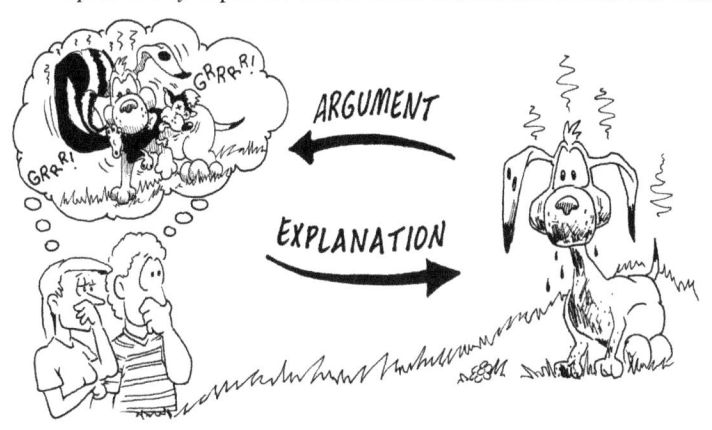

For an explanation "E because of A, B, C, . . ." we can ask what evidence we have for A. Sometimes we can supply all the evidence we need by just reversing the inference. For Zoe's explanation to be good, "Spot killed a skunk" must be plausible, and it is because of the argument Dick gave. They needn't wait until they find the dead skunk.

Explanations and associated arguments
For an inferential explanation: E because of A, B, C, . . .
the ***associated argument*** to establish A is:

  E, B, C, . . . therefore A

An explanation is ***dependent*** if one of the premises is not plausible and the associated argument for that premise is not good. An explanation is ***independent*** if it is not dependent.

156   *How to Reason*

If an explanation is dependent, then it lacks evidence for at least one of its premises that cannot be supplied by an associated argument.

- *Spot chases cats because he sees them as something good to eat and because cats are smaller than him.*
    "Cats are smaller than Spot" is clearly true. But "Spot sees cats as something good to eat" is not. The associated argument is:

    Spot chases cats. Cats are smaller than Spot.
    Therefore, Spot sees cats as something good to eat.

    This is weak. Without more evidence for "Spot sees cats as something good to eat" we shouldn't accept the explanation. The explanation is dependent.

Each premise of an independent explanation is plausible, either because of the associated argument for it or because of independent reasons, such as our knowing that most dogs bark or that Sheila is not a herring. Still, an independent explanation might be bad.

- *Suzy: Why do classes last only 50 minutes instead of an hour?*
  Maria: Because students need time to get from one class to another.
    The premise is certainly plausible, so the explanation is independent. But it's not a good explanation because it's not strong. Why not have classes that last 45 minutes? What follows is only that there should be some time between classes.

Comparing explanations

Given two explanations of the same claim, which is better? If one is good and the other is bad, the good one is better. If both are acceptable, we prefer the one that doesn't leave us asking a further "Why?". Then we prefer the **simpler explanation**:

- Its premises are more plausible.
- It is more clearly strong or valid (unstated premises are obvious and more plausible).
- It has fewer steps in the deduction.

- *Zoe: How was your walk?*
  Dick: Spot ran away again just before we got to the yard.
  Zoe: We better get him. Why does he run away just before you come home?
  Dick: It's just his age. He'll outgrow it. All dogs do.
    This sounded like a good explanation until Dick and Zoe found that Spot chased a cat up a telephone pole in the field behind their house.

The explanation that Dick gave is not bad. Perhaps in a year or two when Spot is better trained, he won't run away even to chase a cat. But there's a better explanation: Spot ran away because he likes to chase cats and he saw a cat nearby to chase. It's better because it's stronger.

- *Harry: Amazing. Zoe and Dick got into a fight and . . .*
  Maria: Zoe's so mad she won't talk to him anymore.
  Tom: How do you know that?
  Suzy: She has ESP!
  Harry: C'mon. She must have heard it from someone else.
  Which is the better explanation? The second because it's more plausible.

Some people think that if they have an explanation that explains a lot and is the best anyone's offered, then it must be true. But being the better or even the best explanation we have doesn't make the claims doing the explaining any more plausible. We judge whether an explanation is good by whether its explanatory claims are plausible; we don't judge the explanatory claims plausible because the explanation is good. That would be arguing backwards: from the premises we can deduce true claims, so the premises are true.

- *Me: Why do I have such pain in my back? It doesn't feel like a muscle cramp or a pinched nerve.*
  Physician: A kidney stone would explain the pain. Kidney stones give that kind of pain, and it's in the right place for that.
  When I went into the emergency room one night, the doctor gave me this explanation. It would have been a good one if he'd had good reason to believe "You have a kidney stone." But at that point the only reason he had was the associated argument, and that wasn't strong. Still, it was the best explanation he had.

  So the doctor made predictions, reasoning by hypotheses: "A kidney stone would show up on an X-ray," "You'd have an elevated white blood cell count," "You would have blood in your urine." He tested each of these and found them false. He then reasoned by reducing to the absurd that if the explanation were true, these would very likely be true; they are false; therefore, the explanation is very likely false.

  Nothing else was found, so by process of elimination the doctor concluded that I had a severe sprain or strain, for which exercise and education were the only remedy.

  If the doctor had believed "You have a kidney stone" just because that was the best available explanation, there would have been no point in doing tests. And then I would have undergone needless treatment or even surgery.

• *The AIDS epidemic was started by the CIA. They wanted to get rid of homosexuals and blacks, and they targeted those groups with their new disease. They started their testing in Africa in order to keep it hidden from people here. The government once again tried to destroy people they don't like.*
That the AIDS epidemic was started by the CIA would explain a lot. But that's no reason to believe it's true. The only evidence we have for it is the associated argument, which is weak. Every conspiracy theory depends on thinking that what explains a lot is true.

> **Fallacy of inference to the best explanation** It's a mistake to reason that since these claims give the best explanation of this obviously true claim, they're true.

• *Dick: There. See! The sign for the western menswear store. "Real Men Don't Browse"*
Zoe: Yeah. So?
Dick: It's true. We're genetically programmed that way. Long ago when humans were evolving, men were stronger and went out to hunt. The women gathered fruit and berries. When we're hunting we take the first thing we can get, maybe just a rabbit, even if we're looking for a mastodon, 'cause we don't know if there'll be another chance that day. When women went out to get berries there were lots of choices, so they'd pick the best and discard ones that weren't quite so good. That's why women like to shop and men just go in and buy the first thing that looks good and then leave.
This explains why men don't browse and women do. But it doesn't explain it well. It's an example of the fallacy of inference to the best explanation, an evolutionary *just-so story*, like Kipling's "How the Leopard Got Its Spots."

Here are the ideas in this chapter that will help you recognize and begin to evaluate explanations:
- Inferential explanation.
- Explanatory claims.
- Circular explanation.
- Necessary conditions for an explanation to be good.
- The Guide to Repairing Inferential Explanations.

- Causal explanation.
- Inadequate explanation.
- The relation of arguments to explanations:
  A good explanation is not a good argument.
  An associated argument can establish an explanatory claim.
- A claim that explains everything explains nothing.
- Dependent and independent explanations.
- Simpler inferential explanation.
- Fallacy of inference to the best explanation.

Before you try your hand at evaluating some examples, we need to look at another kind of explanation that often gets mixed up with inferential ones.

24 Functional Explanations

One day while cleaning out the small pond in my backyard I asked myself, "Why is there a filter on this wet-dry vacuum?" The vacuum had a sponge-like filter, but the vacuum sucked up water a lot faster without it. I wondered if I could remove the filter.

I wanted to know the function of the filter. A causal explanation could be given starting with how someone designed the vacuum with the filter, invoking what that person thought would be its function. But most of that explanation would be beside the point. I didn't want to know why it's true that there's a filter on the vacuum, even though the truth of that claim is assumed in the question. I wanted to know the function of the filter. Some explanations should answer not "Why is this true?" but "What does this do?" or "Why would he or she do that?"

> **Functional explanations** A *functional explanation* is an explanation that invokes goals or functions or uses claims that can come true only after the claim(s) doing the explaining.

Functional explanations are often called **teleological** explanations.

- Wanda: *Why is the missile going off in that direction?*
  Lee: *Because it wants to hit that plane.*

  It's a bad anthropomorphism to ascribe goals to a missile. People, not missiles, have goals. We should replace this functional explanation with an inferential one: "The missile has been designed to go in the direction of the nearest source of heat comparable to the heat generated by a jet engine. The plane over there in that direction has a jet engine producing that kind of heat." Often a functional explanation is offered when an inferential one should be used.

There are serious problems with functional explanations. If an explanation uses claims that can be true only after the claim being explained becomes true, it can't be causal (the cause has to precede the effect) and it would seem that the future is somehow affecting the past.

Moreover, a request for a functional explanation assumes that the object has a function or that the person or thing has a goal or motive. That's part of what's being assumed. But often there is simply no motive, no function, no goal, or at least none we can discern. The right response, as to a loaded question, is to ask why we should believe there is a function or motive.

> • Dick (picking his nose): *Why do humans get snot in their nose that dries up and has to be picked away? I can't understand what good it does.*
> Zoe: *What makes you think there's a purpose? Can't some things just be? Maybe it just developed along with everything else.*
> Zoe correctly points out Dick's dubious assumption.

> ***The functional fallacy*** is to assume that because something occurs in nature, it must have a purpose.

A bigger problem with functional explanations is that we don't have criteria for what counts as a good one. That's because we don't have a clear idea how to judge what counts as the function of something. At best, we can say that for a good functional explanation:

- The claim being explained should be highly plausible.
- The explanation should answer the right question.
- The explanation is not circular.
- The explanation does not ascribe motives, beliefs, or goals to something that doesn't have those.

> • *Why do we dream? Dreams serve as wish fulfillments to prevent interruption of sleep, which is essential to good health.*
> According to Freudians, this is a good explanation. And it's functional. There seems to be no way to construe it as inferential, at least not in accord with the rest of Freud's theory.
>
> Opinion now divides. Either this is an example of a good explanation that is truly functional, or this example shows that Freudian theories of the unconscious are no good because they yield only functional explanations.

> • *Why does the blood circulate through the body?*
> *(1) Because the heart pumps the blood through the arteries.*
> *(2) In order to bring oxygen to every part of the body tissue.*
> The first explanation is a good causal one, if it answers the right question. The second is a good functional one, if it answers the right question.

Try your hand at these!
For the following, say if it is an explanation, and if so whether it is inferential or functional, whether it is causal, whether it is dependent or independent, and whether it's good.

162 *How to Reason*

1. Zoe: How did Tom get strep throat?
   Dick: Suzy had it last week.
2. (Heard on National Public Radio) Birds sing in the morning because it keeps other birds away, to announce their territory.
3. Lee: Why did Mr. Johns, the owner of that fast-food restaurant where your mom works, lower prices on all the meals?
   Suzy: It's because he's got a good heart and wants poor people to be able to enjoy his food.
   Zoe: I don't think so. He was the one who opposed soup kitchens in town.
   Suzy: He's just covering up. He's afraid of being thought a nice guy. He can't face his unconscious wish to be loved.
4. Zoe: I wish I could help Wanda. What's the reason for her weight problem?
   Dick: Gravity.
5. Dogs eat meat because they are carnivores.
6. Dick: Darn. My bread landed butter-side down.
   Flo: You buttered the wrong side of the bread.
7. Why are there valves in our veins? So the blood can flow only one way in them.
8. Lee: Why don't you support affirmative action for entry to universities?
   Tom: Because the minorities in this country have it too easy already.
9. Suzy: Why are students required to take a foreign language to get a degree here?
   Prof. Zzzyzzx: Because the faculty senate passed the regulation.
10. Zoe: Why is Spot crouching in front of that hole?
    Dick: So he can catch a mouse.
11. Willie Sutton was a notorious bank robber. When asked why he robbed banks, he replied, "Because that's where the money is."
12. Dr. Smyrn: Now to check your heart. Do you feel that?
    Dr. E: Ow! But what has pricking my finger got to do with heart disease?
    Dr. Smyrn: The heart is on the left side of the body, and in heart attacks the victim will normally get a pain in his left arm.
    Dr. E: Gee, that hurts, too.
    Dr. Smyrn: I believe that we can predict heart disease by testing the little finger of the left hand for pain sensitivity. So I compare reactions to pricking the little finger of the left hand to pricking other fingers.
    Dr. E: Really? Ouch. That sounds wacky.
    Dr. Smyrn: I have been sending patients with unusual sensitivity in that finger to a cardiologist to follow up.
    Dr. E: And? Ow!
    Dr. Smyrn: So far he has found indications of heart disease in only 3 of the 32 people I have sent. But that is because my test is more sensitive than his. I can spot that there is incipient heart disease before any other known test.
13. Harry: You know that because of global warming the ice is melting in the Arctic?
    Dick: Right. And the polar bears are dying off.
    Harry: So I saw on the internet that they've transported one polar bear to Antarctica, to see if she can survive there.
    Dick: Did it work?
    Harry: I saw the video. At first all she did was run around and chase penguins,

never stopped for two days and never caught one. Then she laid down and slept or just didn't move for a whole day. Then she got up and ran around again, aimlessly. They can't figure out what's happening with her.
Tom: Simple. It's because she's the first bi-polar bear.

Answers
1. If it's asking *how*, then it's not inferential. But Dick's answer could be construed as inferential: Suzy had strep throat last week, *therefore* Tom has strep throat now. We might take that to be a good causal explanation if we knew more. Dependent.
2. Functional explanation. Not causal. How could we tell if it's good?
3. Inferential and causal. Dependent. Zoe's comments suggest that the explanatory claim is false. What Suzy says could be true, but there's no way to test whether that's Mr. Johns' motive, since Suzy says he's either hiding it or it's unconscious. Untestable explanations are not good.
5. Either a bad circular explanation or a definition.
7. Functional explanation. Not causal. As an inferential one it would be weak. Blood can flow only one way in our veins, so we have valves in our veins. Even if you accept teleological explanations, you'd have to come up with more claims to show why valves are there rather than some other mechanism.
8. Inferential, dependent, causal. Bad. The sentence doing the work of the explanatory claim is either too vague or implausible. However, if we interpret it as "Tom believes that the minorities in this country have it too easy already," then the explanation would be good.
9. Causal explanation. But it's inadequate: we want to know why they passed the regulation.
10. Teleological. This is as good as the evidence for "Spot wants to catch a mouse." Right now we have only the associated argument to establish that.
11. A good explanation to the wrong question.
12. This is not an explanation. It's a cause-in-population claim. It could be used to make a causal claim, but no claim is being explained here. Dr. Smyrn's last comments suggest that he does not satisfy the Principle of Rational Discussion, for it looks as if he won't accept any evidence that he's wrong.

Making Decisions

The skills you've learned are meant to help you make better decisions, how to find your way in life. To do so, you need to be able to recognize risks and how to evaluate them.

25 Evaluating Risk

> A *risk* is a possibility in the future that we deem bad and that would be a consequence of some action we take or don't take.

Weighing risk

• Dick likes to let Spot run free when they go for a walk, and a risk associated with doing so is that Spot could chase a cat into traffic and get hit by a car. Perhaps Dick never thought of that risk, in which case he's not very thoughtful about what he does. But he has considered it, and he's decided that letting Spot run free is **worth the risk**: *the good that might come from it outweighs by a lot the bad that might come from it.* If Dick doesn't let Spot run free, Spot never gets a chance to get any real exercise, and Dick doesn't think it's very likely that Spot will run out into traffic. He's a good dog.

Tom disagrees. He's seen Spot go crazy around cats, and he knows that's not the only reason Spot might run into traffic. Tom knows, too, that there are other ways for Spot to get exercise: Dick could lead him on a leash while he's bicycling or jogging, or Dick could take Spot to the countryside a few times a week to run free. Tom is weighing the likelihood of the risk differently and is seeing more choices for accomplishing the good that Dick wants.

> *Evaluating risk* To evaluate a course of action we need to:
> - Weigh how likely the risk is.
> - Weigh how likely a good outcome is.
> - Weigh how much we want to avoid the risk versus how much we want the possible good outcome that might come from our action.
> - Weigh how hard it would be to accomplish the good by other means.

Only rarely can we put numbers to these evaluations. How much we want to avoid a risk or get a good outcome is a subjective or at best an intersubjective evaluation.

• *Harry is a hard-working student and he'd really like to make $5,000. He knows a stock that he's sure is undervalued that he could buy for $5,000* and make at least that much in a few months. But he doesn't want to make money so much that he's willing to risk losing almost all his savings. In comparison, for Bill Gates losing $5,000 would be a negligible risk, while making $5,000 would be OK but hardly worth the trouble.

How hard it would be to accomplish the good by other means usually depends on subjective criteria, too.

- *It would be easy for Tom to jog or bicycle with Spot at his side on a leash because Tom plays football and enjoys exercise. But for Dick, who doesn't get much exercise, that would be hard to do. It would be easier for Dick to ask Tom to take Spot for a run, since it was Tom's idea anyway.*
- *Dick: Zoe! Did you hear the weather report? There's a 40% chance of a tornado in the next hour.*
  Zoe: We better open some windows and get into the basement. Grab a flashlight and the radio.

  A tornado is certainly bad, but it's not a risk, for it's not a consequence of something we do or don't do. Insurance companies call a tornado a "natural disaster" or an "act of God." What is a risk here is what might happen to Dick and Zoe if they don't go into the basement.

- *The Union of Scientists Worried about Nuclear War estimates there's a 10% chance of a nuclear war somewhere in the world this year.*

  Many people view the possibility of a nuclear war as if it were a natural disaster, completely out of their control. But whether it happens or not depends on what we do, all of us from a person who doesn't vote, to a diplomat, to the president. To think of nuclear war as an act of God is to imagine ourselves powerless in the face of unseen forces, when the forces are really of our own creation.

How likely is the risk?

Sometimes we have a pretty good sense of how likely the risk is.

- *Tom thinks it's not at all unlikely that Spot will run off into traffic if Spot's not on a leash, and his evaluation seems more accurate than Dick's wishful thinking. In comparison, Harry can't even begin to guess how likely it is he could lose most of his money if he invests in that stock.*

Evaluations of likelihood of a risk or of a good outcome are evaluations of how likely possibilities are, which we've been doing all along in evaluating arguments, causal claims, and explanations. We evaluate the strength of the inference from premises describing the situation now to conclusion describing the outcome we're worried about.

- *Tom thinks that the inference from "Dick lets Spot run free on a walk" to "Spot runs into traffic and gets hit by a car" is much stronger than Dick does. On the other hand, Harry doesn't have a clue how strong the inference is from "I invest $5,000 in a stock, and the stock appears to me to be undervalued" to "I lose most of my money."*

Sometimes we can make a very good estimate of how likely the risk is.

- *Dick: I'll bet you $5 on the next flip of this coin.*
  Tom: You're on.
  Tom knows that the likelihood he'll lose $5 is 50% and the likelihood he'll win $5 is 50%.

- *Zoe: You're buying a lottery ticket?*
  Dick: Sure. Why not?
  Zoe: Can't you do the math? There's less than one chance in 200 million that you'll win.
  Dick's chances of losing $1 is almost certain; his chance of winning is only a tiny bit better than not buying a ticket at all. Yet he still buys a ticket. He reckons that the possible good that can come from buying a ticket, which includes a week of daydreams, outweighs what he considers the minimal loss. He also consoles himself that the money he loses will go to college scholarships, though very little of it does. Others, however, would classify as a bad outcome Dick passing his time daydreaming what he'd do with millions of dollars.

- *Dick: You thought I was crazy to buy a lottery ticket, yet you just bought six of them.*
  Zoe: Yes, but the jackpot is up to $460 million!
  Buying six tickets gives Zoe six times more chances to win than buying one ticket. But still that's only a miniscule chance. Either knowing the numbers associated with the risk doesn't matter to Zoe, or else she considers the outcome of winning so much money, versus the usual $25 million, to be many million times more good to her. It isn't that the lottery is a tax on people who don't understand mathematics; rather, people motivated by greed are willing to weigh a positive outcome much more than the risk, if the risk doesn't cost much.

Examples of mistakes in evaluating risk

- *Tom: I'm thinking of joining the Army.*
  Zoe: That's really dangerous.
  Tom: No it isn't. The death rate for soldiers in Iraq is lower than the death rate in New York City.

Tom is comparing apples and oranges. The death rate for people in New York includes all the old people there, all the sick people, all the homeless. To evaluate the risk, Tom should compare the death rate for healthy New Yorkers who are of military age to that for soldiers in Iraq and then factor in the rate of serious injury, particularly brain injury or suicide, for those two groups.

• *Zoe: Look in the newspaper! There was a plane crash in New York and all 168 people on board died. When we go to visit my mom this year, let's drive and not fly. It'll be a lot safer.*
This is a case of selective attention. The likelihood of being killed in an auto accident per miles traveled is much higher than for flying. It's just that we don't read about so many people dying all at once. There's also the illusion that because we're driving we can control the risk more than in a plane. But an airplane pilot is much better trained and careful at flying than most of us are at driving.

• *Dick: I read that most car accidents occur within three miles of the driver's home. So if we do drive to see your mom, we don't need to be so careful once we're out of town.*
Of course most car accidents happen within three miles of the driver's home because that's where people drive the most. It's the rate of accidents per mile that indicates the likelihood of the risk.

• *Tom: The price of gas is way too high. We need to open up the Arctic for drilling, and all along the coasts, too, and even in the national parks. We'll have more oil then, and the price will go down.*
Tom's right that if we open up all those places to drilling there will be more oil. And yes, it might bring the price down, but not much. There's so much demand now, and the amount of oil that would be produced is so small in comparison to that growing demand, there's no reason to think the price would go down much. Tom's fallen into the **size doesn't matter fallacy**: saying that some consequence of a proposed action would be good (or bad) without considering the size of the consequence. Worse, Tom is looking at only the good consequences of drilling in all those places: lower prices for gas for him. He's not considered the risks: destroying parts of the country that cannot be reclaimed for generations and encouraging people not to conserve energy.

• *Zoe: You drink the tap water here? Don't you know that it's high in arsenic?*
Zoe's mother: It hasn't killed me yet.
Sure Zoe's mom hasn't died yet. Too much arsenic in drinking water won't kill you instantly. Its effect is cumulative. If you drink too much

over a long period of time you'll get cancer. Zoe's mother is confusing short-term risk with long-term risk.

• *Lee's grandfather: It's been 30 years since I smoked, and I still crave a cigarette. I'm 75 now, and that's the life expectancy of a man. So I might as well start smoking. The worst it can do is kill me.*
Lee's grandfather's fatalism is misplaced. That the life expectancy of a man is 75 means a newborn male will, on average, live that long. But if a man is 75, on average he'll live another 10.5 years. And by saying that the worst it can do is kill him he's choosing to ignore the other risks of smoking: it'll make it harder for him to breathe and make his last years much worse even if it doesn't kill him.

• *Maria: The doctor told me that if my knee starts hurting I should take one of these tablets. It's really hurting now, so I'll take two of them.*
Twice as much isn't necessarily twice as good. The extra tablet could hurt her kidneys, or it could start her on the road to addiction, or it could leave her confused the whole day. Maria has fallen into the **fallacy of scale**: the effect will be proportional to the cause, so that if something is good, more is better. The next day if her knee hurts only a little, she might take just half a tablet, and find out that it doesn't affect her pain at all.

Evaluating risk in health-care decisions

In decisions about our health we're often given figures that seem to make clear exactly what the likelihood of the risk is versus a good outcome. But how we understand those numbers and whether those numbers really do tell us what we need to know are crucial for us to make good decisions.

• *Suppose major league baseball has a test to detect steroid use that correctly identifies users 95% of the time and misidentifies nonusers 5% of the time. 400 players are tested, and Ralph's test comes out positive. Should he be suspended?*
Sure, we think, there's a 95% chance he's using steroids. But that's not right. Previous testing showed that only about 5% of baseball players use steroids. So of the 400 players who were tested:
20 (5%) are users.
380 are not users.
Of the 20 users, 19 (95%) are likely correctly identified as users.
Of the 380 nonusers, 19 (5%) are likely incorrectly identified as users.
So there's only a 50% chance that Ralph, one of the 38, tested positive because he uses steroids. It isn't just the accuracy of the test, but also

what proportion of players who use steroids that determines how likely a positive test is right. That's why they repeat the test before suspending someone. After a second test for these 38, of the 19 false positives at most we'd expect one false positive again (5%), while of the ones that were users, 17 would likely test as being users (95%). After a third test, there's almost no chance that a person who isn't a user will be classified as one, and it's almost certain that someone who tests positive is a user.

To evaluate the outcome of a test, we need to consider not just how reliable the test is but also what we know about what proportion of the population actually is or does what's tested.

• *Doctors report that, in treating men with cancer that has started to spread beyond the prostate: Survival is significantly better if radiation is added to standard hormone treatments.*

  The new study assigned 1,200 men to get hormones plus radiation or hormones alone. After seven years, 74 percent of the men receiving both treatments were alive versus 66 percent of the others.

  Those on both treatments lived an average of six months longer than those given just hormones. —*Albuquerque Journal*, June 7, 2010

Suzy's grandfather has prostate cancer that's begun to spread. After she read this, she urged him to get radiation therapy along with hormones. She told him, "You'll live six months longer!"

Her grandfather pointed out that men live six months longer on average, which is no guarantee he'll live that much longer. And he pointed out that the report doesn't talk about the bad effects of taking radiation therapy, which could make a man wish he hadn't lived six months more. Considering only the possible good is no basis for making a decision.

• *Zoe: I can't believe you're taking St. John's wort!*
Zoe's mom: They say it's good for depression. It helped my friend Sally. And besides, it can't hurt. They sell it at the natural foods store.
Evaluating risk is evaluating reasoning. Who's "they"? Is Zoe's mom just repeating what she heard somewhere? That it helped her friend Sally could be coincidence, and even if it weren't, at best it would be anecdotal evidence. And it's nonsense to think that something can't hurt you if it's sold at a natural foods store. With a little searching on the internet, Zoe can show her mom that researchers at Duke University Clinical Research Institute have found that St. John's wort can interfere with other medications. And even if it were harmless, taking it instead of seeking professional help for depression can be harmful. Saying "Oh well, it can't hurt" is just a way to avoid thinking seriously about bad consequences.

- *Women are generally informed that mammography screening reduces the risk of dying from breast cancer by 25%. Does that mean that from 100 women who participate in screening, 25 lives will be saved? Although many people believe this to be the case, the conclusion is not justified. This figure means that from 1,000 women who participate in screening, 3 will die from breast cancer within 10 years, whereas from 1,000 women who do not participate, 4 will die. The difference between 4 and 3 is the 25% 'relative risk reduction.' Expressed as an 'absolute risk reduction,' however, this means that the benefit is 1 in 1,000, that is, 0.1%. Cancer organizations and health departments continue to inform women of the relative risk reduction, which gives a higher number—25% as compared to 0.1%—and makes the benefit of screening appear larger than if it were represented in absolute risks.*

U. Hoffrage and G. Gigerenzer, "How to improve the diagnostic inferences of medical experts" in *Experts in Science and Society*

Evaluating risk uses all our reasoning skills. It's an important part of making good decisions. You need to know how to use these ideas:

- Risk.
- Worth the risk.
- Act of God.
- Fallacy of scale.
- Relative risk reduction.
- Absolute risk reduction.

Try your hand at these!

1. On February 27, 2011, Melissa Jones, a senior on the Baylor women's basketball team, injured her eye in a basketball game. She hit her head on the floor, damaging her optic nerve, and she lost her sight in one eye for a while. Apparently there is a good chance she'll be able to regain her sight. But she wants to finish her basketball career. As quoted by the *Dallas Morning News* (March 24, 2011), she said:

    "I don't tend to live my life in a glass box. I feel like you have the same opportunity getting hurt crossing the street that you do in a skydiving accident. I feel that you want to live your life, do what you want to do and have fun with it."

    Suppose you were a friend of Melissa Jones. What would you tell her about how she's evaluating risk?

2. Suzy: I'm going to bet $5 on Wily Nag to win in the seventh race.
    Dick: Why? He's at 100 to 1. There's so little chance of winning.
    Suzy: But if I win, it'll be a lot. And if I bet 100 times on horses like him, I'm sure to win at least once.

a. What risk is Suzy taking?
b. What fallacy is Suzy making that affects her evaluation of risk?
3. Zeke got tested for HIV last week and it came out positive. The test is 99% accurate: when someone has HIV, the test detects it 99% of the time. The test has a false positive rate of 1%: 1 out of 100 times when someone who doesn't have HIV is tested, the result will say that he or she does have HIV. Reliable public health statistics estimate 0.6% of the population is HIV positive.
   a. What's the probability that Zeke is HIV positive?
   b. If Zeke tests positive on a second test, what's the chance he has HIV?
4. In 1997, the *Cassini* spacecraft was scheduled to be launched from Florida for a mission to Saturn. The power for the spacecraft, once it left the Earth, was to be provided by the heat from a core of plutonium. There was an outcry about this from the public because, though the plutonium was not the type that could cause an explosion, if the launch failed and the spacecraft reentered and broke up in the atmosphere, the plutonium would be dispersed widely, causing many cases of cancer from its inhalation. In one scenario prepared by scientists, the plutonium would be spread over about 2,000 square kilometers, causing 2,300 cancer deaths over 50 years. Other scenarios were for somewhat fewer cancers. In the end, *Cassini* was launched. The mission has been a success.

Mark E. Eberhart, a professor of chemistry and an expert in materials science, evaluates the risk of this mission in his book *Why Things Break*.

"When I awoke on the morning of August 15, 1997, I was confronted with many potential hazards. If I had considered these and ranked them from most probable to least probable, the list would look something like this:

1. Suffering an injury while riding my bicycle during lunch hour.
2. Being in an automobile accident while commuting either to or from work.
3. Having an accident at home—slipping in the shower or falling down stairs.
4. Daily exposure to toxins from the polluted air of Denver.
5. Exposure to second-hand smoke.
6. Exposure to radon.
7. Eating fatty foods.
8. Becoming a victim of crime.
9. Having a work-related accident.
10. Being struck by lightning.
11. Getting caught in a flash flood.
12. Being injured by a tornado or high winds.
13. Suffering an attack by a mountain lion or bear.
14. Inhaling plutonium from the reentry of *Cassini* during earth fly-by.

I am not opposed to minimizing risk, but if I am to approach the problem of minimizing risk as a scientist, those things that pose the greatest risk to life and health should receive the greatest portion of our attention."

Explain what is wrong with Eberhart's analysis.

Answers
2. a. She'll lose $5.
   b. The gambler's fallacy (p. 118).

3. a. ON AVERAGE:
   Of every 1,000 people tested, 6 will have HIV and 994 won't.
   Of the 994, 1% will test positive even though they don't have HIV = 10 will test positive who don't have HIV.
   Of the 6 who test positive, 99% will have HIV = 6 will test positive and have HIV.
   So 16 people will test positive. Of those, 6 actually have HIV. So there's a 6/16 = 37.5% chance that Zeke really is HIV positive.
   b. They test the 16 people. Of the 10 false positives, there's a 1% chance that they'll test positive again—that's fewer than 1 of them. Of the 6 who tested positive and do have HIV, 99% will test positive again, which is 6 of them. So ON AVERAGE of the 16 who people tested positive, only 6 will test positive a second time, and they will all have HIV. So if Zeke tests positive a second time, it's almost certain he is HIV positive.
   Let's hope Zeke doesn't test positive a second time.
4. Eberhart wants to convince us that the risk of getting cancer from the reentry of the spacecraft is not worth our attention. What's wrong with that?
   First, it's an example of a perfectionist dilemma. If you can't stop bigger risks, don't bother to stop a small one.
   Second, Eberhart does not distinguish between risks we voluntarily assume, such as riding a bicycle in downtown traffic; risks we cannot avoid, such as being injured by a tornado; and risks that are imposed on us, such as some politicians and scientists deciding for us that it's O.K. if some of us die to further the space exploration program.
   This is a clear example of why we don't want scientists making policy decisions, for such decisions depend on reasoning skills and ethical sense, which are not what scientists are normally trained in.

26 Making Decisions

We can't make decisions all the time. Imagine every day deciding whether to put your left shoe on first or your right shoe. Imagine every day deciding which side of the bed to sleep on. Imagine every time you go to the supermarket deciding which brand of toothpaste, and then which one of the six varieties of that brand you'll buy. There are people who do try to do that—they have had brain injuries and cannot decide what's important to worry about and what's not important. We must act by habit in most of our lives or we would be paralyzed, unable to act, unable to have time to make decisions that are important.

So the first and most important decisions you have to make are about what is important in your life to bother making decisions about. Buying a car, taking a vacation, where to live, which jobs to apply for, which job to take, what to spend money on when there's almost none left, whether to date someone who has a cat. These are the kind of issues we need to decide in some way. And not just by the state of our digestion and how well we slept last night. Not just by impulse or neglect. Doing nothing is a choice, too, a choice that can have serious consequences.

But there's another kind of paralysis that comes in making decisions. If we have too many choices, we just can't go forward. There are eight different schools you could go to. There are fourteen different cars you could buy. Frustration sets in and you act on impulse. The first step in making a decision about a serious issue for you is to winnow out what are the serious alternatives. This cannot be done by reason alone. And indeed, not even reason. Emotion must inform your decisions or you'll make no decisions. But after you've got down to just two, or three, or four choices, stop. Think about whether your emotions have misled you. Should I take heroin, spice, amphetamines, marijuana, or alcohol? All would give me a high, and emotionally that may be satisfying. But what about the choice of not taking any drugs at all?

Making a decision is deciding if you should or shouldn't do something.

Behind that "should" or "shouldn't" there's a standard, whether you've thought of that or not. So before you even begin to weigh up the alternatives, you better know how you're judging that "should" or "shouldn't". Examine your assumptions. Partly that will come from looking at alternatives and trying to figure out why you think they're good, or bad, or just O.K. And in all this, you are reasoning: trying to decide what to believe, what's true.

* * * * * * * *

Now that your reasoning has been sharpened, you can understand more, you can avoid being duped. And, we hope, you will reason well with those you love and work with and need to convince, and you will make better decisions. But whether you will do so depends not just on method, not just on the tools of reasoning, but on your goals, your ends. And that depends on virtue.

Try your hand at these!
1. Decide whether you should cook dinner at home tonight.
2. Decide whether and what kind of dog you should get.
3. Decide whether you should buy a car next year.
4. Decide whether you should recommend this book to a friend.
5. If you're not married, decide whether you should ever get married.
   If you are married, decide whether you should get divorced.
6. If you're doing drugs, decide whether you should stop.
7. Decide whether you should be honest for the rest of your life.
8. Decide whether you should try to be rich and famous or be known for having a good heart.

Writing Well

First comes clear thinking. Then comes clear writing.

You know how to evaluate claims, arguments, causal reasoning, and explanations. When you want to present your own ideas, use these skills to evaluate your own writing.

Writing well requires practice, unlearning many of the tricks of padding out essays. You'll have lots of opportunities in your studies and your work. Here's a summary of some points that will be helpful.

- If you don't have an argument, literary style won't salvage your essay.

- If the issue is vague, use definitions or rewrite the issue in order to present a precise claim to deliberate.

- Don't make a clear issue vague by appealing to some common but meaningless phrase, such as "This is a free country."

- Slanters turn off those you might want to convince; fallacies just convince the careful reader that you're dumb or devious.

- Beware of questions used as claims. The reader might not answer them the way you do.

- Your argument won't get any better by weaseling with "I believe that" or "I feel that." Your reader probably won't care about your feelings, and your feelings won't establish the truth of the conclusion.

- Your reader should be able to follow how your argument is put together. Indicator words are essential.

- Your premises must be highly plausible, and there must be glue, some claim that connects the premises to the conclusion.

- Don't claim more than you actually prove.

- There is often a trade-off: You can make your argument strong, but perhaps only at the expense of a rather dubious premise. Or you can make all your premises clearly true, but leave out the dubious premise that is needed to make the argument strong. Given the choice, opt for making the argument strong. If it's weak, no one should accept the conclusion. And if it's weak because of an unstated premise, it's better to have that premise stated explicitly so it can be the object of debate.

- In making an argument, you might think you have a great one. All the premises seem obvious and they lead to the conclusion. But if you imagine someone objecting, you can see how to give better support for doubtful premises or make it clearer that the argument is valid or strong. Answering counterarguments in your writing also allows the reader to see that you haven't missed some obvious objections. Just make a list of the pros and cons. Then answer the other side. Your argument must be impervious to the questions "So?" and "Why?".

- Sometimes the best argument may be one which concludes that we should suspend judgment.

Use the critical abilities you've developed to read your own work. Learn to stand outside your work and judge it as you would judge an argument made by someone else.

If you reason calmly and well, you will earn the respect of others, and you may learn that others merit your respect, too.

Reasoning in the Sciences

When scientists reason, they make arguments, they make definitions, they deduce from hypotheses, they generalize, they look for cause and effect, they offer explanations.

The language that scientists use is intimidating, so it's hard to see that you already have the skills to understand and evaluate much of what they're doing. In the first chapter here you'll get some practice with how scientists talk.

Then you'll see how scientists use experiments to establish claims and how those relate to the theories and models they build.

When you finish these chapters, you'll be ready to begin any science course, and you'll be able to understand much of what you read about science in the popular press or on the internet.

Have fun!

27 Some Examples to Start

• *The feeding strategies of amphibians include their choice of prey and the ways in which they locate, capture, and ingest prey. Amphibians generally are considered to be feeding opportunists with their diets reflecting the availability of food of appropriate size. This may be true for some, but results of field and laboratory studies show that some species are selective in their feeding.*
— W.E. Duellman and L. Trueb, *Biology of Amphibians*

The authors of this textbook intend for you to believe what they're saying. But they present no argument here, no reason to believe the claims they are making beyond their supposed authority.

• *The causative agents of some diseases may be found in all parts of the carcasses of animals dying from those diseases. Therefore, carcasses should be disposed of as quickly and thoroughly as possible, by burning, sterilizing with heat, or burying deeply to prevent feral animals from disturbing the carcasses and further spreading the disease.*
— J.H. Galloway, *Farm Animal Health and Disease Control*

This is an argument; the word "therefore" cues us to that. The conclusion is "Carcasses (of animals dying from those diseases) should be disposed of as quickly and thoroughly as possible, by burning, sterilizing with heat, or burying deeply." You can pick out the premises.

• *I wish that everybody could feel the confidence of being alive in a fairly benign world, because I know that most of the advice and conclusions that scientists—scientists not being very scientific about it—have made concerning our planet and the perilous journey we're on, is all bullshit. Because the place is very good at taking care of itself. We don't have to take care of it. And only by being able to read and understand the articles in places like* Science *and* Nature *and* Scientific American *can you really come to that conclusion. You're surrounded by this total barrage of faulty information that's been driven for economic reasons, information that's been basically made up for purposes of getting grants.*
— Kary Mullis, 1993 Nobel laureate in chemistry, *Annals of Improbable Research*, vol. 5, no. 2, 1999

This guy is a Nobel laureate, so he's an expert. So now we can stop worrying about climate change? No. Mullis is making an argument, and we can use our critical thinking skills to see that it's weak, the premises are implausible, and there's no obvious repair. Scientists can be as prejudiced and full of hot air as anyone else.

• *Species are groups of interbreeding natural populations that are reproductively isolated from each other.*
— E. Mayr, *Populations, Species and Evolution*

There are two kinds of crows in Europe: the black crow and the hooded crow. The former is completely black, while the latter is part black and part gray. These used to be called different species, but some intermediate forms occur due to interbreeding in various places. Biologists now classify those kinds as subspecies. It seems that they take the word "isolated" in Mayr's definition to mean "total isolation"; by that definition species can't interbreed. Other biologists point to species that are highly isolated but do interbreed, just in very restricted areas and only rarely. They are interpreting Mayr's definition in terms of relative isolation. For them, species can interbreed. The "deep" question about whether species can interbreed turns into a question about how to define "species."

Agreeing on a good definition in science is an important step to starting research.

Try your hand at these!
For 1–5, identify whether it's a claim. If it is, give a contradictory for it.

1. If some laboratory rat lives longer than four years, then a paper will be written about it.
2. What a wonderous spectacle is the complex and highly evolved chemistry of the living world!   — M. Olomucki, *The Chemistry of Life*
3. Butterflies go through the following stages in their lifetime:
   egg ⟶ caterpillar ⟶ pupa ⟶ adult ⟶ butterfly.
4. When a steady current is flowing through a conductor, the strength of the current is proportional to the potential difference between its ends.
5. (Mendel) When a large number of pea plants having round, yellow seeds are crossed with a large number of pea plants having wrinkled, green seeds, the second generation of round to wrinkled and of yellow to green is approximately 3:1.

For the following, say whether it's an argument. If it is, evaluate it.

6. Vaccination has been a practical method of protection against transmissible disease since Pasteur developed vaccines against some of the common diseases of livestock and poultry, among them some of the diseases which are most important today. No vaccine is absolutely safe or completely effective all the time; however, the practical value of vaccines has been demonstrated in many millions of protected animals.
        — J. H. Galloway, *Farm Animal Health and Disease Control*
7. The universe began with a big bang. Therefore, there was an instant when all matter was energy.
8. Our atmosphere is unique in the solar system. It is composed of 78 percent nitrogen, 21 percent oxygen, and minor amounts of other gases. The earliest atmosphere was much different and consisted largely of hydrogen, carbon dioxide, and water vapor. The present atmosphere began to form as soon as organisms evolved and through photosynthesis developed the ability to extract carbon dioxide from the air and expel

182 *Reasoning in the Sciences*

oxygen. Thus, the oxygen in today's atmosphere is and was produced by life.
— W.K. Hamblin, *Introduction to Physical Geology*

9. In eclipses the outline is always curved: and, since it is the interposition of the earth that makes the eclipse, the form of this line will be caused by the form of the earth's surface, which is therefore spherical. Again, our observations of the stars make it evident, not only that the earth is circular [spherical], but also that it is of no great size. For quite a small change of position to south or north causes a manifest alteration of the horizon. There is much change, I mean, in the stars which are overhead, and the stars seen are different, as one moves northward or southward. Indeed, there are some stars seen in Egypt and the neighborhood of Cyprus which are not seen in the northerly regions; and stars, which in the north are never beyond the range of observation, in those regions rise and set. All of which goes to show not only that the earth is circular in shape, but also that it is a sphere of no great size: for otherwise the effect of so slight a change of place would not be so quickly apparent.
— Aristotle, *On the Heavens*, II.14.297, translated by Richard McKeon

10. The liver is not the seat of the soul, as was believed by many of the ancients. The proof is that the liver can be removed and another transplanted and the person's soul remains the same. Indeed, every part of the human body can be removed, or removed and transplanted, and, except for the degradations of suffering, the person's soul remains unchanged. All that is, save one: the brain. Damage that even a little, and you will see the person's soul in throes. Thus, the brain is the seat of the soul.

11. Every time I or anyone else has looked into my refrigerator, the light is on. Therefore, the light is always on in my refrigerator.

12. Every time I or anyone I know has seen a tree fall in the forest, it makes a sound. Therefore, anytime a tree falls in the forest, it makes a sound.

Answers

1. Claim. Contradictory Some laboratory rat lives longer than four years, but no paper is written about it.
2. Not a claim.
3. Claim. Contradictory: Some butterfly does not go through those stages.
4. Claim. Contradictory: Sometimes when a steady current is flowing through a conductor, the strength of the current is not proportional to the potential difference between its ends.
5. Not a claim: "a large number" is too vague.
6. Not an argument.
7. An argument. Conclusion: There was an instant when all matter was energy. Premise: The universe began with a big bang. Weak. No obvious repair. Bad.
8. Maybe it is an argument or an explanation. But it's really bad. Science does not tell us that some forms are "more perfected" than others; that is a value judgment. Capitalizing the word "nature" and ascribing creativity to it is a bad metaphor and an odd substitute for theology.
9. There are two arguments for the Earth being spherical. The first is by reference to the shape of the form of an eclipse. But that is not valid nor strong: the Earth could be a flat disk. The second is by consideration of the position of the stars. This needs a lot of unstated premises to be good.

10. Pretty good argument *if* you read "personality" for "soul." But as it stands, it needs a definition of "soul" to convince us that such an identification is not all that is meant.
11. Most folks say that the generalization is bad: when you put your finger over the little button the door hits, you can see the light go out. That is, the sample isn't representative. But what if the light is controlled by a metal connection or a magnet that you can't manipulate? Why believe the generalization is false? You can check the wiring diagram to see that the light is designed to go out when the door is shut.
12. Why should we believe this generalization and not the last one? Because our best wiring diagram (our current physics) says the tree does make a sound. Modern science says the laws of physics are the same whether there is an observer or not. But that is an untestable assumption. So all of modern science is based on an untestable, hence unscientific, assumption. Fortunately, it doesn't appear to have any effect on what we deduce about what we can experience. It's just an unnecessary bit of faith added to physics.

28 The Scientific Method

• *I have a waterfall in my backyard. The pond has a thick, rubberized, plastic pond liner, and I have a pump and hose that carry water from the pond along the rock face of a small rise to where the water spills out and runs down more rocks with concrete between them. Last summer I noticed that the pond kept getting low every day and had to be refilled. You don't waste water in the desert, so I figured I'd better find out what was causing the loss of water.*

I thought of all the ways the pond could be leaking: the hose that carries the water could have a leak, the valve connections could be leaking, the pond liner could be ripped (the dogs get into the pond to cool off in the summer), there could be cracks in the concrete, or it could be evaporation and spray from where the water comes out at the top of the fountain.

I had to figure out which (if any) of these was the problem. First I got someone to use a high-pressure spray on the waterfall to clean it. We took the rocks out and vacuumed out the pond. Then we patched every possible spot on the pond liner where there might be a leak.

Then we patched all the concrete on the waterfall part and water-sealed it. We checked the valve connections and tightened them. They didn't leak. And the hose wasn't leaking, because there weren't any wet spots along its path.

Then I refilled the pond. It kept losing water at about the same rate. It wasn't the hose, it wasn't the connections, it wasn't the pond liner, it wasn't the concrete watercourse. So it had to be the spray and evaporation. I reduced the flow of water so there wouldn't be so much spray. There was a lot less water loss. The rest I figured was probably evaporation, though there might still be small leaks.

In trying to find the cause of the water leak at my waterfall and pond, I was using a method scientists often use.

The scientific method

- Conjecture possible causes.
- By experiment, eliminate them by showing they don't make a difference until there is only one.
- Check that one: Does it make a difference? If the purported cause is eliminated, is there still the effect? Is there a common cause?

I assumed there was a cause, then by a process of elimination on some conjectured causes, I fixed on one: when that occurred, the effect always did, too, and it made a difference, and I knew I could fill in the normal conditions.

But why should I assume there is a cause? Does this mean I'm assuming everything has a cause? No, I'm assuming that there is some way to stop the leak, which in this case amounts to assuming that the leak has a cause. The assumption that a particular effect has a cause is sometimes just an expression of our desire to find a way to manipulate the world.

But then doesn't this method rest on a false dilemma?

A or B or C is the cause of E. It's not A. It's not B. So it's C.

No. We also have to check that C satisfies all the conditions for cause and effect, not just that it makes a difference. We must be willing to accept that our experiments will show that none of the conjectured causes satisfies all the conditions. This method cannot find the cause from nothing, but only, if we guess right, isolate it from a range of conjectured causes.

• *Recently Lee found out that he has hepatitis B. None of his friends has hepatitis. He wonders how he could have gotten it.*

He reasons: Since he wants to be a nurse, he volunteers to work at a hospital three times per week. Some of the patients there have hepatitis, and he often washes their bedpans and comes in contact with their body fluids, though he's always careful to wear gloves. Or at least he thought he was. A recent study he read said that 25% of health-care workers exposed to hepatitis B get it. So, he figures, he got hepatitis B from working at the hospital.

How strong is this argument? At best we can say that "Lee contracted hepatitis B from working at the hospital" is a good conjecture. We rule out all other causes we can think of. We can imagine conditions under which he could have gotten hepatitis there, but we can't specify the exact conditions that occurred that would give us the normal conditions. Eliminating all other possible causes (that we can think of) doesn't mean that we can conclude we've found the cause unless we also have:

(*) The only ways Lee could have gotten hepatitis B are P, Q, R, S, and U.

There are very strong arguments that he didn't get it from Q, R, S, or U. Therefore (reasoning by excluded middle), he got it from P. This reasoning to a cause is just as strong as (*) is plausible.

> • *In my backyard, indeed throughout the neighborhood where I live, the abundance of birds is limited. In other neighborhoods there are many more birds. The most important difference I can think of concerns cats. Many cats are around where I live; elsewhere there are less of them. It is probable that there will be other differences between neighborhoods which differ in bird abundance. However, in view of background information it is reasonable to infer that cats will be a causal factor. Cats eat birds and birds are afraid of cats. An experiment could provide more confirmation. If I would shoot the cats near my place and bird abundance would subsequently increase, I would feel confident that cats do influence the abundance of birds. . . .*
>
> *If an experiment of this kind were indeed performed with positive results (for the birds I mean), the evidence would be telling. However, we should realize that the situations compared—before and after the shooting—may differ in other respects. Thus it is possible that, from a bird's point of view, there happens to be a long-lasting improvement of the weather after the shooting.*
>
> *In view of this the following experiment would be more decisive. Suppose we identify ten neighborhoods with many cats. We could remove the cats from five randomly chosen neighborhoods, and let the cats be in the remaining ones. If bird abundance would increase in the cat-free areas, not elsewhere, that would be something. It is improbable that the two groups of neighborhoods will systematically differ in another factor that influences birds.*
>
> Wim J. van der Steen, *A Practical Philosophy for the Life Sciences*

Scientists are usually interested in general causal claims. To get strong arguments for those, they use cause-in-population studies, which experiments are meant to establish.

29 Experiments

What counts as evidence in science?

> ***Observational claim*** An observational claim is one that is established by personal experience or observation in an experiment.
>
> ***Evidence*** Evidence is usually the observational claims that are used as premises of an argument. Sometimes the term refers to all the premises.

What do we mean by "observation in an experiment"?

A physicist may say that she saw an atom traverse a cloud chamber, when what she actually saw was a line made on a piece of photographic film. A biologist may say he saw the nucleus of a cell, when what he saw was an image projected through a microscope. In both cases these people are not reporting on direct personal experience but on deductions made from that personal experience. However, those claims made by deduction from the perceptions arising from certain types of experiments are, by consensus in that area of science, deemed to be observations.

Within any one area of science there is a high level of agreement on what counts as an observational claim. But from one area of science to another that standard may vary. A physicist beginning work in biology may well question why certain claims are taken as "obvious" deductions from experience, such as the reality of what you see through a microscope. But after the general form of the inference—from such direct claims about personal experience to the observational claims—is made explicit once or twice, he's likely to accept such claims as undisputed evidence. If he doesn't accept such deductions, he is questioning the basis of that science.

When new techniques are introduced into a science or when a new area of science is developing, there is often controversy about what counts as an observational claim. Galileo's report of moons around Jupiter was received with considerable skepticism because telescopes were not assumed to be accurate, and indeed at that time they distorted a lot. In ethology, the study of animal behavior in natural settings, there is no agreement yet on what counts as an observational claim, and you can find different journal articles using different standards. For example:

Some would describe this as the first chimpanzee getting angry and chasing the second one away, and then the second returning to pacify and re-establish bonds with the first. That's what they saw. But others say that such a description is loaded with assumptions that have not been established, such as that chimpanzees have emotions sufficiently similar to humans to label as anger and that chimpanzees intend to accomplish certain ends rather than just operating instinctually.

One constraint we impose on reports of observations is that they can be duplicated. We believe that nature is uniform. What can happen once can happen again—*if* the conditions are the same. Scientists typically won't accept reports on observations that they are unable to reproduce.

> **Duplicable experiments and reproducible results** An experiment is *duplicable* if it is described clearly enough that others can follow the method to obtain observations. The *results* of an experiment are *reproducible* if whenever the experiment is duplicated the observations of the new experiment are in close agreement with the observations of the original experiment.
>
> When an experiment has been duplicated and the results reproduced, it's said that the experiment was *replicated*.

The difficulty is to specify exactly what conditions are required and what counts as close enough agreement. It's fairly easy in chemistry and physics, less so in biology, much more difficult in psychology or ethology. It's virtually impossible in history and economics, which means history and economics are not sciences, except to the extent that we can describe very general conditions that may recur.

- *A recipe from a famous coffeehouse*
  Vegetarian Chile
  2 cans each (include liquid): Pinto beans, Chili beans, Great
     Northern beans, Red beans, Kidney beans
  1 # 10 can diced Tomatoes
  Garlic, 6-8 cloves chopped
  Bell Pepper, 1 chopped
  Jalapeño Peppers, 3 chopped
  Chili Powder 2 soup spoons
  Onions, 2 chopped or in food processor
  Paprika, 1 soup spoon

Put in soup tureen and heat to boil for 1 hour. Take care the beans don't stick to the bottom.

Any expert in the subject (any person who has worked in a commercial kitchen) will know what a #10 can of tomatoes is. Though "chopped" and "soup spoon" may be unclear, anyone who saw the chile being made would be able to duplicate the preparation.

- *Feeding behavior of primates*
General Methodology
Data were collected simultaneously on both the activity of the animals and the forest strata at which this activity took place. Counts were made at five-minute intervals of the numbers of individuals engaged in each of the six activities and the level of the forest in which the activity was performed. The following activities were recorded: feeding—the animal actually in the process of ingesting or picking a food item; grooming—mutual and self-grooming were distinguished for certain analyses; resting—no body displacement, or feeding, or grooming, sunning, etc.; moving—movement of an individual, including individual foraging; travel—movement of the group; and other—e.g., sunning, play, fighting. These data were collected only after the animals under observation were reasonably habituated to the observer. Each observation of an animal constituted an individual activity record (IAR) collected in a given five-minute time sample. Because of the focus of the study and the difficulty in keeping continuous contact with an individual animal, no attempt was made to follow individual animals nor to collect statistical data on specific age or sex classes. Statistical analyses of the data were complicated by the fact that some of the activity records were not independent of each other. The methods used for the statistical analyses are reported in Sussman et al.

To determine levels of the forest, I used Richards' (1957) categories of forest stratification as a model and assigned numbers of one to five to the forest layers. Level 1 is the ground layer of the forest; it includes the herb and grass vegetation. Level 2 is the shrub layer, from one to three metres above the ground. This layer is usually found in patches throughout the continuous canopy forest, but is much more dense and is the dominant layer in the brush and scrub regions. Level 3 of the forest consists of small trees, the lower branches of larger trees, and saplings of the larger species of trees. This layer is about three to seven metres high. Level 4 is the continuous or closed canopy layer. It is about five to 15 metres high. The dominant tree of the closed canopy, at all three forests, is the kily (Tamarindus indica). Level 5 of the forest is the emergent layer and consists of the crowns of those trees which rise above the closed canopy. It is usually over 15 metres high.

All three forests in which I made intensive studies were primary forests and the tree layers were quite distinct. In most cases, the particular level in which an animal was observed could be distinguished easily. If I could not determine the forest level unambiguously, I did not record it.

Observations recorded in this manner may be biased because animals that are active in certain levels of the forest may be more difficult to see than those active at other levels. I attempted to minimize this problem by following a relatively small number of animals (usually from five to ten) throughout a period of continuous observation, keeping track of all the animals. For Lemur fulvus this usually included the whole group, which was small and, for the most part, moved together. It was more difficult to do this when observing Lemur catta, for which it was often necessary to follow and observe subgroups of the larger group. The larger group would disperse, especially during foraging and feeding, and during afternoon rest periods.

Day ranges were mapped by following a group from one night resting site in the morning to the time it settled in another night resting site in the evening. The location of the group was plotted throughout the day on a prepared map of the forest and the amount of time the group spent in each location was recorded. Home ranges include the sum of all the day ranges. The data on home ranges are limited, however, and probably do not represent total home ranges of the groups, since the study in each area was limited to a few months.

— R.W. Sussman, "Feeding behaviour of Lemur Catta and Lemur Fulvus" in *Primate Ecology*, ed. T. H. Clutton-Brock

It is difficult to be more precise than this in ethology. The description of the methodology is clear enough to count as duplicable, perhaps even by someone who isn't an expert in the subject. Whether the observations are replicable will depend on how closely we expect them to agree with the ones in this paper.

Note that the author has not stated what time of year the observations were made, nor the percentage of males versus females in the groups he studied. These are not part of the conditions that need to be duplicated; implicitly the author is saying they don't matter. If it turns out in trying to duplicate this experiment that different observations are obtained at different times of the year, then the time of year would have to be added as part of the conditions that are important and that have to be duplicated.

• *The refraction of light rays*

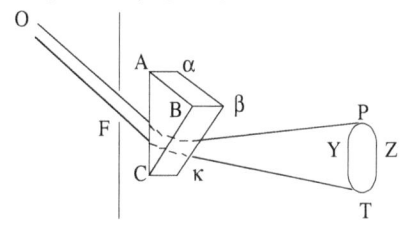

In the wall or window of a room let F be some hole through which solar rays OF are transmitted, while other holes elsewhere have been carefully sealed so that no light enters from any other place. The darkening of the room, however, is not necessary; it only enables the experiment to turn out somewhat more clearly. Then place at that hole a triangular glass prism AαBβCκ that refracts the rays OF transmitted through it toward PYTZ. — Isaac Newton, *Optica*, Part 1, Lecture 1, 1670, translated from the Latin in *The Optical Papers of Issac Newton,* ed. Alan E. Shapiro

This is very clear because of the diagram. It can be and often was duplicated, and the observations were reproduced.

• *Testing for anomalous cognition (ESP)*
The vast majority of anomalous cognition experiments at SRI [Stanford Research Institute] and SAIC [Science Applications International Corporation] used a technique known as remote viewing. In these experiments, a viewer attempts to draw or describe (or both) a target location, photograph, object, or short video segment. All known channels for receiving the information are blocked. Sometimes the viewer is assisted by a monitor who asks the viewer questions; of course, in such cases the monitor is blind to the answer as well. Sometimes a sender is looking at the target during the session, but sometimes there is no sender. In most cases the viewer eventually receives a feedback in which he or she learns the correct answer, thus making it difficult to rule out precognition [knowing the future] as the explanation for positive results, whether or not there was a sender.

Most anomalous cognition experiments at SRI and SAIC were of the free-response type, in which viewers were asked simply to describe the target. . . .

> The SAIC remote-viewing experiments and all but the early ones at SRI used a statistical evaluation method known as rank-order judging. After the completion of a remote viewing, a judge who is blind to the true target (called a blind judge) is shown the response and five potential targets, one of which is the correct answer and the other four of which are 'decoys.' Before the experiment is conducted, each of those five choices must have had an equal chance of being selected as the actual target. The judge is asked to assign a rank to each of the possible targets, where a rank of 1 means it matches the response most closely, and a rank of 5 means it matches the least.
>
> The rank of the correct target is the numerical score for that remote viewing. By chance alone the actual target would receive each of the five ranks with equal likelihood, since, despite what the response said, the target matching it best would have the same chance of selection as the one matching it second best and so on. The average rank by chance would be 3. Evidence for anomalous cognition occurs when the average rank over a series of trials is significantly lower than 3. (Notice that a rank of 1 is the best possible score for each viewing.)
>
> This scoring method is conservative in the sense that it gives no extra credit for an excellent match. A response that describes the target almost perfectly will achieve the same rank of 1 as a response that contains only enough information to pick the target as the best choice out of the five possible choices.
>
> — Jessica Utts, "An Assessment of the Evidence for Psychic Functioning,"
> *The Journal of Parapsychology*, vol. 59, no. 4, p. 289, 1995

What does "All known channels for receiving information are blocked" mean? We need to know the exact layout of the room where the experiment was done. "In most cases the viewer eventually receives feedback" —how often, under what circumstances, exactly when? We need to know how close the "decoys" were to the true target. Who are the judges? This is crucial because different judges from different backgrounds may classify differently.

The experiment is not duplicable. Even if you watched the experiment being done, you couldn't duplicate it, for it's not clear what the author considers important and what she considers irrelevant in the setup.

Even if it were possible to duplicate the experiment and get the same results, it's not clear that by chance alone the actual target would not receive each of the five ranks with equal likelihood. Perhaps this experiment would show the opposite.

• *The growth of living nerve cells in vitro*
The immediate object of the following experiments was to obtain a method by which the end of a growing nerve could be brought under

direct observation while alive, in order that a correct conception might be had regard-ing what takes place as the fibre extends during embryonic development from the nerve center out to the periphery.

The method employed was to isolate pieces of embryonic tissue known to give rise to nerve fibres, as for example, the whole or fragments of the medullary tube or ectoderm from the branchial region, and to observe their further development. The pieces were taken from frog embryos about three mm. long, at which stage, i.e. shortly after the closure of the medullary folds, there is no visible differentiation of the nerve elements. After carefully dissecting it out the piece of tissue is removed by a fine pipette to a cover slip upon which is a drop of lymph freshly drawn from one of the lymph sacs of an adult frog. The lymph clots very quickly, holding the tissue in a fixed position. The cover slip is then inverted over a hollow slide and the rim sealed with paraffin. When reasonable aseptic precautions are taken, tissues will live under these conditions for a week and in some cases specimens have been kept alive for nearly four weeks. Such specimens may be readily observed from day to day under highly magnifying powers. — Ross Harrison, *Proceedings of the Society for Experimental and Medicine Biology*, vol. 4, 1907

This is the first method ever recorded for maintaining living cells outside the body. It is very much like the recipe from the *Dog & Duck*. Even for an expert it would have been difficult to duplicate it from just reading this.

The morals of these examples

- It's hard to describe an experiment clearly enough to duplicate it.
- What is described in an experiment is what needs to be duplicated. What is not described is deemed irrelevant to obtaining similar observations.
- What counts as duplicable is going to be relative to the particular scientific discipline. Expert knowledge in the area may make some descriptions clear.
- What counts as close enough agreement for observations to be deemed replicable is going to depend on the particular scientific discipline.
- New experimental designs are often sketchily described, but they are accepted anyway because people go to the lab, see how it is done, go back to their labs and do the experiment, and then pass that on to other people.

Experiments to Test a Generalization

> • Flo: *Spot barks. And Wanda's dog Ralph barks. And Dr. E's dogs Anubis and Buddy bark. So all dogs bark.*
> Becky: Yeah. *Let's go over to Maple Street and see if all the dogs there bark, too.*
> Flo is generalizing. Relative to her experience it's a pretty good generalization. Becky wants to test the generalization.

Suppose that A, B, C, D are given as inductive evidence for a generalization G. (Some other plausible premises may also be needed, but we'll keep those in the background.) Then we have that G explains A, B, C, D.

But if G is true, we can see that some other claims must be true, instances of the generalization G, say L, M, N. If those are true, then G would explain them, too. For example, Rodolfo barks, Lady barks, . . .

That is, G *explains* A, B, C, D and *predicts* L, M, N, where the difference between the explanation and the prediction is that in the explanation we know that the claim being explained is true, whereas we don't know if the prediction is true.

Suppose we devise experiments and find that L, M, N are indeed true. Then "A, B, C, D + L, M, N therefore G" is a better argument for G than we had before. At the very least it has more instances of the generalization as premises.

But how do more instances of a generalization prove the generalization better? They can if (i) they are from different kinds of situations, that is A, B, C, D + L, M, N cover a more representative sample of possible instances of G than do just A, B, C, and D. And this is usually what happens. We deduce claims from G for situations we had not previously considered.

And (ii) because we had not previously considered the kind of instances L, M, N of the generalization G, we have some confidence that we haven't arrived at G by manipulating the data, selecting situations that would establish just this hypothesis.

One of the best ways to test an hypothesis-generalization is to try to falsify it. Trying to falsify a generalization just means that we are consciously trying to come up with instances of the generalization to test that are as different as we can imagine from A, B, C, D. Trying to falsify is just a good way to ensure (i) and (ii).

In this chapter there are only a few definitions:
- Observational claim.
- Evidence.
- Duplicable experiment.
- Reproducible results.
- Replicable experiment.

The rest is just examples to help you see how to use the ideas. You'll get a chance to do some analysis of your own at the end of the next chapter.

30 What Can Go Wrong with an Experiment?

There are lots of ways experiments and interpretations of experiments can go wrong besides bad sampling or bad causal reasoning.

Experiments Start with a Question

• *Professor Shibokbok asks each of the 103 students in her psychology class to interview at least two people, asking what they've thought during the last two days. Then she and her students examine the answers, going over them again and again, classifying the responses. Eventually they find a correlation—between the weight of the person and his or her view of public transportation.*

There's always some correlation you can find if you look long enough at some mass of observations. But that's going backwards. Unless you start with a question, and have some criteria for what counts as an observation, and follow the usual rules for generalizing and causal reasoning, it's nonsense.

Observations are meant to answer a question, to test an hypothesis, to give some evidence to believe or disbelieve a claim. Otherwise, there would be no justification for the conclusions you'd draw.

> ***The fallacy of mining the data*** It is a mistake in reasoning to comb through a mass of observations looking for some correlation and then claim that the correlation is significant—when the data was not collected for the purpose of studying that correlation

Lying

• *In 2004 the highly respected journal* Science *published an article by Hwang Woo-suk detailing how he and his team had for the first time ever cloned human embryonic stem cells. That had been thought impossible. Hwang, a veterinarian and researcher, was already well-known for having cloned a cow and, for the first time, a dog, Snuppy. In 2006 Hwang admitted that the research papers had faked data. He was convicted by a court in Korea of embezzlement of millions of research dollars and of bioethical violations (taking human eggs from his research assistants).*

- *In 1988* The Lancet, *one of the most respected medical journals, published an article by Dr. Andrew Wakefield and twelve other authors. It said that they had found a link between children receiving the triple vaccine for measles, mumps, and rubella (MMR) and developing autism. The paper did not claim that there was cause and effect. But before it was published, Wakefield held a press conference in which he said that vaccinations using MMR should be suspended until further research was done. A lot of people stopped vaccinating their children. Outbreaks of measles became more common.*

    But no one else was able to reproduce his results. More and more cause-in-population studies showed the safety and efficacy of the MMR vaccinations.

    In 2011 the medical journal The BMJ *published an article showing that Wakefield's study misrepresented or altered the medical histories of the twelve children studied in it. As Brian Deer, a reporter for the* London Sunday Times *said, Wakefield was responsible for "falsifying medical histories of children and essentially concocting a picture, which was the picture he was contracted to find by lawyers hoping to sue vaccine manufacturers." According to* The BMJ, *Wakefield received $674,000 from the lawyers. Wakefield lost his license to practice medicine in the United Kingdom, and* The Lancet *retracted the article.*

Self-Deception

- *In the late 1800s a German mathematics teacher, Wilhelm von Osten, was convinced that animals have reasoning skills and intelligence. He tried to test his hypothesis with cats, but they were indifferent. His horse, Hans, however learned how to answer simple addition and multiplication problems by tapping his hoof the correct number of times. He could even do problems with fractions, which are beyond many high school students. After much skepticism was voiced, Germany's board of education organized a committee of a psychologist, a horse trainer, several school teachers, and a circus manager to investigate. They concluded there was no trickery. Then Oskar Pfungst, a psychologist, was called to study Hans. He found that it didn't matter whether von Osten or others questioned Hans: the answers were always correct. Unless, that is, the person didn't know the answer or was not visible to the horse. Eventually, Pfungst was able to show that each questioner, even when advised not to, showed a slight relaxation of tension when the horse tapped the correct number, which was what cued "Clever Hans" to stop. Clever Hans wasn't doing mathematics; he was clever only in reading people's expressions.*

    Von Osten wasn't deceptive. He continued to believe that Clever Hans could do mathematics. But he was overlooking possibilities. That an animal's behavior can be influenced by subtle and unintentional cues from a questioner is called the **Clever Hans effect**. It also holds for questioning humans, who might not be aware that they're picking up on unintentional cues.

Sometimes, though, the problem is that there is less that is important.

• *Lee is one of 200 students in an experiment on psychic effects done by Professor Shibokbok. She asks each student to predict whether a coin flipped by a machine will land heads or tails. Each student does this 20 times. Most are right about 50% of the time, but 20 of them are right 15 or more times, including Lee. Those, she reckons, are the ones most likely to have psychic abilities. So she tests them again, and 4 of them, including Lee, are right more than 15 times out of 20. She tests those 4 again. Lee gets 16 right, and the others get less than 10. Now Professor Shibokbok wants to know whether Lee has precognition (can predict the future) or whether he's influencing the flip of the coin by telekinesis. The next day she tests Lee again, and he predicts only 6 flips out of 20. Then again, and he predicts only 4 out of 20. Somehow, Professor Shibokbok says, his psychic abilities have deteriorated overnight.*

Lee hasn't lost his psychic abilities because he never had any. With 200 people, it's likely that someone will predict correctly more often than 50% of the time, especially with so few flips. Professor Shibokbok didn't test those who weren't predicting correctly who might have suddenly "gained" psychic powers. In a long enough run of tests, Lee, as the other students, will have a run of correct predictions. But eventually the sum of all his predictions will tend toward 50%, the average (mean) of what is predicted as occurring by chance. Though it's often difficult to rule out chance as an explanation in an experiment, in this case it's not.

Professor Shibokbok couldn't get her work published in a reputable journal because it was obvious to the **referees**, other scientists who judge articles submitted to journals, that she didn't understand probability. She was denied tenure and has now moved to a position in administration.

Regression to the mean When experimental results are found that are far from the average predicted to occur by chance, and in subsequent trials the results tend to that average, it's a case of *regression to the mean*.

The power of suggestion

* *A young psychologist from Hamburg, Germany, named Krüger had been to a market and a gypsy woman gave him a description of his character. He was amazed how well it suited him. He showed it to his colleague, Zietz, without telling him where he'd gotten it and who gave it to him. Zietz thought it applied to himself. Both being of the conviction that they were very different people personality-wise, they decided to investigate the matter more closely. Krüger told the students in one of his psychology classes that he wanted to do a graphological experiment. All the students had to hand in a handwriting sample. To make the experiment look serious, Krüger waited 4 weeks before he gave the students their answers. They were called into a separate room where they were handed a typed version of the character description given to Krüger by the gypsy woman. Not one of the 39 students was dissatisfied with the evaluation of his or her character. Some thought that minor points were a little off, but most were astounded by the accuracy of the description. Afterwards, the students were told that they had all received the same description. The experiment has been repeated many times, with the same result.*

Taking fortune-tellers' predictions seriously or following the daily astrology predictions may seem like intellectual peccadilloes, not serious problems of the power of suggestion. But the power of suggestion can ruin scientific experiments involving humans, especially in testing medications. Special precautions have to be taken to avoid having the expectations of both the subjects and the experimenters skew the results.

* *In studying new drugs, there is a problem that some people will report improvement of symptoms if given only sugar pills. That is why the control group is administered a placebo. Neither the subjects in the experiments nor those administering the drug or placebo are told which is a placebo and which a drug—that's the definition of a double blind trial.*

   The anecdotal and empirical accounts of the potency of the placebo effect are legion. For example, in one study, 30% of a large number of patients reported decreased sex drive, 17% increased headache, 14% increased menstrual pain, and 8% increased nervousness and irritability. These were all side effects of the administration of a placebo in a double-blind study of oral contraceptives [reference given]. In a double-blind study of a cold vaccine, 7% of patients in both groups reported toxic side effects requiring additional medical intervention. Double-blind studies will often list iatrogenic [i.e., induced by medical procedure] side effects found in the placebo group, but these symptoms will differ markedly from study to study. In contrast to the study of oral contraceptives, it is not

> surprising that in double-blind studies with antihistamines, fatigue and sleepiness are reported. Obviously the target symptoms monitored are different. In an antihistamine study, it is unlikely that the investigators would inquire about decreased sex drive and headaches among females.
> — Frederick J. Evans, "Expectancy, therapeutic instructions and the placebo response" in *Placebo,* L. White, B. Trusky, and G. Schwartz, eds.
>
> But the studies Evans cites don't show that the people had those symptoms. The authors show that the subjects reported that they had the symptoms. There's a big difference. And given the looseness of what we count as a headache, people may report what they wouldn't normally call a headache simply in order to have something to report. Wanting to please the researcher can distort responses, too. Further, even a sugar pill can have some effect, perhaps enough to make one a little happier and so have something to report.

It's extraordinarily hard to define "placebo effect" well, but roughly this is what we use.

Placebo A *placebo* is any substance or treatment given to some participants in a controlled cause-to-effect cause-in-population medical study that is assumed to have no effect.

Placebo effect A placebo effect is a reported or experienced change that follows from a person being given a placebo.

Double-blind trial A double-blind trial is a controlled cause-to-effect cause-in-population study in which neither the subjects nor those who administer the drug or placebo are told which is a placebo and which a drug.

With the slipperiness of what really is a placebo, all we can do is use double-blind studies with large enough populations. This allows us to compare the responses of those given the drug or treatment with those in the control group to see if there is a statistically significant difference. If there is, that's taken to be the effect of the drug or treatment.

With uncontrolled cause-to-effect experiments involving people, the expectations of the people involved can result in an unrepresentative sample. No matter how carefully studies are made on the effectiveness of different female contraceptives, they will be only marginally useful in helping women choose which method to use. That's because women who most want to avoid pregnancy choose the contraceptive they think will be most effective. So the women using the pill, which they are told is a highly effective way to avoid pregnancy, will be more motivated to follow the instructions for its use and always use it, while those who use contraceptive foam are likely to be more lax in following the method. According to the people who devise these studies, there doesn't seem to be any way to correct for this bias in the analysis of the data.

> *Self-selection bias* Self-selection bias occurs when those in the sample for a survey or experiment select themselves to participate.

Self-selection bias isn't only with people. When an ethologist studies only the chimpanzees that come to a feeding station, the sample of chimpanzees she's studying is self-selected.

Positive publication bias

• *Professor Fergamitz and Professor Lyle, at different universities and unknown to each other, have each done an experiment to the highest standards. They've examined their observations using the best statistical analyses.*

Prof. Fergamitz: I just found out that there's no correlation between being fat and being left-handed.

Prof. Lyle: I just found out that there's a 12% greater chance of being fat if you're left-handed.

There's no hope that Prof. Fergamitz can get his work published. Who would think that there would be a correlation? However, Prof. Lyle got his work accepted by a respected medical journal because it's such a surprising result.

Journals will publish new positive results but rarely new negative ones—unless, that is, to refute someone's experiment that is famous, like Andrew Wakefield's (p. 197). If Professor Lyle's paper starts lots of research on left-handed people, Prof. Fergamitz will likely be able to get his work published.

Journals—and researchers—tend to take positive results more seriously than negative ones. So when there are many people doing research, and only the positive results are published, we get a skewed picture of what's proved.

- [Dr. Joseph Banks Rhine was a famous ESP researcher from Duke University. He devised an experiment using cards with five easily distinguishable symbols: a square, circle, cross, star, and wavy lines. Used in decks of 25 cards, 5 for each symbol, the person being tested was asked to predict which symbol will be drawn.]

Let us imagine that one hundred professors of psychology throughout the country read of Rhine's work and decide to test a subject. The fifty who fail to find ESP in their first preliminary test are likely to be discouraged and quit, but the other fifty will be encouraged to continue. Of this fifty, more will stop work after the second test, while some will continue, more will stop work after the second test, while some will continue because they obtained good results. Eventually, one experimenter remains whose subject has made high scores for six or seven consecutive sessions. Neither experimenter nor subject is aware of the other ninety-nine projects, and so both have a strong delusion that ESP is operating. *The odds are, in fact, much against the run. But in the total (and unknown) context, the run is quite probable. (The odds against winning the Irish sweepstakes are even higher. But someone does win it.) So the experimenter writes an enthusiastic paper, sends it to Rhine who publishes it in his magazine, and the readers are greatly impressed.*

— Martin Gardner, Fads and Fallacies in the Name of Science

There's no deception here and no self-deception. The one experimenter did his work well. Still, a reputable scientific journal wouldn't publish his results unless they were reproduced by many experimenters, since they contradict so much else we know. Good referees are alert to the possibility of chance being at work.

Still, not every negative result is significant.

- *The famous Michelson-Morley experiment in the 19th century showed that the speed of light did not vary according to whether it was measured in the same path as the Earth's movement or across that path. This was the observation that led Albert Einstein to formulate his theory of relativity based on the assumption that the speed of light is the same for every observer. In the 1920s, 40 years after Michelson and Morley, a reputable physicist named Dayton C. Miller repeated the experiment and found slight variations in the speed of light, sufficient to question the theory of relativity. He repeated the experiment many times, always with the same results. He published articles about his work in scientific journals. But no one accepts that his experiment refutes the claim that the speed of light is constant.*

The Michelson-Morley experiment has been duplicated many times in virtually all technologically advanced countries, at differing altitudes, with different kinds of equipment. Except for Miller's work, the results always show that the speed of light, at least to the accuracy of the instruments involved, is the same. Even now no one knows why Miller's observations were different. It isn't bias toward positive results to conjecture that there was something odd in his equipment or that he, perhaps unconsciously, made errors recording the observations. Yes, it's possible that in that one place, at those particular times, there were differences in the speed of light. But no reputable scientist would accept that, not because he or she would be intimidated by the scientific community but because all the weight of evidence is against it.

Should we ever believe scientists?

One experiment is published; another contradicts its results. Should we just suspend judgment? Is there no standard we can use?

Some say that because scientists differ in evaluating some experiments and because there is no clear line between good work and bad work, between science and pseudoscience, we should suspend judgment on all scientific theories: the theory of evolution is no more to be trusted —or discounted—than astrology. That's a drawing-the-line fallacy. In the extremes, and those extremes are not far from the middle muddle, we can clearly distinguish between a theory that is very likely to be accurate and one that is very likely to be wrong.

Work in science is distinguished by constant testing. No observation, no result, no theory will long be accepted as both correct and important until it has been tested again and again. Yes, scientists make mistakes. Like all of us, they are sometimes careless, sometimes self-deceived, sometimes misled by mistaking chance for significance, and sometimes seduced by hope of money and power. But the community as a whole acts as a skeptical audience. Some call the testing, checking, and revising in science the "scientific method." But that's just a fancy name for all that scientists do, from their first training as students in how to reason to their laboratories and theoretical analyses. Testing, checking, and revising is what all of us would do for all the important decisions in our lives if we had the time and money—and energy.

In this chapter you've learned how to better evaluate experiments by looking for what can go wrong, using these ideas:
- The fallacy of mining the data.
- Clever Hans effect.

204 *Reasoning in the Sciences*

- Referee.
- Regression to the mean.
- Placebo.
- Double-blind trial.
- Self-selection bias.
- Positive publication bias.

Yet you also saw that we normally do have good reason to accept claims that scientists make if those claims have been tested by other scientists.

Try your hand at these!

1. List all the mistakes about data mining in the story "The Exaggerated Promise of So-Called Unbiased Data Mining" at <https://www.wired.com/story/the-exaggerated-promise-of-data-mining/>.
2. Explain why it is just as safe to jump from an airplane without a parachute as with one (see https://www.kanw.com/post/researchers-show-parachutes-dont-work-theres-catch).

Evaluate the following experiments and arguments about experiments.

3. We should take claims about extrasensory perception seriously. Look, suppose no one in the world had a sense of smell except one person. He would walk along a country road where there is a high stone wall and tell his friend, "There are roses there." Or he would walk into a home and say, "Someone cooked onions here yesterday." These would seem extraordinary extrasensory perceptions to his friends and acquaintances. Similarly, just because we don't understand and can't imagine a mechanism that would explain extrasensory perception, we shouldn't stop the investigation.
4. Thus it is observed by the easy experiment of opening an artery at any time in living animals that blood is contained in the arteries naturally.

    In order that on the other hand we may be more certain that the force of pulsation does not belong to the artery or that the material contained in the arteries is not the producer of the pulsation, for in truth this force depends for its strength upon the heart. Besides, we see that an artery bound by a cord no longer beats under the cord, it will be permitted to undertake an extensive dissection of the artery of the groin or of the thigh, and to take a small tube made of reed of such thickness as is the capacity of the artery and to insert it by cutting in such a way that the upper part of the tube reaches higher into the cavity of the artery than the upper part of the dissection, and in the same manner also that the lower portion of the tube is introduced downward farther than the lower part of the dissection, and thus the ligature of the artery which constricts its calibre above the cannula is passed by a circuit.

    To be sure when this is done the blood and likewise the vital spirit run through the artery even as far as the foot; in fact the whole portion of the artery replaced by the canula beats no longer. Moreover, when the ligature has been cut, that part of the

artery which is beyond the cannula shows no less pulsation than the portion above.
— Andreas Vesalius, *Fabrica,* VII. 19, written in 1543, translated by S. Lambert (also in *The Origins and Growth of Biology,* ed. Arthur Rook, p. 120)

5. Cyclic Variations in Grass Growth
Grass exhibits a cyclical growth pattern surprisingly different from any other known plant. In this study, average grass blade heights have been measured, on a daily basis, over a 10 week period. Measurements were taken, utilizing vernier calipers, of the height of one hundred individual grass blades randomly chosen in a 10 foot square area positioned in front of an apartment complex in the Lexington, Kentucky area. (Measurements were also repeated with a different set of calipers to ensure reproducibility on a different apparatus.) The average of these measurements was computed and experimental error was taken as the standard deviation of the mean divided by the square root of the number of grass blades in the average. The procedure was repeated on a daily basis for a period of 10 weeks.

Figure 1: Experimental measurements of average grass height are plotted versus time. Solid line represents experimental data. Short dashed line indicates a 'constant grass height' calculation and is normalized to the experimental data to produce the best fit.

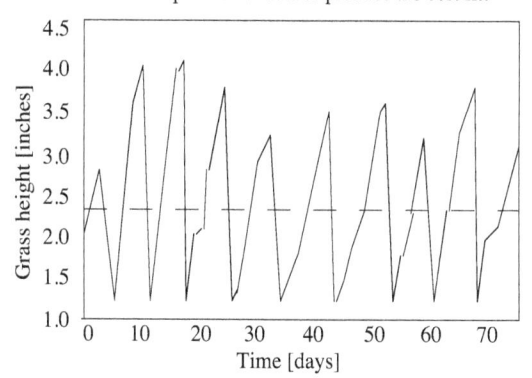

Results and Discussion: The average grass heights, measured in this work, are plotted as a function of time in Figure 1. As one can readily see, there exists a periodic variation in average grass height with an approximate cycle of 7 to 10 days. Another intriguing observation is that there exists a minimum grass height, or 'grass baseline,' of about 1.3 inches.

Since the cyclic period of the grass is 7 to 10 days, one may conclude that grass height varies on a 'week-about' basis. The physical mechanism responsible for this cyclic grass height phenomenon is not clearly understood at this time.

— V.D. Irby, M.S. Irby, Department. of Physics and Astronomy, University of Kentucky, *Annals of Improbable Research,* vol. 1, no. 4, 1995

6. Several studies indicate that people who smoke cigarettes have an increased risk for low back pain and prolapsed disk [references given]. Individuals who have not smoked for more than a year, however, do not appear to have an increased risk, at least for prolapsed lumbar disk [reference given]. Table 6 shows that current smokers

have almost twice the risk for prolapsed lumbar disk as those who have never smoked or who are former smokers. In the same study [reference given] it was estimated that the risk in current smokers is increased by about 20% for every 10 cigarettes smoked per day on the average. Possible mechanisms for the association between smoking and low back pain and prolapsed disk include decreased diffusion of nutrients into the intervertebral disk among smokers [reference given], and increased pressure on the low back from the frequent coughing experienced by many smokers.

Table 6. Estimated Relative Risk for Prolapsed Lumbar Intervertebral Disk According to Cigarette Smoking Status, Connecticut

Smoking Status	Estimated Relative Risk	95% Confidence Limits
Never smoked (referent group)	1.0	—
Current smoker (smoked in past year)	1.7	1.0–2.5
Former smoker (smoked, but not in past year)	1.0	0.6–1.7

*Relative risk = risk in those exposed to factor divided by risk in those not exposed (referent group).
— Jennifer L. Kelsy, Anne L. Golden, Diane J. Mundt, *Rheumatic Disease Clinics of America*, vol. 16, no. 3, 1990

7. *Sleepwalking and spontaneous parapsychological experiences: a note*

Two studies were conducted in which a questionnaire in Spanish with a true and false response format was used. It included, among other items, five questions about parapsychological experiences (waking ESP, dream ESP, apparitions, out-of-body experiences, and auras) and one question about somnambulism as follows: Some people have told me that I have sometimes walked in my sleep. The studies were conducted at the Centro Caribeno de Estudios Postgraduados, a private institute of graduate psychology studies in San Juan, Puerto Rico. In the first study, 120 questionnaires were collected by masters and doctoral students taking a graduate psychology course offered by the author. The students collected questionnaires from family, friends, and acquaintances outside the institution. In the second study, 52 questionnaires were collected by a colleague in two of his graduate courses. To measure frequency of psi [parapsychological] experiences, an index was formed from the above-mentioned five questions, assigning a score of 1 for true and a score of 0 for false answers.

The composite parapsychological experiences measure produced scores with the following characteristics: Study 1 (N = 120, M = 2.03, Range: 0–5, SD = 1.59); and Study 2 (N = 52, M = 1.48, Range: 0–4, SD = 1.23). The frequency of positive replies to the sleepwalking question was 17% for Study 1 (N = 119) and 24% for Study 2 (N = 51).

In the first study, those participants who replied affirmatively to the sleepwalking question (N = 20) obtained a mean of parapsychological experiences of 2.60, as compared to a mean of 1.94 for those who replied negatively, (N = 99), t(117) = 1.70, p = .045 (one-tailed), r = .16. In the second study, those with sleepwalking experiences (N = 12) obtained a mean of parapsychological experiences of 2.00, as compared to a mean of 1.28 for those without, N = 39, t(49) = 1.80, p = .039 (one-tailed), r = .25. The combined assessment of the p values in both studies produced a Stouffer z of 2.45, p = .01 (one-tailed). The combined effect size, using a Fisher z transformation [reference given] was .21. The difference between the effect sizes of Study 1 (r = .16) and Study 2 (r = .25) was not significant, z = –.52, p = .603 (two-tailed).

The results support the idea that sleepwalking is related to the frequency of parapsychological experiences. This, in turn, provides further evidence of a low-magnitude association between parapsychological experiences and dissociation. Further work should be conducted using better measures of sleepwalking, probing for both the frequency of experiences and for the stage in the experiencer's life in which sleepwalking took place or was most frequent. Habitual sleepwalkers should also be compared to nonsleepwalkers in future studies. . . .

— Carlos S. Alvarado, *Journal of Parapsychology*, vol. 62, no. 4, 1998

8. Every species of plant or animal is determined by a pool of germ plasma that has been most carefully selected over a period of hundreds of millions of years.

We can understand now why it is that mutations in these carefully selected organisms almost invariably are detrimental. The situation can be suggested by a statement made by Dr. J.B.S. Haldane: my clock is not keeping perfect time. It is conceivable that it will run better if I shoot a bullet through it; but it is much more probable that it will stop altogether. Professor George Beadle, in this connection, has asked: "What is the chance that a typographical error would improve *Hamlet*?"

— Linus Pauling, *No More War*

9. *Ethics of using animals for experimental studies*

Every year we slaughter over 4 billion animals for meat and euthanize more than 10 million as unwanted pets. We have distanced ourselves far enough from the farm to forget that chicken, beef, fish, leather, and other animal products were once living, feeling beings. This distance allows us to behave irresponsibly, and to be influenced by extreme and inappropriate opinions. On one hand, we tend to dehumanize all animals and at the opposite extreme we treat other species as human surrogates.

The mythical garden of Eden in which there are no predators and consequently no prey does not exist on this planet. While the relationship between a snake and a mouse may seem ruthless and cruel, it is a part of the biology that supports the complex ecosystems of this planet. It is not a matter of choice. Every living animal costs other living things something, somewhere in their ecosystem.

Ethical convictions need not be logical, but when we put them into practice they at least need to be adaptive. Both dogs and monkeys were used in the development of the rabies vaccine, and that vaccine protects both owners and pets worldwide. The cost-benefit ratio of such research is favorable from most points of view. To not conduct the research is to put all who live in the future at avoidable risk.

Research should not be wasteful and it should be conducted with care, empathy, and respect. Primates should be used only for subjects that cannot be studied in more inexpensive species. However, if one wishes to learn about the specific biology of a particular primate, that species must, of course, be investigated.

Investigators do make mistakes, they have the same human foibles as the rest of the populace. Consequently, institutional monitoring, critical proposal reviews, and national standards of care are important to prevent abuse, waste, or neglect.

Primatologists, especially interested in behavior, have a reputation among researchers as animal advocates in their institutions.

Captive breeding is the only alternative for species that no longer have a natural habitat, and with sponsorship from Conservation International, there is a global captive action plan formulated by the International Union for Conservation of Nature and Natural Resources. Funding for captive breeding is minimal, and the reality is that financial resources tend to be invested in those species that are in demand as research subjects. Habitat loss due to the expansion of the human population is the most serious threat to many, if not all nonhuman primate species. We must understand our world and ultimately make compromises between short-term and long-term sustainability if we are to be intelligent, responsible custodians.

— Claud A. Bramblett, *Patterns of Primate Behavior,* 2nd edition.

Answers
3. This analogy breaks down. The person with the sense of smell will be right most of the time, in many different situations, and clearly so. No magician is going to find him out. Eventually, using brain scans and physical examinations, we could determine to some extent the mechanism behind his predictions, even if we ourselves couldn't experience them. But to date, claims about ESP can't be duplicated, even by the person claiming to have the powers; they are often debunked; they aren't right almost always but at best just a bit more than average. It's not just that we have lost motivation to investigate ESP because of so many false claims about it. We haven't even found a good candidate to study.
4. An argument. Conclusion: The force of pulsation (of the blood) does not belong to the artery, and the material contained in the arteries is not the producer of the pulsation. Additional premise needed to make it valid or strong: If when the artery is cut and replaced by a tube, the blood still pulses through the cannula and the part of the artery that is still connected above but not below does not pulse, then neither the blood nor the artery is what is causing the pulsation. Vesalius uses the experiments to show that the other person's claim is false directly. The argument is as good as the unstated premise and the experimental results are plausible.
5. The authors take great care that their experiment can be duplicated, and almost certainly it is reproducible. But you should have figured out by now that this doesn't make it a good experiment.
6. The authors suggest that the cause-in-population studies they cite show smoking causes lower back pain. But they could have cause and effect reversed: people who have back pain might want to smoke to take their minds off the pain or possibly even to alleviate the pain. Or there could be a common cause: people who do manual labor might smoke more, and the manual labor also causes back problems. Unless further cause-in-population studies can rule out those possibilities, this is just a correlation-causation fallacy.
7. Did you go glassy-eyed and get wowed by the statistics? They are meaningless. You should be able to note that the sample was not chosen randomly and has lots of room for bias. And even if the statistics did show a correlation between the responses, all that shows is that there is a correlation between the *responses people give on a*

questionnaire to whether they sleepwalk and whether they have parapsychological experiences. Or rather to whether someone has *told* them they sleepwalk. His conclusion assumes that there is a correlation between people saying they have parapsychological experiences and actually having those experiences. Even in this journal that takes for granted that there are parapsychological experiences, the correlation between reporting that you've had such an experience and actually having one has to be established. The whole study is nonsense.

8. Argument by analogy. Conclusion: Mutations in plants or animals are almost invariably detrimental. Comparison: Shooting a bullet through a clock that doesn't keep perfect time is like a mutation in the germ plasma of a plant or an animal. Making a typographical error in *Hamlet* is like a mutation in the germ plasma of a plant or animal. The dissimilarities are much too great for this to be a good analogy. Clocks and *Hamlet* are man-made and are designed in advance to perform some function or achieve some goal. To change them is to tinker with their design, whether that design is good or bad. But the whole point of evolutionary theory is to replace design and goals and purposes as the causes of why plants and animals are like they are now.

9. This is not an argument! The only possible conclusion would be the last sentence, but that is way too vague. Either you agree with what he says or you don't. Or perhaps you accept what he says because of his authority. But you shouldn't, because an animal researcher is not an expert on ethics. This is a good example of a scientist putting forward his views with authority, where he has no expertise, nonetheless expecting to be believed.

31 Models and Theories

What is a model? How do we determine if a model is good? How can we modify a model in the light of new evidence?

- *A map of Minersville, Utah—reasoning by analogy*

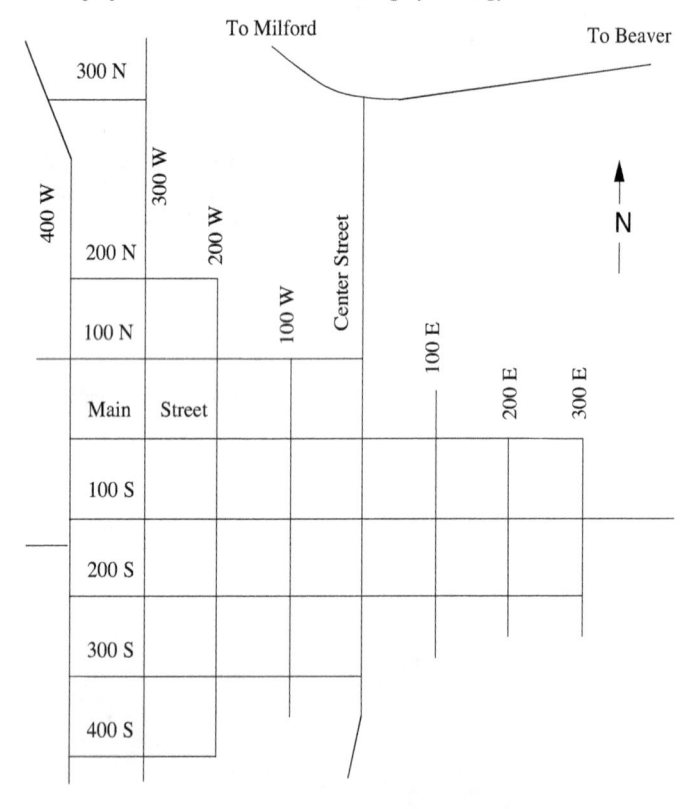

This is an accurate map of Minersville, Utah. Looking at it we can see that the streets are evenly spaced. For example, there is the same distance between 100 N and 200 N as between 100 E and 200 E. The last street to the east is 300 E. There is no paved road going north beyond Main Street on 200 E.

That is, from this map we can deduce claims about Minersville, even if we've never been there. But there is much we can't deduce: Are there hills in Minersville? Are there lots of trees? How wide are the streets? How far apart are the streets? Where are there houses?

The map is accurate for what it pays attention to: the relative location and orientation of streets. But it tells us nothing about what it ignores.

The differences between the map and Minersville aren't important when we infer that the north end of 200 W is at 200 N. In contrast, a scale model of a city or a mountain abstracts less from the actual terrain: height and perhaps placement of rivers and trees are there. The map of Minersville *abstracts more* from the actual terrain than a scale model of the city would—that is, *it ignores more*.

To use this model is to reason by analogy: we can draw conclusions when appropriate similarities are invoked and the differences don't matter. The general principle, in this example, is not stated explicitly. The discussion above suggests how we might formulate one, but it hardly seems worth the effort. We can "see" when someone has used a map well or badly.

• *Models of the solar system*

Here is a sketch of the model of the universe the Egyptian astronomer Ptolemy proposed in the second century A.D.

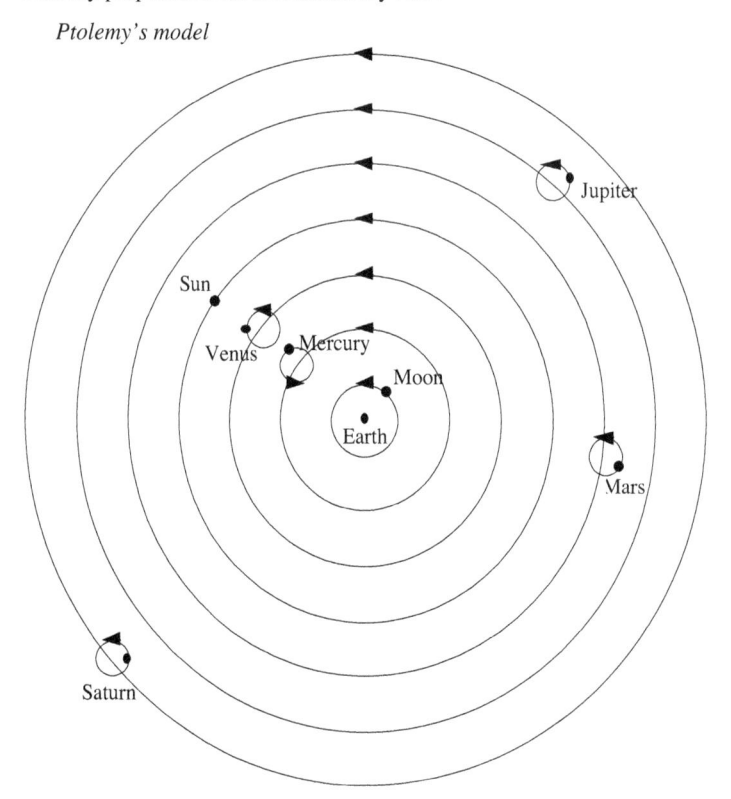

Ptolemy's model

It's meant to show the relative positions of the planets, sun, and moon, and the ways they move. We can't deduce anything about, say, the size of the planets, the distances between them, nor the speeds at which they move, because this model ignores those. According to this model, the moon, sun, and each of the planets revolves around the Earth in a circular orbit, all moving in the same direction. Along that orbit, each planet also revolves in a smaller circle, called an "epicycle." The sun, Earth, and Venus are always supposed to be in a line as shown in the picture.

Ptolemy made a lot more claims about the planets, Earth, and sun that were to be used in making predictions, but for our purposes this sketch will do.

Ptolemy's model accorded pretty well with observations of the movements of the planets and was the generally accepted way to understand the universe for many centuries. But in 1543 the Polish astronomer Copernicus published a book with a different model of the universe.

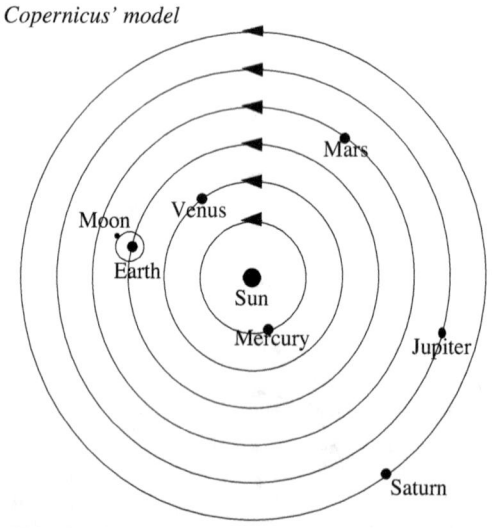

Copernicus' model

This sketch, too, abstracts a lot from what is being modeled. The sun is shown to be larger than the planets, but that's all we see about their relative sizes. We can't tell from the picture whether the orbits are all on the same plane or on different planes. We do see that the planets all revolve in the same direction and that the Earth, sun, and Venus do not always stay in line.

Ptolemy accounted for the motion of the sun, planets, and stars in the sky by saying they revolved around the Earth every 24 hours. Copernicus accounted for those motions by saying that the Earth revolved around its own axis every 24 hours. How could someone in the late 16th century decide between these two models? Both were in accord with the observations that had been made.

In the early 1600s the telescope was invented, and in 1610 Galileo built his own telescope with a magnification of about 33 times, using it to study the skies. One of his students suggested an experiment that might distinguish between the Ptolemaic and Copernican models. Venus was too far from the Earth to be seen as anything other than a spot of light. But according to Ptolemy's model, viewed from the Earth, at most only a small crescent-shaped part of Venus will be illuminated by the sun. From Copernicus' model, however, we can deduce that from the Earth, Venus should go through all the phases of illumination, just like the moon: full, half, crescent, dark, and back again. Galileo looked at Venus through his telescope for a period of time and saw that it exhibited all phases of illumination, and this he took to be proof that Copernicus' model was correct.

Not a lot of other people were convinced, however. Telescopes were rare and not very reliable: they introduced optical illusions, such as halos, from the imperfections in the glass and the mounting. Why should astronomers have trusted Galileo's observations?

It was more due to Newton that something like Copernicus' model of the universe was finally accepted. Newton deduced from his laws of motion that the orbits of the Earth, sun, and the planets would have to be ellipses, not circles. And the distances between them would have to be much greater than supposed. Using Newton's laws, Edmond Halley predicted correctly the return of a comet that had been observed in 1682. Telescopes were better, with fewer optical illusions, and they were common enough that most astronomers could use one, so better and better observations of the planets and stars could be made. Those observations could be deduced from the Copernican-Newtonian model, while new epicycles had to be invented to account for them in the Ptolemaic model.

Note that each model is supposed to be similar to the universe in only a few respects, ones that would have an effect on how we could see the objects in the universe from the Earth. Differences, such as whether Venus is rocky or gaseous, are not supposed to matter for those observations. If the model is correct, then reasoning by analogy—very precise analogy—certain claims can be deduced.

• *The kinetic theory of gases—getting true predictions doesn't mean the model is true*
This theory is based on the following postulates, or assumptions.
1. Gases are composed of a large number of particles that behave like hard, spherical objects in a state of constant, random motion.

2. The particles move in a straight line until they collide with another particle or the walls of the container.

3. The particles are much smaller than the distance between the particles. Most of the volume of a gas is therefore empty space.

4. There is no force of attraction between gas particles or between the particles and the walls of the container.

5. Collisions between gas particles or collisions with the walls of the container are perfectly elastic. Energy can be transferred from one particle to another during a collision, but the total kinetic energy of the particles after the collision is the same as it was before the collision.

6. The average kinetic energy of a collection of gas particles depends on the temperature of the gas and nothing else.

— J. Spencer, G. Bodner, and L. Rickard, *Chemistry*

Here is a picture of what is supposed to be going on in a gas in a closed container. The molecules of gas are represented as dots, as if they were hard spherical balls. The length of the line emanating from a particle models the particle's speed; the arrow models the direction in which the particle is moving.

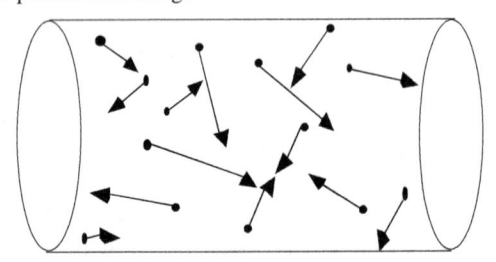

The kinetic energy of a particle is defined in terms of its mass and velocity: kinetic energy = .5 mass x velocity^2. The model defines what is meant for a collision to be elastic. In contrast, here is a picture of what happens in an inelastic collision between a rubber ball and the floor.

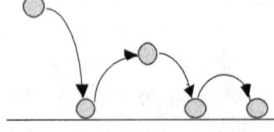

Each time the ball hits the ground, some of its kinetic energy is lost either through being transferred to the floor or in compressing the ball.

What are we to make of these assumptions? Some are false: molecules of gas are not generally spherical and are certainly not solid; the collisions between molecules and the walls of a container or each other are not perfectly elastic; there is some gravitational attraction between the particles and each other and also with the container. How can we use false claims in a model?

The model proceeds by abstraction, much like in analogy: to the extent that we can ignore how molecules of gases are not spherical, and ignore physical attraction between molecules, and ignore . . . we can draw conclusions that may be applicable to actual gases. To the extent that the differences between actual gases and the abstractions don't matter, we can draw conclusions. But how can we tell if the differences matter?

The model suggests that the pressure of a gas results from the collisions between the gas particles and the walls of the container. So if the container is made smaller for the same amount of gas, the pressure should increase; and if the container is made larger, the pressure should be less. So the pressure should be proportional to the inverse of the volume of the gas. That is, the model suggests a claim about the relationship of pressure to volume in a gas. Experiments can be performed, varying the pressure or volume, and they are close to being in accord with that claim.

Other laws are suggested by the model: Pressure is proportional to the temperature of the gas, where the temperature is taken to be the average kinetic energy of the gas. The volume of the gas should be proportional to the temperature. The amount of gas should be proportional to the pressure. All of these are confirmed by experiment.

Those experiments confirming predictions from the model do not mean the model is more accurate than we thought. Collisions still aren't really elastic; molecules aren't really hard spherical balls. The kinetic theory of gases is a model that is useful, as with any analogy, when the differences don't matter.

• *The acceleration of falling objects—an equation can be a model*
Galileo argued that falling objects accelerate as they fall: they begin falling slowly and fall faster and faster the farther they fall. He didn't need any mathematics to show that. He just noted that a heavy stone dropped from 6 feet will drive a stake into the ground much farther than if it were dropped from 6 inches.

He also said that the reason a feather falls more slowly than an iron ball when dropped is because of the resistance of air. He argued that at a given location on the Earth and in the absence of air resistance, all objects should fall with the same acceleration. He claimed that the distance traveled by a falling object is proportional to the square of the time it travels. Today, from many measurements, the equation is given by:

$$d = 1/2 \; 9.82 \text{ meters }/\text{sec}^2 \cdot t^2 \quad \text{where } t \text{ is time in seconds}$$

This equation is a model by abstraction: we ignore air resistance and the shape of the object, considering only the object's mass and center of gravity. If the differences don't matter, then a calculation from the equation, which is really a deduction, will hold. But often the differences do matter. Air resistance can slow down an object: if you drop a cat from an airplane, it will spread out its legs and reach a maximum velocity when the force of the air resistance equals the force of acceleration.

With this model there is no visual representation of that part of experience that is being described. There is no point-to-point conceptual comparison, nor are we modeling a static situation. The model is couched in the language of mathematics; equations can be models, too.

- *Newton's laws of motion and Einstein's theory of relativity—how a false theory can be used*

Newton's laws of motion are taught in every elementary physics course and are used daily by physicists. Yet modern physics has replaced Newton's theories with Einstein's and quantum mechanics. Newton's laws, physicists tell us, are false.

But can't we say that Newton's laws are correct relative to the quality of measurements involved, even though Newton's laws can't be derived from quantum mechanics? Or perhaps they can if a premise is added that we ignore certain small effects. Yet how is that part of a theory?

A theory is a schematic representation of some part of the world. We draw conclusions from the representation (we calculate or deduce). The conclusion is said to apply to the world. The reasoning is legitimate so long as the differences between the representation and what is being represented don't matter. Newton's laws of motion are "just like" how moderately large objects interact at moderately low speeds; we can use those laws to make calculations so long as the differences don't matter. Some of the assumptions of that theory are used as conditions to tell us when the theory is meant to be applied.

- *Ether as the medium of light waves—a prediction can show that an assumption of a theory is false*

In the 19th century light was understood as waves. In analogy with waves in water or sound waves in the air, a medium was postulated for the propagation of light waves: the ether. Using that assumption, many predictions were made about the path and speed of light in terms of its wave behavior. Attempts then were made to isolate or verify the existence of an ether. The experiments of Michelson and Morley showed those predictions were false. When a better theory was postulated by Einstein, *one that assumed no ether and gave as good or better predictions in all cases where the ether assumption did, the theory of ether was abandoned.*

- *Euclidean plane geometry—a model that can't be true*

Euclidean plane geometry speaks of points and lines: a point is location without dimension, a line is extension without breadth. No such objects exist in our experience. But Euclidean geometry is remarkably useful in measuring and calculating distances and positions in our daily lives.

Points are abstractions of very small dots made by a pencil or other implement. Lines are abstractions of physical lines, either drawn or sighted. So long as the differences don't matter, that is, so long as the size of the points and the lines are very small relative to what is being measured or plotted, we can deduce conclusions that are true.

No one asks (anymore) whether the axioms of Euclidean geometry are true. Rather, when the differences don't matter, we can calculate and predict using Euclidean geometry. When the differences do matter, as in calculating paths of airplanes circling the globe, Euclidean plane geometry does not apply, and another model, geometry for spherical surfaces, is invoked.

Euclidean geometry is a deductive theory: a conclusion drawn from the axioms is accepted only if the inference is valid. It is a purely mathematical theory, which taken as mathematics would appear to have no application since the objects of which it speaks do not exist. But taken as a model it has applications in the usual way, arguing by analogy where the differences don't matter.

Models, analogies, and abstraction

We've seen models of static situations (the map) and of processes (acceleration of falling objects). We've seen examples of models that are entirely visual and of models formulated entirely in terms of mathematical equations. We've seen models in which the assumptions of the model are entirely implicit (the map), and we have seen models in which the assumptions are quite explicit (Galileo's laws of acceleration).

In all the examples either the reasoning is clearly reasoning by analogy or can be seen to proceed by abstraction much as in reasoning by analogy. We do not ask whether the assumptions of a theory or model are true, even if that was the intention of the person who created the theory. Rather, we ask whether we can use it in the given situation: do the similarities that are being invoked hold and do the differences not matter? Even in the case of Newton's laws of motion, where it would seem that what is at stake is whether the assumptions are true, we continue to use the model when we know that the assumptions are false in those cases where, as in any analogy, the differences don't matter. In only one example (the ether) did it seem that what was at issue was whether a particular assumption of the theory was actually true of the world

The assumptions of theories in science are false when we consider them as representing all aspects of some particular part of our experience. The key claim in every analogy is false in the same way. When we say that one side of an analogy is "just like" the other, that's false. What is true is that they are "like" one another in some key respects that allow us to deduce claims for the one from deducing claims for the other.

The term **model** is typically applied to what can be visualized or made concrete, while **theory** seems to be used for examples that are fairly formal with explicitly stated assumptions. But in many cases it is as appropriate to call an example a theory as to call it a model, and there seems to be no definite distinction between those terms.

> *The atomic model of matter has gone through many refinements. At one time or another, atoms were imagined to be tiny spheres with hooks on them (to explain chemical bonding), or as tiny billiard balls continually bouncing against each other. More recently, the "planetary model" of the atom visualized the atom as a nucleus with electrons revolving around it, just as the planets revolve around the sun.*
>
> — D.C. Giancoli, *Physics,* 2nd edition, 1985

Giancoli describes various models of the atom as they were used to help visualize the working of something we can't see. What isn't mentioned, however, are all the other claims about the workings of the atom that were made in conjunction with those pictures, claims from which predictions about the behavior of chemical compounds could be made. Those claims, along with the similarities between atoms and the models that were proposed, constituted the atomic theory of that time.

Confirming a theory

From theories we can make predictions. When a prediction turns out to be true, we say it **confirms** (to some degree) the theory.

This is not to say that the claims that make up a theory—the assumptions of the theory—are true or false. Verifications of the relation of pressure, temperature, and volume in a gas do not confirm that molecules are hard little balls and that all collisions are completely elastic. Fitting a carpenter's square exactly into a wooden triangle that is 50 cm x 40 cm x 30 cm does not confirm the theorem of Pythagoras. Nor can we say that finding a tree at the corner of 100 W and 100 S in Minersville disconfirms the model given by the map. We can only say of a theory such as Euclidean plane geometry or the kinetic theory of gases that it is **applicable** in a particular situation we are investigating.

To say that a theory is applicable is to say that, though there are differences between the world and what the assumptions of the theory state, those differences don't matter for the conclusions we wish to draw. We use the theory to draw conclusions in particular cases, claiming that the differences don't matter. If the conclusions—the predictions—turn out to be true (enough), then we have some confidence that we're right. If a prediction turns out false, then the model is not applicable there. We do not say that Euclidean plane geometry is false because it cannot be used to calculate the path of an airplane on the globe; we say that Euclidean plane geometry is inapplicable for calculating on globes.

When we make predictions and they are true, we confirm a **range of application** of a model. When we make predictions and they are false, we disconfirm a range of application—that is, we find limits for the range of application of a model. More information about where the model can be applied and where it cannot be applied may lead to our describing more precisely the range of application of a model. In that case, the claims describing the range of application can be added to the theory. We often use mathematics as a language to make this art of analogy precise. But in many cases it is difficult to state precisely the range of application. Reasoning using models is reasoning by analogy, which is likely to require judgment.

Sometimes it's said that a theory is valid, or is true, or that a theory holds. These are just different ways to assert that a particular situation or class of situations to which we wish to apply a theory is within the range of that theory.

Theories are tools, not statements of fact.

Modifying theories in the light of new evidence

Consider what we do when we discover that a prediction made from a theory is false.

When Newton's laws of motion result in inaccurate predictions for very small objects, we note that the theory had been assumed true for all sizes and speeds of objects, so we restrict the range of application. But when the theory of the ether resulted in false predictions, no modification was made to the theory, for none could be made. That theory did not abstract from experience, ignoring some aspects of situations under consideration, but postulated something in addition to our experience, which we were able to show did not exist. The theory was completely abandoned.

If a theory has been made by abstraction—that is, many aspects of our experience are ignored and only a few are considered significant— then tracing back along that **path of abstraction** we can try to distinguish what difference there is between our model and our experience that matters. What have we ignored that cannot in this situation be ignored? If we cannot state generally what the difference is that matters, then at best the false prediction sets some limit on the range of applicability of the model or theory. We cannot use the theory here—where "here" means this situation or ones that we can see are very similar.

But our goal will be to state precisely the difference that matters and try to factor it into our theory. We try to devise a complication of our theory in which that aspect of our experience is taken into account. As with Einstein's improvement of Newton's laws, we get a better theory that is more widely applicable and that explains why the old theory worked as well as it did and why it failed in the ways it failed. We improve the map: by adding more assumptions, we can pay attention to more in our experience, and that accounts for the differences between the theories.

Sometimes we are confronted with two theories that both yield good predictions for a class of situations and both of which have a clear path of abstraction. In that case, we say that one theory is **better** than another if:

- Its assumptions are simpler.
- It yields clearer derivations of the claims it is meant to explain.
- It has a wider range of application.

• *Consider the density of leaves around a tree. I suggest the hypothesis that the leaves are positioned as if each leaf deliberately sought to maximize the amount of sunlight it receives, given the position of its neighbors, as if it knew the physical laws determining the amount of sunlight that would be received in various positions and could move rapidly or instantaneously from any one position to any other desired and unoccupied position. Now some of the more obvious implications of this hypothesis are clearly consistent with experience: for example, leaves are in general denser on the south than on the north side of trees but, as the hypothesis implies, less so or not at all on the northern slope of a hill or when the south side of the trees is shaded in some other way. Is the hypothesis rendered unacceptable or invalid because, so far as we know, leaves do not 'deliberate' or consciously 'seek,' have not been to school and learned the relevant laws of science or the mathematics to calculate the 'optimum' position, and cannot move from position to position? Clearly, none of these contradictions of the hypothesis is vitally relevant; the phenomena involved are not within the 'class of phenomena the hypothesis is designed to explain'; the hypothesis does not assert that leaves do these things but only that their density is the same as if they did. Despite the apparent falsity of the 'assumptions' of the hypothesis, it has great plausibility because of the conformity of its implications with observation. We are inclined to 'explain' its validity on the ground that sunlight contributes to the growth of leaves and that hence leaves will grow denser or more putative leaves survive where there is more sun, so the result achieved by purely passive adaptation to external circumstances is the same as the result that would be achieved by deliberate accommodation to them. This alternative hypothesis is more attractive than the constructed hypothesis not because its 'assumptions' are more 'realistic' but rather because it is part of a more general theory that applies to a wider variety of phenomena, of which the position of leaves around a tree is a special case, has more implications capable of being contradicted, and has failed to be contradicted under a wider variety of circumstances.*

— Milton Friedman, "The Methodology of Positive Economics"

Friedman's hypothesis about leaves seeking to maximize the amount of sunlight they receive cannot be used for reasoning by analogy or abstraction. It does not begin by either (a) looking at a real situation and comparing it to the growth of leaves, allowing us to distinguish the similarities and the differences, or (b) abstracting from experience to state the points of similarity that are supposed to hold, ignoring all else.

Rather, what he has posited is not an abstraction, but the addition of properties to a given situation. We are asked to suppose that leaves behave anthropomorphically with the skills of a terrific calculator. And then we are asked to ignore that as well. This doesn't make sense as a method of reasoning: why should we have confidence that predictions made from such a hypothesis will be accurate? That some of the predictions turn out to be accurate cannot be enough, any more than they are in astrology. We need to know why they turn out accurate in order to have confidence in the theory or model.

The alternative hypothesis of passive adaptation that Friedman presents is better, but not for the reasons he gives; rather, it is better for the reason he says is not meaningful. Namely, we have better reason to accept the alternative hypothesis precisely because we can see that in this case it is reasonable to believe it is true. No clearly false assumption incapable of fitting into reasoning by analogy or abstraction has been made.

Constructing models and theories and evaluating them are the basic work of science. Doing that well depends on understanding the following ideas:

- Model.
- Theory.
- A model is an analogy.
- An equation can be a model.
- A prediction confirms a theory.
  But a true prediction does not show that the assumptions of a theory are true.
- Range of application of a theory.
- Modifying a theory in light of new evidence.
- Path of abstraction.
- One theory is better than another.

32 Explanations in Science

Is a theory an explanation?
Sometimes it's said that a theory gives a good explanation of some claim. It's said, for example, that Einstein's general relativity explains why there's no difference in speed between light moving with the direction of the earth and light moving across the path of the Earth. But that's a loose way of talking. A theory does not explain; a deduction from a theory can be an explanation.

> • *The new theory, although it has to explain what the old theory explained, corrects the old theory, so that it actually contradicts the old theory: it contains the old theory, but only as an approximation. Thus I pointed out that Newton's theory contradicts both Kepler's and Galileo's theory —although it explains them, owing to the fact that it contains them as approximations; and similarly Einstein's theory contradicts Newton's, which it likewise explains, and contains as an approximation.*
> — Karl Popper, *Objective Knowledge*

Wrong. You can't explain anything using false claims, and you certainly can't explain a claim that contradicts the claim doing the explaining. Here, as with many theories, it makes no sense to say that the premises are true but rather that the theory as a whole is applicable. Popper is conflating theories with explanations.

> • *Consider the explanation offered by Torricelli for a fact that had intrigued his teacher Galileo; namely, that a lift pump drawing water from a well will not raise the water more than about 34 feet above the surface of a well. To account for this, Torricelli advanced the idea that the air above the water has weight and thus exerts pressure on the water in the well, forcing it up the pump barrel when the piston is raised, for there is no air inside to balance the outside pressure. On this assumption the water can rise only to the point where its pressure on the surface of the well equals the pressure of the outside air on that surface, and the latter will therefore equal that of a water column about 34 feet high.*
>
> *The explanatory force of this account hinges on the conception that the earth is surrounded by a "sea of air" that conforms to the basic laws governing the equilibrium of liquids in communicating vessels. And because Torricelli's explanation presupposed such general laws it yielded predictions concerning as yet unexamined phenomena. One of these was that if the water were replaced by mercury, whose specific gravity is about 14 times that of water, the air should counterbalance a column*

about 34/14 feet, or somewhat less than $2^1/_2$ feet, in length. This prediction was confirmed by Torricelli in the classic experiment that bears his name. In addition, the proposed explanation implies that at increasing altitudes above sea level, the length of the mercury column supported by air pressure should decrease because the weight of the counterbalancing air decreases. A careful test of this prediction was performed at the suggestion of Pascal only a few years after Torricelli had offered his explanation: Pascal's brother-in-law carried a mercury barometer (i.e., essentially a mercury column counterbalanced by the air pressure) to the top of the Puy-de-Dôme, measuring the length of the column at various elevations during the ascent and again during the descent; the readings were in splendid accord with the prediction.

— Carl G. Hempel, *Aspects of Scientific Explanation*

Torricelli offered an explanation, but the only evidence he had for the explanation, which was a generalization, was the claim being explained. So he made predictions of further instances of the generalization or of consequences of the claim doing the explaining; those were shown to be true. The claim doing the explaining thus became more plausible because the associated argument for it was strengthened.

Insight and general laws

An explanation is not meant to convince that the claim doing the explaining is true. It's meant to give us some insight into why what's being explained is true. But what do we mean by "insight"?

• *From accounts given by gunners, I was already aware of the fact that in the use of cannon and mortars, the maximum range . . . is obtained when the elevation is 45° . . . ; but to understand why this happens far outweighs the mere information obtained by the testimony of others or even by repeated experiment.*

— Galileo, *Dialogues Concerning Two New Sciences*

The insight, it's often said, is a law that connects the claim being explained to other experiences. But what's a "law" or "general principle"? It's a claim that's needed to strengthen an inferential explanation that must somehow link what's being explained to other claims we know to be true, somehow place what's being explained within our general knowledge. A good inferential explanation must show what the claim being explained follows from and must lead us to a place where we can stop asking "Why?". That often is the role of a theory, connecting many explanations into one general view of a part of the world.

The best explanation
Some scientists think that if you have the best explanation, one that explains a lot, it must be true.

> • It can hardly be supposed that a false theory would explain, in so satisfactory a manner as does the theory of natural selection, the several large classes of facts above specified [the geographical distribution of species, the existence of vestigial organs in animals, etc.]. It has recently been objected that this is an unsafe method of arguing; but it is a method used in judging of the common events of life, and has often been used by the greatest natural philosophers.
> — Charles Darwin, *On the Origin of Species*, p. 476

If Darwin was right, why did scientists spend the next hundred years trying to confirm or disprove the hypothesis of natural selection? Only now do we believe that a revised version of Darwin's hypotheses are true. Darwin fell into the fallacy of inference to the best explanation.

Scientists have high hopes for their hypotheses and are motivated to investigate them if they appear to provide a better explanation than current theories. But the scientific community will soon correct a scientist if he or she thinks that just making an hypothesis establishes it as true. Torricelli had more sense than that.

> *this is the best explanation we have*
> = *this is a good hypothesis to investigate*

Try your hand at these!
1. Evaluate the following argument for why we should believe the law of gravitation and the laws of Galileo and Kepler.

   If you accept the law of gravitation, the laws of Galileo and Kepler, the lunary motions and the tides will, as a matter of course, be systematically explained and cast into a universal mechanics.
   But why should I? The empirical truth of the law is not directly obvious, nor can what it asserts be easily grasped.
   Because if you accept it all these things will, as a matter of course, be systematically explained and cast into a universal mechanics. What could be a better reason?
   — Russell Norwood Hansen, *Patterns of Discovery*

   For 2–4, decide if it is an explanation. If it is one, say whether it's inferential, teleological, and whether it's causal, and then evaluate it.
2. The gas has temperature 83° C because it has pressure 7 kg/cm^2 and volume 807 cm^3.
3. The call of a male Majorcan midwife toad keeps females ripening their eggs in anticipation of sex, a new study shows.

Jerry Lea, a postgraduate student at the Open University in Milton Keynes, has studied three groups of female Majorcan midwife toads, *Alytes muletensis*. All the toads had ripening eggs in their ovaries. To one group, Lea played a synthesized version of the male calls. A second group heard the call of a different species, while the third heard no calls.

After a month, females from the first group had many eggs that were ripe and ready for ovulation, while the females in the other two groups had hardly any ripe eggs. Lea speculates that stimulation of the female's auditory nerve fibres causes hormone release in the part of the brain that controls reproductive behavior.

The finding makes sense given the sex roles of Majorcan midwife toads, says Lea. The males are in short supply because after fertilising the eggs they are celibate for a month while they raise the brood on their own. "The males carry the eggs down the cliff faces to the pools where they develop into tadpoles," says Lea.

Meanwhile, females squabble over remaining males, who advertise their readiness to mate by calling. Some females don't find a partner for the entire breeding season.

There's no point in wasting energy ripening eggs that have no hope of being fertilised, Lea says. —Alison Motluk, *New Scientist*, May 15, 1999

4. Like multiple sclerosis, poliomyelitis in its paralytic form was a disease of the more advanced nations rather than of the less advanced ones, and of economically better off people rather than of the poor. It occurred in northern Europe and North America much more frequently than in southern Europe or the countries of Africa, Asia or South America. Immigrants to South Africa from northern Europe ran twice the risk of contracting paralytic poliomyelitis than South-African-born whites ran, and the South-African-born whites ran a much greater risk than nonwhites did. Among the Bantu of South Africa paralytic poliomyelitis was rarely an adult disease. During World War II in North Africa cases of paralytic poliomyelitis were commoner among officers in the British and American forces than among men in the other ranks. At the time various wild hypotheses for the difference were proposed; it was even suggested that it arose from the fact that the officers drank whiskey whereas men in the other ranks drank beer!

We now understand very well the reason for the strange distribution of paralytic poliomyelitis. Until this century poliomyelitis was a universal infection of infancy and infants hardly ever suffered paralysis from it. The fact that they were occasionally affected is what gave the disease the name "infantile paralysis." With the improvement of hygiene in the advancing countries of the world more and more people missed infection in early childhood and contracted the disease for the first time at a later age, when the risk that the infection will cause paralysis is much greater.

This explains why the first epidemics of poliomyelitis did not occur until this century and then only in the economically advanced countries.

— G. Dean, "The multiple sclerosis problem," *Scientific American*, 1970

5. "Why do birds fly? Because it was a useful trait that helped them survive."
   a. This is an example of a teleological explanation. What unstated assumptions are needed?
   b. How does the theory of evolution avoid invoking a guiding intelligence in its (apparently) teleological explanations?

6. In the 17th century it was believed that worms and flies were spontaneously generated from mud and rotting or putrefying material. Here is how Francisco Redi argued against that:

> I began to believe that all worms found in meat were derived directly from the droppings of flies, and not from the putrefaction of meat, and I was still more confirmed in this belief by having observed that, before the meat grew wormy, flies had hovered over it, of the same kind as those that later bred in it. Belief would be in vain without the confirmation of experiment, hence in the middle of July I put a snake, some fish, some eels from the Arno and a slice of milk-fed veal in four large wide-mouthed flasks; having well closed and sealed them, I then filled the same number of flasks in the same way, only leaving these open. It was not long before the meat and fish, in these second vessels, became wormy and flies were seen entering and leaving at will; but in the closed flasks I did not see a worm though many days had passed since the dead flesh had been put in them. Outside on the paper cover there was now and then a deposit, or a maggot that eagerly sought some crevice by which to enter and obtain nourishment. Meanwhile the different things placed in the flasks had become putrid and stinking.
>
> — Francisco Redi, *Experiments in the Generation of Insects* (1688), translated by Mab Bigelow, 1909, in *The Origins and Growth of Biology*, ed. Arthur Rook

a. What other explanation could there be for why there were no worms in the sealed containers?

b. What other experiment(s) could you perform to show whether Redi is right? Remember that in Redi's time reliable microscopes were not available.

(See Redi's paper for the other possibilities that Redi thought of.)

Answers

1. This is an example of the fallacy of inference to the best explanation.
2. This is a good explanation if the claims are true. But it's not causal because the pressure, volume, and temperature all occur at the same time. Explanations that invoke a law that gives a correlation, such as this one that assumes Boyle's law, are inferential but not causal.
3. The cause-in-population claim "The call of a male Majorcan midwife toad keeps females ripening their eggs in anticipation of sex" is not the explanation; it's what needs to be explained. If all that the text says is true, then it might be a good teleological explanation. Possibly it could be rewritten in terms of some evolutionary fitness inference, but it's hard to see how.
4. Did you spot that Dean says he's explaining "The first epidemics of poliomyelitis did not occur until this century and then only in the economically advanced countries", yet if his premises are true, they show that there must have been *more* cases of nonparalytic polio previously. So at best he explains why there were more cases of *paralytic* polio.

    However, he also explains "Paralytic poliomyelitis was much more prevalent in advanced nations than in less advanced ones." That explanation is inferential and causal, and it's fairly strong if supplemented by some plausible premises. So it's as good as the plausibility of the claims doing the explaining. And we need evidence

for those, unless you're willing to rely on this author's word and the reliability of the magazine, which is in doubt since he missed so badly on the first explanation.
5. The theory of evolution is not teleological. Instead, the basic premise is that mutations occur. Most mutations are either not expressed or lead to a form that does not survive. Sometimes, however, a random mutation leads to an organism that is better able to survive and lives long enough to reproduce. Organisms that have a better chance of reproducing are likely to spread their genes. There is no invocation of a guiding intelligence but only a process that relies on random occurrences.

33 Ways of Knowing

There are many ways of knowing. Science claims to be the best. But religions claim insights known only through revelation that science cannot lead us to. The Zen master claims to teach without words, by actions, an insight deeper than words can give. The shepherd training his dog learns from his dog and knows the nature of his dog and sheep in a way that science cannot describe. There are many ways of knowing.

But there are also ways of pretense and confusion. The charlatan preys on the gullibility of the many to convince them she knows the spirits of the dead. The ESP researcher has so much faith in what he wishes to show that he convinces himself that what is accidental is sure.

Why do scientists claim pride of place in the ways of knowledge? Because they are willing to test every belief they have. No claim is above suspicion. Even the rules of logic can and have been challenged. To be a scientist is, above all, to make claims that you are willing to test, to leave open to disproof, to make public. Science is a public kind of knowledge, and a verbal kind of knowledge.

Religion differs. Some claims are beyond challenge. You cannot hope to gain insight through the religion if you do not accept those claims. And those claims cannot be tested. Or, in the case of Zen and the roads of mysticism, knowledge comes only when all claims have been thrown away.

Magic seeks a middle way, invoking powers that cannot be shown through the methods of science. Magic, not the magic of the circus or Las Vegas but magic that believes, attempts to control the universe. That is what science does, too. But science attempts control through understanding the mechanisms via experiments, arguments, and explanations. Magic attempts to control through rituals and incantations. Any failure of an attempt to control is explained away.

Science is supposed to lead to understanding, prediction, and control of the world in which we live. Religion is supposed to lead to understanding, but control is only in the hands of higher powers. Magic is supposed to lead to control, but understanding is only understanding of the rituals that work to control. The lines between science, magic, and religion are not so clearly drawn that we cannot doubt that science ending at points beyond its understanding does not merge with religion, or that religion that leads to nonverbal understanding does not share many methods with science. And magic shares so many traits with both that we have a spectrum, not a division of ways of knowing. But it is the fallacy of drawing the line to say that because we cannot make a sharp division between science, magic, and religion, there is no difference.

We've seen that to reason well we must imagine the possibilities. Yet there are possibilities that science and reasoning will not countenance because they are not verbal or cannot be tested, either directly or through their consequences, and it is a narrow mind that ignores too many possibilities.

The insight—more than feeling—that strikes us on a quiet riverside at dusk when birds are settling in the trees, the sun setting above the leaves of the oaks, is not to be discounted because it cannot be replicated or even expressed. The insight that strikes suddenly on a crowded street in traffic, in the midst of pushing and bright lights, that changes a life in an instant is not to be derided for being ineffable. There are good reasons to believe that are not public, that are not verbal, that are not in the path of science—this is beyond doubt. Even science itself in psychology can establish that there are tasks we cannot perform, such as driving, if we reflect and try to say what we are doing.

But to wish to know is not to know, and to wish to believe is not good reason to believe. The false ways of knowing, the charlatans, the self-duped, the too eager to be convinced, their ways we can avoid, and the methods of this book are useful tools in the fight to avoid self-deception.

There are many ways of knowing. Here we've learned one of them.

Index

Abd-el-Kader, 44
abstracting in science, Chapter 31
　abstracting more, 211
　path of —, 220–222
absurd, reducing to the, 64–67, 79
accepting/rejecting a claim, Chapter 8
　criteria for, 37
act of God, 167
ad hominem. *See* mistaking the person for the argument; mistaking the person for the claim.
advertising, 38
affirming the consequent, 77
"all"-claim, 83
　contradictory of, 85
"almost all"-claim, 87–88
alternatives, 70
ambiguous sentence, 4–5
analogy, 108
　generalizing and, 109, 124, 142
　legal reasoning and, 112–113
　refuting an argument by —, 66, 111
　science models and —, Chapter 31
　steps in evaluating, 110
anecdotal evidence, 120
antecedent of a conditional, 72
anthropomorphism, 160
appeal to authority, bad, 41
　scientists, 61
appeal to common belief, 42
appeal to emotion, 56–57
appeal to fear, 56
appeal to pity, 56
appeal to spite, 57
appeal to vanity, 57
apples and oranges comparison, 96
application, range of, 218
applying a theory, 218–219

arguing backwards, 52. *See also* affirming the consequent; backwards reasoning; inference to the best explanation.
arguing backwards with "all", 85, 87
arguing backwards with "no", 86, 88
argument, 26
　associated — of an explanation, 154–156
　bad — tells us nothing, 29, 53, 110
　explanations and, 150, 154–156
　good —, 25
　tests for, 28
　checking for validity/strength, 27
　strong, 26
　unrepairable, 53. *See also* fallacy.
　valid, 26
　weak, 35
associated argument of an explanation, 154–156
astrology, 123–124, 199, 203, 222
authority,
　accepting a claim because of, 36, 37, 44
　bad appeal to, 41–42, 61
　scientist is —?. *See* scientist as authority.
average (mean), 94
　regression to the —, 198

backwards reasoning, 52, 78, 85, 87, 86, 88, 123, 157
base of a comparison, 92–93, 96, 98, 101,
begging the question, 28
behavioral explanation, 153
belief, right to, 61

232 Index

believing a claim, choices for, 34
bell-shaped graph, 95–96
bias, positive publication, 201–202
bias, self-selection, 201
biased sample, 117
burden of proof, 19, 153

causal claim, 127
causal explanation, 153–153
    teleological isn't, 168
causal factor, 135
cause and effect, Chapter 21
    a cause, 135
    assuming there is one, 185
    coincidence and, 132
    common cause, 130
    conjecturing a 184–185, ???
    correlation isn't —, 133, 135, 136
    false dilemma and —, 185
    foreseeable consequence, 135
    general causal claim, 127
    intervening cause, 136
    joint cause, 135
    looking too hard for, 132–133
    necessary conditions for, 130
    normal conditions for, 129
    particular causal claim, 127
    post hoc ergo propter hoc, 133
    reversing —, 132
    scientific method and —, 184–185
    subjective causal claim, 134
    testable claims and, 136
    tracing too far back, 131–132
cause in a population, Chapter 22
    definition of, 141
cause-in-population controlled
    experiment, 142
circular explanation, 151
claim, 2. *See also kind of claim,*
    e.g. subjective claim.
Clever Hans, 197–198
Clever Hans effect, 198

coincidence, 128, 132–133
common belief, appeal to, 42
common cause, 130
composition, fallacy of, 110–111
compound claim, 70
conclusion, 22
    follows from premises, 27
    indicator, 30
conditional claim, 72
    contradictory of, 73
    hypothesis and, 79–80
confidence level, 122
confirming a theory, 216–217
consequent of a conditional, 72
constant conjunction. *See* cause
    and effect, correlation isn't.
conspiracy theory, 42, 158
contradictory,
    of a conditional, 73
    of a general claim, 85
    of an "and" claim, 72
    of an "or" claim, 72
contrapositive, 74
control group, 141
controlled cause-in-population
    experiment, 141–142
correlation-causation fallacy, 133
counterarguments, 63–67

Darwin, Charles, 225
decisions, Chapter 26
definition, 7
    criteria for good, 8
    in science, 181
    persuasive, 8, 17
    steps in making, 9
    too broad or too narrow, 8
deleting a premise, 48, 52, 53
democracy, 47
denying the antecedent, 78
dependent explanation, 155
descriptive claim, 15–16

direct way of reasoning
  with "all", 85
direct way of reasoning with
  conditionals, 77
direct way of reasoning with
  with "no", 86
direct ways of refuting
  an argument, 65
disjunction. See "or"-claim.
disjunctive syllogism. See
  excluding possibilities.
double-blind trial, 199–200
downplayer, 18
drawing the line fallacy, 3–4
dubious claim, 27
duplicable experiment, 188
dysphemism, 17

economics is a science?, 188
effect. See cause and effect.
effect-to-cause experiment, 142
Einstein, Albert, 202, 216–217,
  220, 223
emotion, appeal to, Chapter 11
ESP, 191–192, 202, 203, 206–207, 229
ethology, 187–188, 189–191, 201
euphemism, 17
Evans, Frederick J., 199–200
evidence,
  anecdotal, 120
  inductive, 116
  lack of — ≠ false, 34
evolution, theory of, 203, 209,
  228–229
excluding possibilities, 70
excuse, explanation not an, 154
experience as basis for accepting
  a claim, 34–35, 37–38
experiment, Chapter 29
  duplicable, 188
  replicable, 188
  results reproducible, 188

should start with a question, 196
what can go wrong, Chapter 30
See also cause in population.
explanation, functional, 160–161
explanation, inferential, 149
  arguments compared to —s,
    150, 154–156
  associated argument of —,
    154–156
  behavioral, 153
  best, better, 157–158, 225
  causal, 152
    teleological — isn't, 168
  circular, 151
  comparing —s, 156–158
  dependent, 155
  excuses and, 154
  explains everything, 153
  good, 151
  Guide to Repairing —s, 152
  hypothesis, — serves as, 225
  inadequate, 153
  independent, 155
  inference to the best, 158
  repairing an —, 152
  science —, Chapter 31
  simpler, 156
  teleological —. See
    functional explanation.
  theories and, 223–224
  untestable, 153
explanatory claims, 149

factor, causal, 135
fallacy, 3. See also name
  of the fallacy.
false dilemma, 71
  causal reasoning and —, 185
falsifying a generalization, 194
fear, appeal to, 56
"few", 87–88
"follows from", 27

foreseeable consequence, 135
fortune tellers, 199
Franklin, Benjamin, 42
Friedman, Milton, 220–222
function of an object, 159–160
functional explanation, 160–161
functional fallacy, 161

Galileo, 187, 213, 215, 217, 223, 224
gambler's fallacy, 118
Gardner, Martin, 202

general causal claim, 127
general claim, Chapter 16
generalization(s), 116
    analogies and, 109, 124, 142
    experiment to test a —, 194
    hasty, 120
    premises needed for a good —, 122
    statistical, 116
geometry, Euclidean, 217, 219
Giancoli, D. C., 218
glue (in an argument), 46, 50, 137
graph, Chapter 18
    as implicit argument, 105
    base line, 101. *See also* base
        of a comparison.
    bell-shaped, 95–96
    spacing of measure on axes, 102
Guide to Repairing Arguments, 48
Guide to Repairing Inferential
    Explanations, 152

haphazard sampling, 117, 119
Harrison, Ross, 192–193
hasty generalization, 120
health-care decisions, 170–172
Hempel, Carl G., 223–224
history as a science?, 188
Hwang, Woo-Suk, 196
hypotheses, reasoning from, 79–80
hypothesis in science, 194, 196, 225

imagination, 26, 133
implying, 53–54
inadequate explanation, 153
independent explanation, 155
indicator words, 30,
indirect way of reasoning with
    conditionals, 78
individual vs. group ambiguity, 5
inductive evidence, 116
inference to the best explanation, 158
inferential explanation. *See*
    explanation, inferential.
inferring, 53–54
insight, 224, 230
internet, 38–39
intersubjective claim, 13
intervening cause, 136
Irrationality, Mark of, 48
irrelevant premise, 51–52
"is does not imply ought", 60

joint cause, 135
journal as reliable source, 36

Keynes, John Maynard, 118

law, general, in science, 224
law of large numbers, 118
legal reasoning, 112–113
Levi, Edward H., 113
Lincoln, Abraham, 8, 47
loaded question, 17, 149, 161
looking at only one end
    fallacy, 136
lying, 46–47
    in science, 196–197

magic and science, 229–230
margin of error, 122
Mark of Irrationality, 48
Martin Luther King, Jr., 51
Marx, Chico, 34

mean (average), 93–95
  regression to the —, 198
media, 37
median, 93–95
memory, 35, 37
Michelson-Morley experiment,
  200–201, 216–217
mining the data fallacy, 196
misdirection, 19
mistaking the person for
  the argument, 43
mistaking the person for the claim, 41
mode, 93–95
model, , Chapter 31, 218
  assumptions true?, 213–214,
    217–220
  equation can be a —, 215—216,
modus ponens. See direct way
  of reasoning with conditionals.
modus tollens. See indirect way
  of reasoning with conditionals.
Mullis, Kary, 180
mysticism and science, 229

necessary condition, 74
Newton, Isaac, 191, 213, 216–217,
  219–220, 223
"no"-claim, 85–86
"none", 84
normal conditions, 129
"nothing", 84

objective claim, 11–13
observational claim, 187–188
"only"-claim, 84–85
"only if "-claim, 74
opinion, 13
"or"-claim, 70
ought from is, 60

Pachauri, Rajendra K., 61
particular causal claim, 127

path of abstraction, 220–222
percentages, 92–93, 97,
persuasive definition, 8, 17
phony precision, 97
phony refutation, 43, 66
pity, appeal to, 56
placebo, 199–200
placebo effect, 200
plausible claim, 27
Popper, Karl, 223
population, 116
positive publication bias, 201–202
possibility ≠ plausibility, 42,
post hoc ergo propter hoc, 133
precision, phony, 97
prediction(s), 194, 199, 218–220,
  229
premise, 22
  adding a —, 48
  criteria to accept/reject, 37
  deleting a —, 48, 52, 53
  — indicator, 30
  irrelevant, 51–52
prescriptive claim, 15–16
  scientist makes a —, 61
  standard for, 59–60
proof substitute, 18
pseudoscience. *See* ESP.
putting words in someone's
  mouth, 23, 51, 67,

random sampling, 117, 119
range of application of a theory,
  218
Rational Discussion, Principle of,
  46–48
reasoning from hypotheses, 79–80
reasoning in a chain with "all", 85
reasoning in a chain with
  "almost all", 88
reasoning in a chain with
  conditionals, 78

reasoning in a chain with
    "some", 85
reducing to the absurd, 65–67, 79,
    154, 157
referee, 198
reference source, 36
refutation, phony, 43, 66
refuting an argument, 43, 64–67
    by analogy, 66, 111
    direct ways, 65
    indirect way. *See* reducing
        to the absurd.
    strawman, 67
regression to the mean, 198
relativist, 60
religion and science, 229–220
relevance, 52
Repairing Arguments, Guide to, 48
Repairing Explanations, Guide to, 152
replicated experiment, 188
representative sample, 117
reproducible results of
    an experiment, 188
reversing cause and effect, 132
Rhine, Joseph Banks, 202
ridicule, 18–19, 66–67
risk, 123, 166
    evaluating, 166
    short term vs. long term, 170

sample, 116
    biased, 117
    haphazardly chosen, 117, 119
    randomly chosen, 117, 119
    representative, 117
    size of —, 119–120
scale, fallacy of, 170
scientific method, 184–185, 203
scientist as authority, 61, 180, 203, 209
selective attention, 123
self-deception, 197–198, 230
self-selection bias, 201

shifting the burden of proof, 19, 153
single cause fallacy, 136
size doesn't matter fallacy, 169
slanter, 17
    why not to use, 19
slippery slope argument, 79
"some"-claim, 83
    contradictory of, 85
    standard for a prescriptive claim,
        59–60
statistical generalization, 116
strawman, 67
strong argument, 26
subjective claim, 11–13
    can't conclude from objective
        claims, 52
    causal —, 134
    moral claims are —?, 60
subjectivist fallacy, 12
sufficient condition, 74
suspending judgment, 34–39,
    44, 48
    wrong —, 41–42
Sussman, R.W., 189–220

teleological explanation,
    160–161
teleological fallacy. *See*
    functional fallacy.
testable claim, 136, 153. *See also*
    experiment.
theory, Chapter 31, 218
    applicable, 219
    assumptions of — are true?,
        213–214, 217–220
    better —, 220
    confirming, 216–217
    explanations and, 223–224
    modifying in the light of
        evidence, 219–220
    path of abstraction, 220–222
    range of application, 218

Torrecelli, 223–224
tracing a cause too far back, 131–132
two times zero is still zero comparison, 96
two wrongs make a right, 57

uncontrolled cause-in-population experiment, 142
unnamed source, 37
unrepairable arguments, 53. *See also* fallacy; *name of fallacy*.
unsupported claims, judging, 37
untestable claims, 136, 135
up-player, 178
usually reliable sources, 37
Utts, Jessica, 191–192

vague generality, 87
vague sentence, 2–5
  subjective claim is?, 11
valid argument, 26
value judgment, 15, 60, 61
Van der Steen, Wim J., 186
variation in a population, 120
Vesalius, Andreas, 204–205
"very few"-claim, 87–88
virtue, 176

Wakefield, Andrew, 197
weak argument, 25
weaseler, 18
Wikipedia, 38–39
winning an argument, 63–64
wishful thinking, 57
worth the risk, 166

Richard L. Epstein received his B.A. from the University of Pennsylvania and his Ph.D. from the University of California, Berkeley. He was a Fulbright Fellow to Brazil and a National Academy of Sciences Scholar to Poland. He is the author of *An Introduction to Formal Logic, Propositional Logics,* and *Predicate Logic.* Since 1999 he has been the head of the Advanced Reasoning Forum in Socorro, New Mexico. He has also translated and edited *The BARK of DOG,* and directs The BARK of DOG Foundation.

Other books by Richard L. Epstein published by ARF in the series *Essays on Logic as the Art of Reasoning Well*

The Fundamentals of Argument Analysis

Cause and Effect, Conditionals, Explanations

Prescriptive Reasoning

Reasoning in Science and Mathematics

Reasoning and Formal Logic

The Advanced Reasoning Forum is dedicated to advancing the study and teaching of critical thinking, formal logic, philosophy of language, linguistics, and ethics.

www.AdvancedReasoningForum.org

CPSIA information can be obtained
at www.ICGtesting.com
Printed in the USA
FFHW010846270319
51178206-56672FF

9 781938 421402